Spirituality and the Occu

'This is a truly excellent book. The scholarship is sound and the subject timely, and the style is clear and approachable. The material is well-chosen, well-presented and the argument is convincing.'

Juliette Wood

'This study is extraordinarily learned . . . accurate in its account of the occult tradition in Western civilisation, and it adduces substantial evidence to support its claim that occultism is a significant presence in many aspects of the modern world.'

John Mebane, *University of Alabama*

Spirituality and the Occult is a clear and convincing argument for a reappraisal of the marginal status of occult spiritualities in relation to Western intellectual and cultural history. B. J. Gibbons shows the esoteric tradition to have contributed much to the development of many and diverse branches of European culture from the Renaissance onwards.

The continued presence of esoteric mystical movements in Western culture is demonstrated, and their relevance to the history of medicine, science, philosophy, Freudian and Jungian psychology, radical political movements and imaginative literature is illustrated. Laying particular emphasis on the secularisation of occult spiritualities in the Romantic movement and beyond, and stressing the social role of occult faiths as counter-culture, B. J. Gibbons illuminates the influential role of the occult in much of what is taken to be typically 'modern'.

B. J. Gibbons is Lecturer in Literature and Cultural History at Liverpool John Moores University. His main research interests are occult spiritualities and seventeenth-century English Radicalism. He is the author of *Gender in Mystical and Occult Thought: Behmenism and its Development in England* (1998).

Spirituality and the Occult

From the Renaissance to the Modern Age

B. J. Gibbons

London and New York

First published 2001
by Routledge
11 New Fetter Lane, London EC4P 4EE

Simultaneously published in the USA and Canada
by Routledge
29 West 35th Street, New York, NY 10001

Routledge is an imprint of the Taylor & Francis Group

Typeset in Times by BC Typesetting, Bristol
Printed and bound in Great Britain by Clays Ltd, St Ives plc

British Library Cataloguing in Publication Data
A catalogue record for this book is available from the British Library

Library of Congress Cataloging in Publication Data
A catalogue record for this book has been requested

ISBN 0–415–24448–X (hbk)
ISBN 0–415–24449–8 (pbk)

Contents

Acknowledgements

All academic work is essentially collaborative, and this book has been formed and shaped by many minds other than my own. I owe a great deal to people I have never met, and I hope my debts in this respect are sufficiently acknowledged in the notes sections. This work first took shape while I was working at the University of Durham, and it reflects many conversations with friends and colleagues in both the History and English Departments. I would particularly like to thank Sean Burke for his friendly criticism and encouragement. The book was completed while working at the University of Northumbria and Liverpool John Moores University. At both institutions I have received nothing but support and encouragement, and it has been a privilege to work with the fine scholars, both staff and students, of these universities. For most of my life I have enjoyed the friendship of David Napthine and David Campbell who, more than anyone, have helped to develop my thinking on most topics, including many of the issues dealt with in this book.

1 Introduction

The term 'occult spiritualities' may be misleading to the modern reader. It popularly conveys a notion of devil-worship, a misperception which is not fortuitous. Esoteric thought represents a heterodox theology which orthodox thinkers demonised because they sincerely, but mistakenly, believed it to be demonic. A spurious justification could be found for this mistake in the fact that occult thinkers tended to believe not only in the possibility, but also in the legitimacy, of various forms of magic. Early modern occultism flourished at a time when magic was being redefined as a heresy constituted by the renunciation of God in favour of the Devil.[1] The archetypal image of the occult philosopher is Faustus, the semi-legendary German magus who sold his soul to the Devil in order to gain 'a world of profit and delight'.[2] Marlowe's English version of the Faust legend may in fact have involved a conscious attack on one of the earliest and most popular of Renaissance occult philosophers, Agrippa von Nettesheim.[3]

Most of the victims of the early modern repudiation of magic had only a tenuous link with the occult philosophy as such. The popular mentality involved what has been called an 'untutored Spinozism' or 'a simple, unintellectual type of neo-Platonism'.[4] The village wisewomen who were condemned as witches may have shared much of the world-view of esoteric thinkers, since the underlying principles of magical practice are identical to those of occult thought in general. Magic, as Marcel Mauss argued, depends on the laws of contiguity, similarity and opposition,[5] which also happen to be the structural principles of esotericism. What differentiates the witch from the occultist is that whereas in the case of traditional witchcraft it is necessary to infer these basic principles of magic from observed behaviour, the occult philosophers developed them quite consciously within the context of their theological system.[6]

Mauss's argument, that 'on the whole it is the men who perform the magic while the women are accused of it',[7] may not be quite true in terms of who practised magic in early modern Europe, but it was certainly women who were most persecuted.[8] Occult thinkers themselves seem to have been remarkably free from persecution. Some ended their days as martyrs for their faith, like the Behmenist poet Quirinus Kuhlmann, who met his death at the stake in Moscow in 1689. As late as 1795 we find Cagliostro dying in a Roman dungeon after falling foul of the Inquisition.[9] Many, like Jacob Boehme, doubtlessly suffered from the petty harassment of their more orthodox neighbours. Boehme's case also shows the flip-side of the coin, since in his later days he was surrounded by admiring members of the petty nobility and the urban élite.[10] Increasingly, however, the occult philosophers had little to fear except the ridicule of their contemporaries. The biting sarcasm of Butler and Swift may not have been pleasant, but it was surely preferable to the more savage wit of the hangman.[11]

With Butler and Swift we are rapidly approaching the Enlightenment. That supposed Age of Reason may not have been as dedicated to the rational as is sometimes assumed, or indeed as the *lumières* themselves liked to pretend.[12] It is no coincidence that the centres of the German Enlightenment were also ones of Pietism, a religious movement thoroughly permeated by occult mentalities. Both the Pietists and the *Aufklärer* emphasised individualism, tolerance and the primacy of ethics over dogmatic theology.[13] Despite the assumption that the magical world-view entered into terminal decline after the seventeenth century,[14] the occult philosophy continued to exert its influence throughout the eighteenth century,[15] and it was to enjoy a notable recovery in nineteenth-century Romanticism, which was largely 'a revival and secularization of the earlier occult religious philosophy of the Renaissance'.[16] But if the occult philosophy survived the Enlightenment intact, and even revitalised, it was not unscathed. Ridicule takes its toll, and the eighteenth century witnessed the beginning of the process whereby the occult philosophy came to be seen as marginal to mainstream culture. Since the nineteenth century, its marginality may in fact have constituted its most important social feature for both its adherents and its opponents, transforming it into a protest against the hegemonic culture. In the early modern period, however, the occult philosophy was a central expression of both élite and popular mentalities. It was not without its opponents, who certainly carried the day as far as history is concerned. Nevertheless, it has left a lasting imprint on our own culture, so much so that it can be regarded as one of the major sources of modern understandings of what it means to be human.

This assertion is most obviously true in a purely negative sense. Any group of people gains its sense of identity and coherence not merely by asserting its own positive values and assumptions, but also by defining itself in terms of what it is not. We might say the same of the Other as Voltaire said of God: if it did not already exist, a culture would have to invent it. Mainstream Christianity in early modern Europe was constituted partly by constructing others (including occultist *illuminés*) as heretical. Similarly, the accreditation of Enlightenment rationalism was achieved in part through its distance from supernaturalism and superstition; the *philosophe* was a *lumière* because he was not an *illuminé*. This argument can be broadened to encompass the intellectual origins of Western Christian civilisation as a whole. After all,

Christian orthodoxy and the canon of books that legitimated it were established in contradistinction to Gnosticism,[17] a world-view which happens to be one of the more important ancestors of early modern occult philosophy.

This does not mean that there was a direct influence of Gnosticism on early modern occultism. The ancient Gnostic texts had been successfully suppressed after the Emperor Theodosius I established the spiritual monopoly of Christian orthodoxy in AD 381.[18] Gnostic texts were known to the occultists of the sixteenth and seventeenth centuries through the fragments preserved by heresiographers like Irenaeus, but this context in itself made it difficult for purely Gnostic thought to be adopted openly. The taint of heresy was less pronounced in relation to a related body of pagan writings, those attributed to Hermes Trismegistus.[19] Composed mostly in Greek between the second and third centuries of our era, the Hermetic writings incorporated both Gnostic and Neoplatonic elements. The Hermetic texts were recovered for use in the West by Marsilio Ficino in the 1460s, and they were henceforth to be one of the major sources of European occultism.[20] By this time, another offspring of ancient Gnosticism was beginning to exert its influence on Christian intellectuals: the Jewish Cabala. Christian interest in Cabalism can be found from the thirteenth century onwards, in the writings of men like Joachim of Fiore and Alfonso Sabio, but it was really Giovanni Pico della Mirandola in the 1490s and subsequently Johann Reuchlin who introduced a thoroughgoing Christian Cabalism.[21] Throughout the early modern period, it has been argued, 'some knowledge of cabala was part of the equipment of every scholar in every part of Europe'.[22] Another means of transmission of Gnostic thought can be found in alchemy. From its first appearance in Egypt onwards, alchemy involved mystical elements alongside the attempt to transmute base metals into gold. Much of the ancient Greek alchemical tradition was lost to early Western Christendom, but it was preserved and developed by Arabic alchemists like Jabir ibn Hayyan (Geber). From the twelfth century, Arabic alchemical works began to be translated into Latin, and there was a consequent revival of alchemy in Western Europe.[23] Despite Titus Burckhardt's opinion that alchemy after the Renaissance 'had a fragmented character' and that 'as a spiritual art, the metaphysical background was lacking',[24] from the sixteenth century the mystical aspects of alchemy became more pronounced, and a purely spiritual alchemy evolved.[25]

Another source of early modern occultism can be found in the Christian Neoplatonic tradition, especially in the writings of the pseudo-Dionysius.[26] Platonism was a vital aspect of much Christian thought throughout the early Middle Ages, and later esoteric thought has much in common with writers like John Scotus Eriugena.[27] Apart from his own writings, Eriugena can be credited with the Latin translation of the works of the pseudo-Dionysius, making them accessible to later Western thinkers.[28] This Platonic Christianity suffered something of a set-back after the recovery of Aristotle's works in the twelfth century, but elements of the earlier outlook were preserved in the writings of Albert the Great. After Albert, this tradition was reinforced in the thought of Johannes Eckhardt.[29] Although Eckhardt was condemned as heterodox, his work was continued by other Rhenish mystics, notably by Heinrich Suso, Johannes Tauler and the unknown author of the *Theologia Germanica*. This mystical tradition underwent a revival during the Reformation. Luther himself published an edition of the *Theologia Germanica*, and this was to become a major text in sixteenth-century Protestant spirituality.[30]

Christian Neoplatonism takes us back to a final set of influences on occult thought: ancient Greek philosophy.[31] Plato has an obvious importance here, especially Plato seen through the eyes of Plotinus.[32] The Presocratic thinkers were also of some significance. Empedocles bequeathed the idea of the four elements to Western culture as a whole; more particularly, his notion of the cosmos as an eternal process of constitution, dissolution and reconstitution, governed by the opposing forces of Aphrodite (love) and Ares (strife), finds echoes in esoteric thought.[33] This aspect of Empedoclean thought harmonises with Heraclitus's concept of reality as flux, an idea which also found an afterlife in the occult philosophy.[34] In Parmenides the occult philosopher could find the counterbalancing doctrine of the One as the only true reality.[35] Of the Presocratics it was Pythagoras who had most impact on esoteric thought.[36] Reuchlin's *De arte cabalistica*, after all, is as concerned with recuperating Pythagoreanism for Christianity as it is with developing a Christian Cabala.

These Presocratic thinkers expounded different and contradictory systems, but the illuminists tended to regard them as complementary. Occultists took a thoroughly eclectic attitude to their sources, constructing their own philosophies with the debris of ancient thought. It was without any apparent embarrassment that Reuchlin wrote about the Cabala in order 'to make Pythagorean doctrine better known to scholars'.[37] It has been argued that 'when Hermeticism is used to mean a particular attitude of mind towards nature or a particular intellectual sensibility, it is just too vague a term with which to come to grips'.[38] The objection would seem to be all the greater when talking about an 'occult philosophy' which somehow embraces not only Hermeticism, but also Neoplatonism, alchemy, Cabala and so on. Offensive as this might be to those with tidily organised minds, the fact is that there was such a philosophy, and its untidiness and vagueness are not a licence for supposing it out of existence. What has been called (in reference to Giordano Bruno) 'an apparently haphazard eclecticism'[39] is part of the data to be analysed, not a reason for refusing analysis.

These, then, are the major sources of early modern occultism. It is, however, slightly misleading to speak of a single occult philosophy in early modern Europe. We can (in principle at least) distinguish traditional alchemy from Hermeticism, or Cabalism from Neoplatonism, even if these jumbled themselves together in most occultists' minds. The occult philosophy had a distinct Northern and Southern inflection, and had a different character in

Eastern Europe than it did in the West. It inevitably assumed a slightly different complexion under the hands of a Lutheran, a Calvinist or a Catholic. Sometimes we find the sages toadying in the courts of emperors, and a stone's throw away discover them busily turning the world upside down. The occult philosophy, moreover, undoubtedly changed over time. William Blake's thought was not identical to Jacob Boehme's, nor Boehme's to that of Paracelsus, however much the three men may have had in common. This is true even if we confine ourselves to a single writer. The Boehme of 1624 is not quite the same man as the youth who, a quarter of a century earlier, apprehended God in the shimmering of a pewter dish. I shall confine my attention to Western Europe, although it is clear that the occult philosophy, especially in its Behmenist form, was widely influential in nineteenth-century Russia.[40] My sources have tended to come more from Northern Europe than the South; more from England than the Continent; and more from the Behmenist tradition than any of its rivals. Although many historians tend to subsume the whole occult philosophy under the catch-all title of 'Neoplatonism', the Northern tradition (and Behmenism in particular) tends not to be Neoplatonic in according ontological primacy to the divine will rather than the divine intellect. As Urszula Szulakowska has recognised, 'Alchemy, ultimately, was not a Neoplatonic body of thought.'[41] My neglect of the Southern tradition can only be excused by my relative ignorance; the concentration on Behmenism may be justified by the fact that Boehme was undoubtedly the most influential occult thinker in the seventeenth and eighteenth centuries, not only in his native Germany, but also in England, the Netherlands and France.

We might say the same of occult mysticism as Schenk remarked of Romanticism: its unity 'can perhaps best be characterised as contradictoriness, dissonance and inner conflict'.[42] There is, however, a unity in the occult philosophy, and one which for the most part it shared with its Gnostic antecedents. It was itself a gnostic system in the broadest sense of the term, a religion whose basic soteriological principle was knowledge (gnosis) rather than forensic notions of vicarious atonement. As with ancient Gnosticism, gnosis for early modern occultists was not a matter of 'propositional knowledge' or assent to a particular set of doctrines, although a clearly defined doctrinal creed can be found in their works. The esotericists' concept of salvific knowlege referred to the notion of direct contact with the underlying structure of reality, which was God.[43] It was as much conative as noetic, involving the whole of one's being in an intuitive apprehension of the true ground of being as the godhead itself. It functioned as a soteriological principle because, in revealing the ultimate identity of the soul with its source, it reunited them.

There is, however, an important difference in this respect between ancient Gnosticism and early modern occultism. We can distinguish two sorts of gnosis. On the one hand we have an anticosmic system, in which the material world is understood to be alien to the godhead. It was created by either a malevolent or a bungling demiurge, rather than by the divine being itself. The soul is a portion of the transcendent godhead that has become trapped in the material creation, and the Gnostic's goal is to release the soul from its cosmic fetters. There is another form of gnosis which involves a positive attitude to the universe, one in which the cosmos is seen as a manifestation of the godhead. Here the Gnostic's task is one of recognising the divine impulse which throbs not only through his own soul, but also through the material universe.[44] Both the negative and positive forms of gnosis can be found from antiquity through to modernity, but in general, ancient Gnosticism can be seen as gravitating to the negative pole, while early modern occultism tended to revolve around its more positive antipodes.[45]

Ancient Neoplatonism developed a similar, if less pronounced, anticosmic system to Gnosticism. In Plotinus's *Enneads* we learn that there is a single supreme reality, the One or the Good. Because of its own plenitude, there is a spontaneous overflow of being from the One, progressing through mind and soul to the material universe. Each successive stage in this process is represented as a deprivation of being. The evil which prevails in the material universe is not a positive quality, but simply a result of this ontological deficiency. To overcome evil it is necessary to reverse the emanational process and return to the undifferentiated plenitude of the One. M. H. Abrams has suggested that 'a distinctive Romantic innovation' in the Neoplatonic tradition was the repudiation of a simple return to the One: 'when the process reverts to its beginning the recovered unity is not, as in the school of Plotinus, the simple, undifferentiated unity of its origin, but a unity which is higher, because it incorporates the intervening differentiations'.[46] As we shall see, the early modern occult interpretation of creation in terms of divine manifestation had in fact already anticipated this aspect of Romantic thought.

Giordano Bruno in the sixteenth century thought that Nature was 'none other than God in all things', and if God 'is not Nature herself, then he is certainly the nature of Nature, and is the soul of the Soul of the World, if he is not the Soul herself'.[47] 'The bird does not really sing and fly', wrote Sebastian Franck, 'it is sung and flown into the air. God it is which in the bird sings, lives, nests and flies.'[48] According to Jacob Boehme in the seventeenth century, 'all things are arisen from the eternal spirit, as a likeness of the eternal'; 'this world, with the sun, stars, and elements, and with every creaturely being, is nothing else but a manifestation of the eternity of the eternal mind and will'.[49] God is substantially present in the universe: 'he is through all and in all, his birth is everywhere and besides him there is nothing else'.[50] Richard Coppin asserted that 'God hath sown the Image of himself in the whole world of things.'[51] In the eighteenth century, George Cheyne believed that God was 'infinitely present, with every single *Atom* of Matter'.[52] Cheyne thought of the relationship between God and the creation in terms of that between soul and body; the universe is 'GOD's Body, or his *Sensorium*'.[53] For Louis de Saint-Martin, 'The creatures are only the frameworks, the vessels or the active envelopes, where this lively and true essence

[God] comes to enclose itself in order to manifest itself through their means.'[54]

The occult philosophy can be reduced to a single principle, which is given its classic expression in *The Emerald Tablet* of the legendary Hermes Trismegistus: 'whatever is below is like that which is above, and whatever is above is like that which is below'.[55] The doctrine of 'as above, so below' means that everything that exists is related through a series of correspondences. There is, in particular, a tripartite correspondence between God, the world and humanity. Man is the central term in this cosmic analogy, since he is not only a microtheos or 'a complete image of God',[56] but also an image of the world or microcosm. In Paracelsus's words, 'the sun and the moon and all the planets as well as all stars and the whole chaos are in man. . . . For what is outside is also inside, and what is not outside man is not inside.'[57] This idea of the correspondence of all things is expressed in the doctrine of signatures. The cosmos is a semantic system, pregnant with meaning. Everything is a signature, pointing beyond itself to an ultimate and interior reality: 'The whole outward visible world with all its being is a signature, or figure of the inward spiritual world.'[58] Permeating all occult thought, this idea was to survive in Coleridge's belief that 'Each exterior is the physiognomy of the being within it, its true image reflected and thrown out from the concave mirror.'[59] Charles Fourier, the nineteenth-century utopian socialist, thought that 'everything, from atoms to stars, is an image of the properties of the human passions'. His 'science of analogy', positing 'a unified system of movement for the spiritual and material world', is simply a restatement of this concept of cosmic isotropy.[60] The doctrine of signatures also survived in nineteenth-century scientific circles. In 1852, for example, the Duke of Argyll denied the possibility of separating science and religion, since 'Every outward visible thing has some inward invisible meaning; and if the true one be not seen, a false one will be invented.'[61]

As a consequence of the doctrine of signatures, the natural world becomes the Book of Nature, another Scripture. The idea of the Book of Nature is not confined to occult thought, and it can be found in theological writings that pretend to the strictest orthodoxy. Calvin believed that 'In every part of the world, in heaven and on earth', God 'had written and as it were engraven the glory of his power, wisdom and eternity'. For Calvin, however, the knowledge of God attainable through nature is just sufficient to deny man 'refuge in the plea of ignorance';[62] it was never, as it became in some occult thought, adequate for salvation. In writers like Calvin, the Book of Nature demonstrates God's providence and provides the argument for God's existence from design, but that is all. The occult thinkers give the notion of a Book of Nature an immanentalist emphasis which more orthodox Christians mistook for pantheism.[63] This is understandable, given the incautious statements occasionally made by the occult-minded. Peter Sterry, for example, said that the creation was 'a kind of Incarnation', since in it 'Naturall things are shadows of Spirituall.'[64] It was only in the Enlightenment, however, when the occult philosophy was radically secularised by writers like John Toland, that a genuine pantheism emerged in esoteric thought.[65]

The relationship between the transcendent godhead and the world is one of emanation. According to ancient Gnosticism, the divine being unfolds itself through a series of Aeons, and it is a crisis in the last of these (Sophia) which leads to the production of the material world.[66] The function of the Aeons in Gnosticism is to place the godhead at the furthest possible remove from the world; this is why the number of Aeons in Gnostic thought gradually increased, until some writers posited the existence of several hundred.[67] Later esotericism retains the idea of emanations, but uses it for a diametrically opposed purpose: to show how the godhead becomes manifest in the creation. Divine immanence replaces transcendence, and a structure of thought created in the service of a world-negating religion is co-opted for the purposes of a world-affirming one.

There are several emanational systems in occult thought. The medieval Zoharic Cabala described a series of ten powers or *sefiroth*, culminating in Malkuth, who is the Shekhinah or divine presence on earth.[68] The *sefiroth* form the body of Adam Kadmon, the original cosmic man.[69] A crisis involving Malkuth leads to her alienation from the world, which constitutes a cosmic Fall.[70] Already in this system we can detect a distinct shift from the anticosmic stance of ancient Gnosticism. For the latter, the Fall originates in Sophia's immersion in the material creation, but for the Cabala it is constituted by the Shekhinah's alienation from the world. The Gnostic project is consequently one of disentangling the divine from the mundane order, while the Cabalist seeks to reunite the creation with its divine source.

Another important system is Jacob Boehme's idea of the seven 'fountain spirits' (*Quellgeister*) which constitute reality. The *Quellgeister* are the means whereby the Abyssal Will of Boehme's transcendent godhead becomes manifest in the creation. In a strict sense this is not an emanational system at all, since the seven fountain-spirits coexist in each other at all times; Boehme expressly states that, although he describes them in a temporal succession, one emerging from the other, this is only because of the inadequacy of human language to describe them as they really exist. None of the fountain-spirits 'is the first, neither is any of them the last',[71] but they are nevertheless pictured as generating each other in a dialectical process. The first fountain-spirit is an impulse of contraction, the second a counterbalancing one of expansion. The tension between these two impulses generates the third fountain-spirit, 'the great anguish'. This results in the sudden 'flash' of the fourth fountain-spirit, and the dialectical process of the lower ternary is repeated in the last three fountain-spirits, culminating in the seventh, which is represented as the summation of all the others. The *Quellgeister* also form the three Principles of the Godhead. The first four fountain-spirits constitute the First or Dark Principle, which is one of wrath, associated with the Father in the Trinity. They are also Eternal Nature, the archetype of temporal nature, although some Behmenists identified this with all seven fountain-spirits.[72] The fifth and sixth fountain-spirits constitute the Second or Light Principle, which is one of love, associated with the Son in the Trinity. The Third Principle, the Principle in which the Abyssal Will becomes manifest in the creation, is formed by the seventh fountain-spirit, associated with the Holy Ghost. Man stands in the fourth fountain-spirit, the point of transition between the lower ternary of the natural world and the higher ternary of the spiritual world, capable of turning towards either.[73] As in the doctrine of man as microcosm and microtheos, he is the middle term between God and Nature; or rather, since this is a dynamic construction of this doctrine, he plays a pivotal role between the two. Boehme's three Principles were often identified with the three higher *sefiroth* of the Cabala, and his seven *Quellgeister* with the lower *sefiroth*; the differences between the various systems of occult thought did not impede a vigorous syncretising impulse among the mystics.

Boehme advises his readers 'to know that in Yes and No consist all things',[74] and his thought has a dialectical structure which derives from the doctrine of the coincidence of opposites. The idea of a balance of light and dark in the divine realm was already present in the pre-Zoharic Cabala.[75] Similarly, the *Zohar* itself tells us that 'In the work of the creation there was an antagonism of the Left against the Right' (the *sefiroth* Hesed and Gevurah). The *sefirah* Tifereth 'intervened and allayed the discord between the two sides . . . and the Left became absorbed in the Right, and there was peace over all'.[76] As McGregor Mathers noted, 'the doctrine of equilibrium and balance is a fundamental qabalistic idea': 'Equilibrium is that harmony which results from the analogy of contraries, it is the dead centre where, the opposition of opposing forces being equal in strength, rest succeeds motion.'[77] The opposites and their coincidence are often expressed symbolically in terms of the separation of male and female and their reunion, either sexually (as in the Jewish Cabala), or in the form of a spiritual androgyne (as in Behmenism).[78]

The doctrine of the coincidence of opposites was given its classic statement in the writings of Nicholas of Cusa. Since God is the ground of being, all predicates must somehow exist in him. Many predicates, however, are mutually exclusive, and thus God becomes 'the one being to which contradictory predicates can and must be ascribed'.[79] The search to achieve a coincidence of opposites was a structural principle of all occult thought. For Giordano Bruno, the doctrine of contraries was both a metaphysical and an ethical one.[80] Both contraries are necessary: 'the beginning, the middle, and the end, the birth, the growth, and the perfection of all that we see, come from contraries, through contraries, into contraries, to contraries'.[81] Robert Fludd believed that there were opposites in God, the divine Nullity and Volunty; accordingly, there were also dark and light sides of the creation, conflicting principles of good and evil which would

be reunited in the fullness of time.[82] Romantics like Eckhartshausen and
Azaïs also believed in the existence of two opposing forces in nature, the
one 'expansive', the other 'compressive'; it was in the harmony of these
two forces that nature achieved its perfection.[83] William Blake thought
that without contraries 'there is no progression'.[84] For Charles Fourier,
'a regular clash of contraries' was necessary to achieve 'the equilibrium of
the passions', a precondition of social and cosmic harmony.[85] According
to Schelling, there is a 'polarity and dualism throughout all nature'.
Matter itself is simply an equilibrium between two opposed forces, and is
'brought to life' when the equilibrium is disturbed.[86] Coleridge's 'polar
logic' is another Romantic appropriation of the occult doctrine of contraries,
and his representation of the dialectical structure of the godhead reads like
Behmenism recast in philosophical jargon.[87] Later in the nineteenth century
Eliphas Lévi detected two opposing forces in the Astral Light which he
believed permeated the universe; achieving equilibrium between these was
the first requisite of successful magic; in fact, the Absolute itself was to be
found in 'the harmony which proceeds from the analogy of opposites'.[88]
Papus argued that 'the Ego cannot be realized except through its opposition
to the Non-Ego. . . . But the opposition of the Ego and the Non-Ego
immediately gives rise to another factor; this is the *Affinity* between this
Ego and this Non-Ego.'[89] Papus's patently Fichtean terminology is a
reminder of the close connection between the occult tradition and German
Romantic philosophy; it was the occult doctrine of contraries, in its dynamic
form, which was to become the Hegelian and Marxist dialectic of thesis,
antithesis and synthesis.

This system of thought may well seem alien to many modern readers, and the
notion that it might have been a major contributing factor to the formation
of modern understandings of the human identity would therefore seem
improbable, if not absurd. As Norbert Elias has observed, one of the central
features of the modern sense of personal identity is that the body is seen as
'the vessel which holds the true self locked within it', and that the skin is
'the frontier between "inside" and "outside"'.[90] Such an understanding of
the self is a complete antithesis to that found in the occult philosophy. The
esoteric mystic did not experience the self as something that was closed off
from all that lay beyond a particular boundary, confronting its environment
as 'Other'. On the contrary, the 'Other' is also the substance and essence of
the self. This is the meaning of the microcosm–macrocosm analogy: not that
man is an image of the world as a portrait is a likeness of its sitter, but that
man and the world share an ultimate existential identity. Yet history is sometimes more akin to Fortuna in its caprices than to its tutelary goddess, Clio; it
often appears to unfold through unintended consequences. I shall argue that,
as strange as the occult representation of the human condition may appear,
it was in fact important in forming our own sense of identity. The occult
philosophy still exists in a more or less pure form, and it perhaps has more

adherents than is generally realised. But its real significance was in its trans-formations, in its shift from transcendentalism to immanentalism, and thence to a peculiarly religious type of secularism that might be characterised as mystical humanism. As D. P. Walker observed, 'magic was always on the point of turning into art, science, practical psychology, or, above all, religion'.[91] In the hands of the occult philosophers and their Romantic off-spring, a radically secularised and partly rationalised magic was in fact to become all of these things; and in the modern world magic has played its role as ersatz religion precisely by becoming art, science and psychology. This claim might become slightly more credible if we undertake a preliminary examination of some of the ways in which the occult philosophy has impinged on modern Western culture.

Frances Yates argued that Renaissance Hermeticism encouraged the growth of the scientific world-view.[92] Given the deeply mythopoeic quality of occult thought, it would seem to be an unlikely ancestor of empirical science. The occult philosophers, however, believed that the universe was permeated by hidden forces, and their project involved the discovery and manipulation of these forces. In this way, occultism implied the notion of a law-bound universe. The nature mysticism of esoteric thinkers like Paracelsus, moreover, arguably encouraged an empirical approach to the study of the natural world. The relationship between science and the occult is a complex issue, and Yates's thesis in particular has serious weaknesses. A fuller discussion of this topic will be given in Chapter 3, but we might note that science certainly does not preclude an occult vision of the world. Both Erwin Schroedinger and Werner Heisenberg were interested in the occult, Schroedinger ultimately adopting an Upanishadic philosophy.[93] Similarly, the nuclear physicist John W. Parsons was a follower of Aleister Crowley and one of the links between the occult tradition and Scientology.[94]

Whatever the relationship between esotericism and science, occult mysti-cism certainly exerted a considerable influence on German philosophy,[95] and Jacob Boehme in particular has been seen as the 'spiritual progenitor' of modern philosophies of 'innerworldly fulfillment' from Marxism to Nazism.[96] Hegel regarded Boehme as one of his intellectual ancestors, calling him 'the first German philosopher'.[97] This was to do no more than justice to Boehme's influence. Behmenism was a system which explained how the ineffable godhead became manifest in the creation through a dialectical process, while Hegelianism claimed to show how Spirit became realised in history through a dialectical process. Hegel, however, was referring to another aspect of Boehme's thought: the activist and subjectivist epistem-ology that came to fruition in Kant's *Critique of Pure Reason*. In this, Boehme had been anticipated by another illuminist, Valentin Weigel.[98] Schelling once described Boehme as 'the oddest individual of that species', the theosophers, and he had nothing but contempt for Boehme's French disciple, Louis de Saint-Martin.[99] Nevertheless Schelling's later philosophy was much influenced by Boehme,[100] so much so that we might venture to

call him a Behmenist. The impact of Eastern religious thought on Schopenhauer is well known,[101] but Schopenhauer's ideas can also be given a Western
occult context. He commended Boehme's *Signatura Rerum*, and his concept
of the Will as the ground of all being is comparable to Boehme's understanding of the First Principle of the godhead.[102]

Boehme's influence in philosophy did not end with the nineteenth century.
When Lewis White Beck remarked ironically that 'existentialists looking
for venerable ancestors have not yet rediscovered' Boehme, he was in fact
mistaken; Paul Tillich cited him as a source of existentialism in 1942.[103]
Like existentialism, Behmenism is preoccupied with the problem of authenticity and freedom in a world characterised by facticity, and it has been
observed that 'Heideggerian religiosity breathes deeply the air of Böhme
and of Pietism'.[104] If, as has been suggested, Coleridge can be regarded as
another forerunner of existentialism,[105] it is largely in terms of those aspects
of his thought most indebted to the occult tradition. The voluntaristic outlook of the occult philosophy made man the master of his condition. Pico
della Mirandola, in a celebrated passage, envisages God as telling Adam
that 'Thou, constrained by no limits, in accordance with thine own free
will, in whose hand We have placed thee, shalt ordain for thyself the limits
of thy nature.'[106] The Behmenist conception of man as poised between the
Light and Dark Principles similarly accords him a freedom to choose; we
might summarise the Behmenist position as 'you are what you imagine'.
Or, to borrow Sartre's classic formulation of existentialism, 'existence
precedes essence'.[107] Sartre's *Existentialism and Humanism* is in many ways
a reprise of Pico's *Oration on the Dignity of Man*. Both are concerned with
the dignity of man, and both discover that dignity in freedom. There are,
of course, important differences. Pico's freedom still operates within a transcendent order of values,[108] and is circumscribed within a finite number of
possible choices: to be a beast or a god. Sartre's freedom rests on a repudiation of all transcendent values, and the possibilities it opens are limitless. On
the other hand, the range of choice offered by Sartre, like Pico's, can be
reduced to just two: authentic existence or living in bad faith. There can be
no question in the case of Sartre of direct influence from the occult tradition.
The similarities are perhaps as much a matter of a common sensibility as
anything else, as with the parallels between existentialism and ancient
Gnosticism.[109] Whatever influence the occult philosophy exerted on French
existentialism was mediated by German philosophy.

There may have been a more particular influence of Behmenism on
German existentialism in Heidegger's philosophy of language.[110] We might
also consider the role of esoteric speculation in the history of linguistics
generally. Language is the basic tool of the magician,[111] and in the Judaeo-
Christian tradition man's first act was one of magical speech: Adam names
the creation, thereby securing his dominion over the things named. It is
not surprising therefore to find a keen interest in linguistics in early
modern occultism. The occultists wished to recover Adam's prelapsarian

Natursprache, the 'Catholique language' in which there was no disjunction between sign and thing signified.[112] Often, as in the case of Jacob Boehme or Thomas Tany, this involved little more than the splendidly Gothic gobble-degook of pseudo-Cabalism (a fitting ancestor for Heidegger); but it also led to a serious attempt to reconstruct the language lost by humanity after the Fall.[113] This search for a mythical *Ursprache* was inevitably futile, but none-theless fruitful in stimulating linguistic studies. The rise of German philology was influenced by Herder's theories of language. Herder repudiated the most obviously occult aspects of Hamann's thought on the subject (his Cabalist belief in the mystical significance of scriptural words), but he followed his master in asserting that language was the basis of culture.[114] Herder's theory of the natural origins of language would seem to be an absolute repudiation of occult linguistics. If language is not a God-given phe-nomenon, but a human convention, it cannot function as a real or non-conventional signifier of the divine. Herder, however, merely shifted the role of divine signifier from language itself to its production in the human spirit: 'The mind has evolved language because it is necessary to its operation as the most perfect image of the Creator.'[115] Here Herder's thought can be seen as prefiguring the transmutation of occult thought effected by Romanticism. The occult emphasis on man as the image of God culminates in the attribu-tion of a divine creativity to the human spirit.

It has been argued that the occult philosophy is a precursor of modern psychology.[116] George Cheyne has been hailed as one of the founders of neurological and epidemiological psychiatry,[117] although his thought in this sphere is only incidentally involved with his mysticism.[118] The role of occult thought in the history of psychology was sometimes one of developing what have subsequently come to be regarded as pseudo-sciences. Both Antoine-Joseph Pernéty and Johann-Caspar Lavater, the most influential proponents of physiognomics, were illuminists.[119] This is hardly surprising; the theory of physiognomics is implicit in the doctrine of signatures, and the idea of reading people's inner characters from the configuration of their faces has Paracelsian roots.[120] Mesmerism also played a role in the history of psychology, and the idea of 'animal magnetism' was used by nine-teenth-century illuminists to give a scientific gloss to their ideas.[121] Both Freudian and Jungian psychology may also be indebted to the occult phil-osophy, a theme that will be considered in greater detail in Chapter 7. More generally, it could be argued that magic stands at the origins of the modern cult of 'self-realisation', which sometimes takes the form of a secular spirituality.[122] Stoddard Martin has observed that 'A first function of magic is to create an effective type of personality.'[123] Magic is essentially a means of concentrating the will and of engaging the imagination. Although most Westerners are inclined to dismiss it as ineffective nonsense, the fact is that magic works – although it may not work in the way the magicians think it does.[124] Magic was also a way of 'turning the magician into a fully realised human being'.[125] The goal of the occult philosophy, after all, is wholeness and harmony with the cosmos.

The illuminists have also left their mark on the plastic arts. This is clearly the case with painters like Botticelli, who worked within the context of the Florentine Neoplatonism established by such writers as Marsilio Ficino and Pico della Mirandola.[126] The influence of esoteric thought is also obvious in the case of William Blake, who might be regarded as the last of the truly great occult thinkers.[127] Esotericism was a prominent aspect of much Symbolist art, especially that of the artists associated with Sâr Péladin's Salons de la Rose+Croix. Fred Gettings has pointed out that the earliest abstract paintings were produced by a group of London artists who were attempting to paint the astral plane, and both Mondrian and Kandinsky seem to have been influenced by occult thought, the latter publishing a book *Concerning the Spiritual in Art* in 1911. As Nadia Choucha has demonstrated, the impact of the occult on Dada and Surrealism was substantial.[128]

Esotericism can also be linked to music, which had a respected place in magical theory from the time of Ficino (to say nothing of Pythagoreanism).[129] Magicians may have gained more from this than musicians, but there was nevertheless a connection. Occultists like Michael Maier, in his *Fugues and Epigrams* (1617), treated music as integral to the alchemical art, and there is an esoteric context to A. J. P. de Vismes' *Pasilogie* (1806), in which music is treated as a universal language of divine origin. Claudio Monteverdi was himself an alchemist, and it is not difficult to discern an Hermetic project underlying Giulio Caccini's belief that music should recreate 'the never-ceasing celestial harmonies whence proceed so many good effects and benefits upon earth'. Mozart's *The Magic Flute*, of course, also has an esoteric-masonic context.[130]

We can also find occultism playing a significant role in literature. Sometimes this involves little more than an attack on esotericism as either fraudulent, as in Jonson's *The Alchemist*, or as hubristic, as in Marlowe's *Dr Faustus*. Poets like George Herbert, John Donne, Andrew Marvell and Robert Southwell borrowed some of their symbolism freely from the alchemical tradition.[131] It has been argued that Shakespeare's *A Midsummer Night's Dream* 'can be interpreted successfully as an alchemical drama', with the mishaps of the star-crossed lovers representing the dissolution and reconstitution of the primal matter.[132] Less persuasively, Charles Nicholl has argued that *King Lear* can also be understood as an alchemical allegory.[133] The occult philosophy in fact forms the background to much English Renaissance drama,[134] and the theme of the 'Mercurian Monarch' can be found in political poetry from Spenser to Pope.[135] If much of this is simply pillaging occultism from the outside, some writers, like Henry Vaughan, stood foursquare within the esoteric tradition itself.[136]

Occult thought had its greatest literary impact on Romanticism. There was, of course, 'a plurality of Romanticisms',[137] just as there was a plurality of occult philosophies. In both cases, however, there were common threads uniting the different strands, and in the case of Romanticism one of the more important of these unifying threads was the relationship to esotericism.[138] Maurice Bowra spoke of the Romantics' 'peculiarly private and individual search for a reality beyond the senses', and of 'their unprecedented speculations'.[139] There are, however, many precedents for the Romantics' religious sensibilities in the occult tradition, not least with regard to the central theme of Bowra's book, the imagination.[140] William Blake, for all his uniqueness, can only be understood from within this tradition, and Coleridge's thought is deeply indebted to esotericism and, like that of the German thinkers he admired, it can be regarded as theosophy decked out in a philosophical frock-coat.[141] Wordsworth shared a similar if less articulated religious vision in his early years.[142]

Esoteric thought did not cease to play a role in English-language literature with the death of the first generation of Romantics. American Transcendentalists like Ralph Waldo Emerson or Amos Bronson Alcott can be related to this tradition, and Walt Whitman's 'I am a cosmos' is an echo of the mystical humanism of the occult. Magic and the occult played an important role in the novels of Sir Edward Bulwer-Lytton, including *Zanoni* and *The Coming Race*. Esoteric spirituality also permeated the writings of *fin-de-siècle* Decadents, and in Ireland the occult philosophy found one of the last of its truly great poets in W. B. Yeats.[143] In a later generation of poets we can find esotericism in the poetry of Kathleen Raine, and occult interests lay close to the surface in the work of Ted Hughes, albeit in an ill-digested form. Esoteric mysticism also forms the background to more recent poetry, as in Hilary Llewellyn-Williams's *Book of Shadows* (1990).

In Germany, according to Heine, 'the endless lauding and praising of Jacob Boehme' was worthy of special remark 'among the madnesses of the Romantic school'.[144] The Hermetic philosophy is certainly one of the contexts in which it is possible to read Goethe.[145] If Novalis (Friedrich von Hardenberg) is 'the most Romantic of the Romantics', this is perhaps because of his deep indebtedness to occult mysticism.[146] Magical themes derived from the occult philosophy permeate much of modern German literature, the most notable example being Thomas Mann's *The Magic Mountain*.[147] Esoteric thought in the form of Anthroposophy was also integral to the poetry of Christian Morgenstern.[148]

Romantic circles in France were permeated by occultism. Esoteric ways of thinking can already be found in the writings of 'pre-Romantics' like Réstif de la Bretonne in the late eighteenth century, and they culminate in the thought of Victor Hugo.[149] By this time Emanuel Swedenborg was becoming as important a source of illuminism as Boehme, and writers like Honoré de Balzac regarded the Swedish seer as 'the Buddha of the North'.[150] Several of Balzac's novels deal with occult subjects: *La Peau de chagrin* or *Séraphîta*, for example. Although he cannot be claimed as an occultist in the fullest sense, Charles Baudelaire incorporated esoteric themes in poems like '*Correspondances*'.[151] Esoteric interests were prominent in the French Symbolist movement, and Arthur Rimbaud exploited occult imagery in several of his poems.[152] In a letter to Paul Demeny, Rimbaud outlined his vatic aesthetics, which is clearly derived from occult thought. The poet must 'become a *seer* through a long, immense and controlled *disordering of all the senses*'. In this way he will become 'the supreme Sage! – For he arrives at the *unknown*'. The poet can then mediate the unknown to others, but to do so he must create 'a universal language' which would sum up 'everything, scents, sounds, colours'.[153] The poet is thus engaged in the same project as occult linguists, the recovery of a language that truly signifies. J.-K. Huysmans was another French writer with a deep interest in the occult, and his novel *Là-bas* was written in the hope of creating 'a work of art of a supernatural realism, a spiritual naturalism'. During his research for the novel, Huysmans became embroiled on the margins of a long feud between various French occultists, a feud waged both magically and by the more conventional means of duelling pistols. After publishing *Là-bas*, Huysmans himself practised occult rituals to defend himself from the 'fluidic fisticuffs' of his magical opponents.[154]

This brief, and far from complete, survey of the literary impact of esotericism might be supplemented by reference to the perennial interest in 'the occult' in its broadest sense, as evinced by the fantasy novels of writers like Ursula Le Guin, the purely sensationalist fiction of such authors as Denis Wheatley, or the popularity of such films and TV series as *Buffy the Vampire Slayer*.[155] These do not have quite the same social cachet as the works of Blake or Yeats, and the 'occultism' they purvey is frequently muddled and vulgarised, but they are nevertheless an important means of popularising notions drawn from the occult philosophy. Fiction has in fact become one of the major ways of disseminating esoteric ideas. Sometimes this has been quite unintentional, as in the case of the fantasy writer H. P. Lovecraft, who was himself a sceptical rationalist, but whose works have given rise to a school of Lovecraftian magic and the 'discovery' of a thoroughly spurious ancient occult text, *The Necronomicon*. On the other hand, several writers with an esoteric vision of the world have used fiction with the conscious intention of enlightening the public: Arthur Maclean, Charles Williams, J. W. Brodie, Aleister Crowley, Dion Fortune and John Cowper Powys are all examples.[156]

There is some truth in William James's assertion that 'we find the same recurring note' in mystical literature throughout the world, so that 'mystical classics . . . have neither birthday nor native land'.[157] It is, however, only a partial truth, and the historian of ideas should pay heed to Anders Nygren's warning that an 'idea or belief can have exactly the same form without having at all the same meaning'.[158] The following account of the occult philosophy, ranging over several centuries, is arranged thematically, and my objective has been to elucidate common aspects of the illuminists' outlook since the

Renaissance. This procedure obviously entails the danger of obscuring both historical change and synchronic diversity. It would be well to stress at the outset that my argument is not that there was a transmission of a single, unalloyed *theologia prisca* from the sixteenth to the twentieth centuries. The occult philosophy underwent several important changes in this period. Until the sixteenth century, the occult philosophy seems to have been organised largely informally; insofar as medieval alchemy had an institutional setting, for example, this was often that of the monastery.[159] From the seventeenth century onwards we find a proliferation of secret societies functioning as a major institutional means for the preservation of the occult tradition. To some extent esotericism began to disintegrate as it lost contact with the established churches and became the property of the sects.[160] With the later eighteenth century we can discern a definite dechristianisation of occult thought. On the one hand, it began to appear in a secularised guise, as 'philosophy' in the modern sense, and by the twentieth century the exultant suprarationalism of the esoteric tradition was giving way to a new would-be rationalism. Occultists have increasingly redirected their attention towards 'things supernormal or paranormal rather than supernatural', and they have become ever more eager to validate their claims in terms of conventional science.[161] On the other hand, there was a distinct paganisation of occultism, and the illuminists began to feel the attraction of the Eastern religions which were eventually to displace the native European Gnostic tradition. As O'Keefe has observed, '*oriental* theosophies came to play in the twentieth-century [occult] revival the role that Neoplatonism and Hermetic gnosticism played in the Renaissance'.[162] From the nineteenth century onwards we encounter with increasing frequency figures like Alphonse Cahagnet, who sought spiritual enlightenment not only in studying Agrippa and Mesmer, but also in taking opium and hashish.[163] Helena Blavatsky also indulged in hashish-smoking, declaring that 'It is a wonderful drug and it clears up a profound mystery.'[164] The New Age announces itself.

Perhaps the most important change undergone by the occult philosophy was its marginalisation. In the sixteenth century the basic premises of occult thought made sense to everyone from the unlettered peasant to the educated élite. The men and women of the Renaissance and Reformation lived in a magical universe, but by the nineteenth century much of the world had become disenchanted. Paradoxically, and unintentionally, the occultists themselves made a substantial contribution to this disenchantment and secularisation of the world through their extreme immanentalism. The marginalisation of illuminism was reflected in the tendency of the sages to squabble among themselves: 'It is as if each were trying to establish his essential soundness in refusing to be linked with what others might regard as spurious'.[165]

It has been suggested that post-Renaissance Hermeticism developed in two ways: there were the 'recidivists' who retained the magical and mystical elements of occultism to the full, and the 'romantics' who were linked to the earlier tradition primarily by their belief that the natural world is meaningful.[166] It would be hard to maintain this as a rigorous distinction, but it does point to one of the ways in which esotericism was losing its coherence as a total world-view. Increasingly it was less a matter of an occult philosophy and more one of a pick-and-mix collection of woolly metaphysical speculations. Along with the marginalisation of the occult philosophy we can discern a certain loss of authenticity in the 'essentially sensation-seeking' occultism of the Romantics and their successors,[167] accompanied as it was by the spiritual quackery of the Cagliostros and the Crowleys of this world. The Romantic marriage of illuminism and poetry sometimes leaves the impression of conscious posing. As Denis Saurat observed, poetry is characterised by its 'lack of intellectual responsibility', opening the question of whether the poet is in earnest or merely engaged in 'artistic diversions'.[168] Whether as a genuine spirituality or merely as a pose, however, the occult philosophy has been interwoven with virtually every aspect of European culture, and its impact could be traced in the last century in such diverse and apparently contradictory phenomena as Nazism[169] and Scientology on the one hand,[170] and New Age spirituality or neopagan witchcraft on the other.[171] Occultism may be, as Theodore Adorno says, little more than 'feeblemindedness with a *Weltanschauung*',[172] but it has nevertheless played a significant role in our history and is a living presence in our own culture.

2   Nature in occult thought

For many people in early modern Europe, the natural world was a threaten-ing and hostile realm, beyond the control of even the most extensive of human powers.[1] 'What care these roarers for the name of king?' asks the boatswain caught up in *The Tempest*.[2] Nature had not always been so refrac-tory. Its awesome, uncontrollable power was the product of a specific event: the Fall. Describing Eve's lapse into temptation, Milton tells us that

> Earth felt that Wound, and Nature from her seat
> Sighing through all her Works gave signs of woe,
> That all was lost.

And when Adam joined his wayward spouse in transgression,

> Earth trembled from her entrails, as again
> In pangs, and Nature gave a second groan,
> Sky lour'd and muttering Thunder, some sad drops
> Wept at completing of the mortal Sin
> Original.[3]

This was not pathetic fallacy on a grand scale, but referred to the belief that Adam's Fall had literally entailed the fall of the whole creation: 'this wretched Carcass of the World' differs from its prelapsarian state 'as a vile Dungeon does, from a Royal and Magnificent Palace'.[4] The belief had scriptural warrant in Genesis 3:17 ('cursed is the ground for thy sake') and such supporting passages as Romans 8:22 ('The whole creation groaneth and travaileth together in pain until now').

By the early modern period, a fairly clear and comprehensive picture had been constructed of what the fall of nature involved. Some of the elements of this picture are to be found in the Bible itself: the existence of weeds and thistles, for example (Genesis 3:18). By a sort of free association, we also have poisonous plants, venomous snakes and insects, 'caterpillars, flies, fleas and bedbugs'.[5] Other aspects of the fall of nature seem to owe more to the classical myth of the decline of the Golden Age.[6] The perpetual spring of Eden gave way to the succession of the seasons, and with the seasons we have intemperate weather. Milton tells us that wind, mist, ice and snow are all products of the Fall.[7]

The myth of the fall of nature was incorporated into the occult tradition. The Behmenist Thomas Tryon agreed with Milton that the Fall had introduced 'turbulent fierce Storms, violent Winds, Rain, Snow and Hail, and all other unkind and unseasonable Weather'. This was the product of the 'evil Center' of the fallen Magia, Boehme's wrathful First Principle, which Adam's Fall released from its proper subordination to the merciful Second Principle. Now 'All things are in pain, seeking and groaning with the highest Desire, to obtain the Eternal Unity, not being capable of Rest, till they are swallowed up in it'.[8] Jacob Boehme described the lamentable condition of the world reduced to ruins by the Fall:

> Untowardness is found to be in all Creatures, biting, tearing, worrying, and hurting one another, and such Enmity, Strife, and Hatred, in all Creatures; . . . every Thing is so at odds with itself, as we see it to be not only in the living Creatures, but also in the Stars, Elements, Earth, Stones, Metals, in Wood, Leaves, and Grass, there is a Poison and Malignity in all Things.[9]

It was clear to William Law that 'the Strife of Properties, of *Thick* against *Thin*, *Hard* against *Soft*, *Hot* against *Cold*, &c had no Existence till Angels fell, that is till they turned from God to work with Nature'.[10] Francis Lee thought that 'all inferior Nature could not but suffer from the original Taint contracted by our first Parents, to whom the same was made subject; and by them subjected, consequently, to Vanity'.[11] Before the Fall animals had tamely done the Protoplasts' bidding, but now they flee from humans:

> The Beasts no longer them obey, if nigh
> They come, they dread them, and away they flye.[12]

Animals, of course, had little to fear from prelapsarian man, who was a vegetarian.[13] With the Fall, animals lost their harmonious relations not only with humanity, but also with each other. Before that catastrophe,

> The Lion with the Lamb did play, the Bear rob'd
> Not the Bees, nor Sheep the Wolf did Fear.[14]

Now, however, animals are 'in bitterness and rage one against another'.[15]

The esoteric understanding of the fall of nature needs to be understood in the context of occult cosmogonies. There are different cosmogonic myths in occult thought, but they are all characteristically procreationist rather than creationist. Everything had originally existed in Chaos, which was

> A Masse confused darkeley clad,
> That in itself all nature had.

This was 'The first matter, mother of all'.[16] Like Paracelsus, most occultists identified this *prima materia* with the waters of Genesis over the face of which the Spirit of God had moved in the creation.[17] According to Philalethes, the creation was an act in which God's Spirit penetrated the primal waters 'with his heavenly quickening power'.[18] Thomas Vaughan thought that light, which 'is properly the life of everything', had impregnated the first matter.[19] The process of creation was like 'the *Incubation* of a *Hen* upon her *Eggs*', in which God 'did . . . hatch the *Matter*, and bring out the *secret Essences*, as a *Chick* is brought out of the *shell*'.[20] There is some disagreement among occultists about whether Chaos was created by God or was coeternal with the divine being; 'the Point', Vaughan conceded, 'is obscure', although he seems to have favoured the latter opinion.[21] For Jacob Boehme, 'CHAOS is God himself',[22] and creation therefore proceeds *ex deo*. Basil Valentine regarded the *prima materia* as part of the created order,[23] a conception which represents creation as *ex nihilo*. According to Paracelsus, this 'Great Mystery' was not itself created, but an eternal feminine counterpart to God.[24] In Paracelsian thought the cosmogonic process proceeds by way of separation, with God separating the elements out from the primal waters.[25] Occultists understood the creation as an ongoing process of generation rather than a single act occurring at a definite point in the past. The forces governing this process were the sun and moon, which were 'two Magicall Principles'. There is 'a little Sun, and a little Moon' in everything,[26] and these solar and lunar principles are 'the conjugall Mystery of Heaven and Earth'.[27] The power of begetting appertained to the sun, but this needed to be 'tempered with the moisture of the Moon his Wife, to make it apt for generation'.[28]

A procreationist idiom was omnipresent in occult writings. According to the *Zohar*, 'When the upper world was filled and became pregnant, it brought forth two children together, a male and a female, these being heaven and earth after a supernal pattern'.[29] Dutoit-Membrini thought that the Elohim were intermediate between God and the creation; each of the Elohim had its own Virgin, through which the Holy Spirit brought the creation into being. Life, according to Restif de la Bretonne, 'is the product of the ineffable copulation of God, firstly and essentially male, with nature, firstly and essentially female'. Restif believed that the planets were sexual beings whose intercourse produced 'cometoplanets'.[30] Similarly, Charles Fourier thought that planets were hermaphroditic creatures whose northern poles produced male fluid, while the southern poles produced female fluid. By means of these fluids a planet copulates either with itself or with other planets.[31]

The vitalist assumptions underlying these bizarre speculations can be found throughout occult thought. The whole cosmos is itself a living creature. Thomas Vaughan tells us that 'the *Texture* of the *universe* clearly discovers its *animation*'.[32] The world around us can be understood as a vast womb in which everything is gestating. Even minerals undergo 'generation and parturation',[33] and metals are in fact 'vegetable things'.[34] Creation is an act of conception, understood in terms of traditional obstetrics: God gives form to Chaos, just as the male seed gives form to the female seed or menses.[35] The Fall is a partial reversal of this process, a return to confusion. Creation is also a nuptial union, represented in a way familiar in early modern conduct books: just as the wife is properly subordinated to her husband, creation should be subordinated to God.[36] The fall of nature is simply a breakdown of this subordination. Alchemy is a sort of cosmic marriage guidance service, enabling the reunion of God and Chaos.

It is with the Fall that matter enters into the world. In Paracelsian thought, the world has fallen from the permanence of the Yliaster, the first realisation of the Great Mystery at the heart of creation, into the materiality and temporality of the Cagastrum, the cosmos as we know it.[37] It was by Lucifer's fall, Saint-Georges de Marsais informs us, that 'chaos was produced, which was the gross matter of which this world was formed'. Cagliostro wrote that 'after the Fall, the harmony of the universe was corrupted, and man plunged into matter'. Matter, according to Bathilde d'Orléans, duchess of Bourbon, was a condensation of Luciferic light.[38] William Law thought that 'all the *Matter* or *Materiality* of this World, is the effect of Sin, and could have its beginning from nothing else'.[39]

There was, however, no absolute distinction between matter and spirit. Francis Mercury van Helmont regarded matter as the result of a 'coalition or clinging together' of spiritual monads.[40] Lady Conway thought that matter was a 'thicker and grosser' form of spirit, the distinction between the two being 'only modal and gradual, not essential or substantial'.[41] A similar understanding of matter recommended itself to George Cheyne, who tells us that 'a *material* Substance is an infinitely condensed, or incrassated, *spiritual* Substance'.[42] Cheyne's views were echoed in the early twentieth century by McGregor Mathers, a leading light of the Order of the Golden Dawn: 'Matter and Spirit are only opposite poles of the same universal substance.'[43] In the eighteenth century, Martines de Pasqually thought that matter was an illusion created by the Fall. Louis de Saint-Martin, on the other hand, suggested that matter had been created by the fallen angels, which would imply its independent reality. Elsewhere, however, Saint-Martin agreed with Martines that 'Matter is deceptive and void . . . spirit is everything.'[44]

Luther thought that the sun had been much brighter before it was tarnished by Adam's sin.[45] On the other hand, there is a sense in which the powers of the heavenly bodies were augmented by the Fall. According to Milton, it was with Adam's transgression that man became subject to the influence of the stars; before then, it was man who ruled the heavenly bodies.[46] This was a commonplace doctrine in occult thought. Jacob Boehme tells us that the Created Spirit of Man . . . rules . . . over and in the Virtue of the Spirit of the Stars and Elements very mightily, as in that which is its proper own. But in the Fall of *Adam* we lost this great Power, when we left Paradise and went into the third Principle, into the Matrix of this World, which presently held us captive in Restraint.[47]

The validity of judicial astrology, according to Mungo Murray, was based on the fact that 'corruption has invaded all & the body of man as others terrestrial became subject to ye celestial power'.[48] Thomas Tryon thought that people 'by their Uncleanness and Sinful Methods attract and draw the venomous Nature and Dispositions out of all the Stars, Elements, and all Undergraduated things'.[49]

Astrology merely reflected the fact that man was a microcosm. As Tryon explained, 'there is an Astrology within Man, as well as without him. A microcosmical Sun and Moon and all the rest of the Planets we carry about us.'[50] The fall of nature was explicable in terms of man's original existential identity with the cosmos. Gerrard Winstanley observed that 'In the beginning of time the whole Creation lived in man, and man lived in his Maker. . . . But when man began to fall out of his Maker . . . the creature fell out of him.'[51] Man is a signature of the world and the world of man. Both originally were signatures of God, but since the Fall neither man nor the world are adequate in signifying the divine being. This disjunction between signifier and signified is the meaning of the Fall in occult thought. Language played an important role in occult understandings of the cosmogonic process. In the *Zohar*, the creation proceeded through an arrangement of the letters of the alphabet, with which God had played for 2,000 years before deciding that *bereshith bara* ('in the beginning') should open the cosmic drama.[52] For Raymond of Sebonde, each creature is a letter made by God, man being the principal letter.[53] Occult linguistics centred on the doctrine of a prelapsarian language of nature in which there was a perfect correspondence between signifier and signified: '*Adam* therefore that gave the first names to things, knowing the influences of the heavens, and properties of all things, gave them all names according to their natures . . . which names indeed contain in them wonderful powers of the thing signified.'[54] For John Webster, the fall of nature is a sort of cosmic dyslexia. Every creature is a letter in 'the great unsealed book of God', 'but alas! who spells them aright, or conjoyns them so together that they may perfectly read all that is therein contained'. Before the Fall, the names Adam gave to the creatures had been fully expressive of their essence, and it was through his linguistic competence that Adam exercised his dominion over the world. Language has subsequently degenerated, and words are now without efficacy. Man's role in the cosmic drama is one of regaining his prelapsarian understanding of the signatures of all things. Hence, care should be 'taken for the recovery and restauration of the Catholique language in which lies hid all the rich treasury of natures admirable and excellent secrets'.[55]

The Fall in Christian thought implies the Redemption; if the creation had fallen with the first Adam, it would be redeemed by the second Adam. At the end of time, 'The creatures shall appear in their primitive beauty and goodness, wherein they were created, being all in subjection, and useful to man.'[56] This restoration of all things to their prelapsarian purity was foretold by Paul: 'the creature itself shall be delivered from the bondage of corruption into the glorious liberty of the children of God' (Romans 8:21). Similarly, in the Book of Revelation 21:1, we are promised 'a new heaven and a new earth'. Despite these scriptural passages and the Reformers' penchant for literalism, the idea of the redemption of nature is not very prominent in mainstream Reformation thought. Although Romans 8:21 had been understood in the Middle Ages to include the whole world, in Reformation thought Paul's 'creature' was often interpreted as simply meaning 'man'.[57] Both Luther and Calvin believed that there had been a literal fall of nature, and both accepted the notion of some sort of restoration. According to Calvin, 'Christ will come to drive away everything hurtful from the world, and to restore to its former beauty the world which lay under the curse.'[58] Nevertheless, in the Reformers' austerely theocentric understanding of the afterlife, everything tended to be absorbed into the beatific vision of God, leaving little room for notions of a renewed earth.[59] Both mentors of Protestant Europe were prone to interpret passages referring to the redemption of nature in a purely allegorical way. For Luther and Calvin, Isaiah's prophecy that the wolf would lie down with the lamb is simply a representation of the harmony that would exist between Christians.[60] Isaiah had foretold that the sun would become brighter at the end of time, but Luther thought that to take this literally was 'the work of insane preachers'.[61]

The idea of a redemption of nature achieved its fullest expression in the less orthodox theology of the occult sciences. Writers like Paracelsus were prepared to understand the redemption of nature literally: 'It is opposed to all true philosophy to say that flowers lack their own eternity. They may perish and die here; but they will reappear in the restitution of all things. Nothing has been created out of the great mystery which will not inhabit a form beyond the aether'.[62] Henry Vaughan addressed God in one of his poems, saying

> Thou shalt restore trees, beasts and men
> When thou shalt make all new again.[63]

This literalism was a result of the occult emphasis on the doctrine of man as microcosm and microtheos. The doctrine was an essential part of the intellectual equipment of the age, but it was applied most thoroughly in alchemical, Hermetic and Cabalist circles. Whereas many writers tended to use the concept as a metaphor, with the Renaissance occult revival there was a move to a more literal understanding.[64] The restoration of nature in occult thought was seen as a magical act on the part of man rather than a forensic act on God's part. The underlying attitude is autoplastic, seeking control over the world by 'self-manipulation' instead of 'by operating directly on the external environment'.[65] Cosmic redemption was simply the most general instance of one of the basic laws of magic, the law of contiguity. In its simplest form, this law suggests that the part contains the whole.[66] It follows from this that an act performed on one part of an organism will produce effects on the whole. Man is a part of the cosmos: an operation performed on or in him will therefore affect the entire universe. Since the great world around us is simply a reflection of the little world within, changes in the spiritual state of man are accompanied by changes in the physical state of the universe.

Thomas Tryon believed that 'The Body of Man is the Human Ground or Earth, which is as it were a Circle; in which is contained all the spiritual Powers, Forms and Principles of Nature'.[67] Since man is a microcosm, it is by turning 'the Eye of the Mind inwardly' that he is to rehabilitate nature:

> when he beholds any Individual Form, Figure or Shape, he Sees and Penetrates into the Center of that thing, and distinguishes the inward Nature and Complexion, and what Form or Quality has the Government and Signature, by which knowledge and true Sight he can put it to that use that God and his Handmaid Nature ordained it.[68]

Valentin Weigel assures us that with our inner heaven, which is the Spirit of God, 'we may shake off and drive away all the provocations of the evill ascendents of naturall stars'.[69] According to Paracelsus 'the stars of the microcosm rule over and govern the stars of heaven. For never forget that God has created the planets and all other stars not to rule over and govern man, but to obey him as do all other created things.'[70] In these terms the redemption of both man and nature involves a restoration of our inner stars to their rightful domination over the outward stars. Although they often used the idiom of astrology, the attitude of occult mystics should not be confused with a simple astrological determinism. In contrast to the 'fatalism and rigidity' of astrology itself, alchemy was based on a 'concept of dynamism and flux'.[71] The dominion of the stars is a function of the depravity of humanity, and underlying the occult position is a radical voluntarism that goes far beyond the traditional astrological formula that *stellae inclinant, non necessitant*. The relationship between the stars and man was one of reciprocal action. According to Paracelsus the cosmos, like man, consisted of body and soul, and it was through the soul of the universe that human beings could influence its body.[72] If man had been subjected to the heavenly bodies by his immersion in material existence, spiritual regeneration offered the possibility of gaining control over the stars, and thereby over nature as a whole.[73] Agrippa insisted that evil did not come from the stars themselves, but from man, who 'by reason of his unlikeness with the heavenly things receiveth hurt, whence he ought to reap benefit'.[74] Saint-Martin thought that 'man has it in him to raise above the astral [powers] everything which belongs to his being as well as his association'.[75]

Whereas mainstream eschatological thinking emphasised the passivity of man's role in the fulfilment of history, the alchemist envisaged man as participating in the redemption of nature. 'Man must bring everything to perfection', Paracelsus tells us, 'This work of bringing things to their perfection is called alchemy.'[76] As Robert Barnes has argued, Paracelsian nature mysticism envisaged 'an inner transformation that would be reflected in the phenomenal world'.[77] The alchemical project is the salvation of both man and nature,[78] and the alchemical process itself is 'a microcosmic reconstitution of the creation, in other words a re-creation'.[79] God himself was a sort of alchemist who, as Sendivogius wrote, 'will one day calcine' the elemental earth and 'create out of it a new crystalline earth'.[80] If alchemy envisaged the regeneration of the world, it did not regard this as an event that would occur only in the future. Cosmic regeneration is an ongoing process, 'For nothing that is created, or born, is at rest, but daily undergoes increase on the part of Nature, until it becomes that which is created and ordained to be the treasure of all mankind.' Thus, 'the suffering, disease and imperfection brought not only upon man, but also upon plants and animals, by the Fall of Adam, found a remedy in that precious gift of Almighty God, which is called the Elixir, and Tincture'.[81]

The elixir, tincture and treasure of all mankind all refer to Christ. The whole creation is said to be becoming the treasure of all mankind, implying its deification through Christ. Since occultists are often mistaken for pantheists, it is perhaps worthwhile to stress the obvious: this is not pantheism, since the world is not seen as being God, but as becoming him. Technically, the occult position is closer to panentheism than pantheism: God contains the world, but not as the totality of his being.[82] 'Panentheism' is a term that was introduced into theology by the Swedenborgian Freemason and Idealist philosopher K. C. F. Krause. For the occultist the world is in God, but only just; since the Fall much of it has spilled out of the divine being. Perhaps more significant than esoteric panentheism, however, is the tendency to what has been called 'panenanthropism', the subsuming of the objective world in the human subject.[83] The result is a mystical humanism which functions as the basis of the redemption of the world. The belief that nature would be redeemed through its correspondence with both man and Christ can be found in the thought of Marsilio Ficino. Christ is a universal *Humanitas*, a sort of Platonic form of humanity. Since man is a microcosm, Christ is also the form of nature, and it is because of this that human beings are able to bring about a cosmic redemption.[84] The deification of nature through Christ is a doctrine which survived in Romantic illuminism. Novalis, for example, suggested the possibility of 'a continuous redemption in nature': 'If God could become man, then he can also become stone, plant, animal, and element.'[85]

In purely alchemical tracts the notion of the deification of the world is hidden in symbolism, but several writers in Interregnum England are more explicit. According to Gerrard Winstanley, 'the body of the first man was a representation of the whole creation, and did corrupt it; so the body of Christ was a representation of the whole creation, and brings all into the unity of the Father again'.[86] Richard Coppin believed that God's image was becoming manifest again in the natural world, renewing the world by transcending the duality of spirit and flesh.[87] Peter Sterry informs us that Christ 'is the Truth of all Things. Every Thing is seen in Him according to its most Right, most Proper, and solidest Appearance.' Just as the soul gives 'Shape, Life, and Lustre' to the body, 'So shall the Heavenly Man sprout forth through the Earth, as an Vniversall Paradise; sending forth all Earthly Formes, as Revived Plants, by a New Growth, out of Himselfe.'[88] For William Law, the fall of nature was constituted by its alienation from Christ: 'Wherever Christ is not, there is the *Wrath* of Nature, or Nature left to itself and its own tormenting Strength of Life, to feel nothing in itself but the vain restless Contrariety of its own working Properties.'[89]

Alongside the tradition of the fall and restoration of nature was another tradition, one which represented nature as already redeemed. Men like the sixteenth-century herbalist John Gerard could discern the shadow of Paradise in the world around them; plants, he thought, 'were such delights as man in the perfectest state of his innocence did erst enjoy'.[90] The redeemed status of nature is implicit in the belief that 'God has stamped his image on every creature.'[91] Nature might be seen as not merely redeemed, but also as redemptive. In the Middle Ages Heinrich Suso was already speaking with the voice that we will hear spoken again by later occultists and Romantics: 'I traverse heaven and earth, the universe and the abyss, forests and fields, mountains and valleys: they all fill my ear with the echo of the vast concert of your infinite praise.'[92] In the seventeenth century, Jacob Boehme believed that 'if we look upon the starry Heaven, the Elements and living Creatures, also upon Trees, Herbs, and Grass, we may behold in the material World, the similitude of the paradisical incomprehensible World'.[93] As John Everard informs us, 'every creature . . . plainly represents and speaks out God with a loud voyce'.[94] For Thomas Tryon, 'The wonderful Creator hath Made and created all things like himself, for He and the whole Off-spring of Heaven and Earth are but One, he is not divided from his Works, but is in the very Center of them, by which he doth support and preserve them.'[95] Thomas Vaughan thought that 'There is nothing on Earth though never so simple, so vile, and abject in the sight of man, but it beares witness of God, even to that *abstruse Mystery*, his *Vnity* and *Trinity*.' The Spirit of God is 'in all the *Great World*', just as it is in the little world of man: 'For God *breathes continually*, and passeth through all things like an *Aire* that refresheth.'[96]

The redemptive possibilities of nature are given one of their finest expressions in the poetry of Henry Vaughan. In one of his poems Vaughan described Adam's first encounter with the world after the Fall:

> Things here were strange unto him: sweat, and till
> 　All was a thorn or weed,
> Nor did those last, but (like himself) died still
> 　As soon as they did *seed*;
> They seemed to quarrel with him; for that act
> 　That fell him, foiled them all,
> He drew the curse upon the world, and cracked
> 　The whole frame with his fall.

This seems like a conventional account of the fall of nature, but Vaughan continues in a way which suggests that the natural world may not be fallen after all:

> 　　　. . . each day
> 　The valley or the mountain
> Afforded visits, and still *Paradise* lay
> 　In some green shade or fountain.
> Angels lay *leiger* here; each bush, and cell,
> 　Each oak, and highway knew them,
> Walk but the fields, or sit down at some *well*,
> 　And he was sure to view them.[97]

Like Blake after him, Vaughan saw a world of angels underlying the phenomenal world:

> My God, when I walk in those groves,
> 　And leaves thy spirit doth still fan,
> I see in each shade that there grows
> 　An Angel talking with a man.[98]

It has been observed that Vaughan 'repeatedly compares humanity's indifference to its Creator with Nature's readier response'.[99] For Vaughan nature still stands in the closest proximity to God: 'Thy other Creatures in this Scene / Thee only aim and mean'. This is why Vaughan longs to be 'some Bird or Star'.[100] Vaughan's environment seemed to sing God's praises constantly:

> There's not a *spring*,
> Or *leaf* but hath his morning-hymn; each *bush*
> And oak doth know I AM.[101]

Vaughan believed that while the rest of nature had its 'set *ascents*' to God, man 'Sleeps at the ladders foot'.[102] This is, of course, a reversal of the traditional use of the ladder image, which generally places man on a higher rung than the rest of the creation.[103] The world is a pathway to the divine, and in nature man is given 'lectures for his eye and ear': 'All things here shew him heaven'.[104] God 'is in all things, though invisibly',[105] and in viewing the natural world

> Thou canst not miss his praise; each *tree, herb, flower,*
> Are shadows of his *wisdom* and his *power*.[106]

Vaughan can see the wonders of the world about him 'And in those weaker glories spy / Some shadows of eternity'.[107] Like Boehme, Vaughan believed in a double Incarnation, Christ being embodied both in his human form and in the cosmos.[108] Vaughan foreshadows both Blake and Wordsworth in his attitude to childhood, which he saw 'as a time when the veil between the material and spiritual worlds is kept transparent by innocence'.[109] This is an attitude which all three poets shared with Boehme.[110] Vaughan is also close to Boehme in his use of the symbolism of light and darkness to express cosmic harmony; like the German theosopher, he regarded darkness as 'necessary for the success of its opposite'.[111]

Georgia Christopher has argued that Vaughan's 'vision of nature's sentience' derives 'from a piety that owes a great deal to Calvin' rather than to the occult tradition.[112] Yet, though Calvinists employed the notion of a Book of Nature, there is nothing in orthodox Calvinism to suggest the intimate spiritual bond between inner self and external world which we find in Vaughan's poetry. English Calvinists were in fact somewhat less favourable to the belief in the redemption of all creatures than was Calvin himself.[113] Vaughan's understanding of such passages as Romans 8:19–22 is thoroughly animistic in a way that surely derives from Hermeticism.[114] Although the Book of Nature image was ubiquitous, Vaughan's contemporaries clearly associated the idea that 'this visible world is but a picture of the invisible' with 'the Philosophy of *Hermes*'.[115] Vaughan's twin-brother, Thomas, was one of the leading Hermeticists of Interregnum England, and though Henry's outlook appears more orthodox, his poems are nevertheless permeated by occult modes of thought.[116] Henry Vaughan translated two works by the Paracelsian Heinrich Nolle, and these were published by the Behmenist Humphrey Blunden.[117] Given his known proximity to the occult tradition, any contextualisation of his work that omits this aspect is surely deficient.

It is impossible to read Vaughan's poetry without being reminded of the Romantics, for whom nature was a major source of both inspiration and consolation. When Beethoven declared that 'Every tree seems to say, Holy, Holy' we are hearing an authentic echo of the occult tradition.[118] Romanticism, however, transformed and added to esotericism as much as it preserved it. Restif de la Bretonne thought that 'there is nothing in the world which more effectively puts man back in his natural state than a free countryside, rustic, surrounded with woods or wastes'.[119] Restif was a dabbler in occult thought, but this sentiment owes more to Rousseau than it does to esotericism. It expresses the well-known Romantic tendency to contrast nature favourably with civilisation, and perhaps indicates how the transition from traditional occultism to Romanticism reflects a changing social orientation: the Romantics are more clearly protesting against the present constitution of society than their esoteric forebears. Already in the early eighteenth century certain attitudes to nature which derive from mystical thought had become detached from their roots, and their presence does not necessarily indicate a close relationship to esotericism. The Earl of Shaftesbury played an important role in popularising the view that nature was 'All-loving and All-lovely, All-divine!'[120] Shaftesbury can be linked tenuously with the esoteric tradition, since his thought was inspired in part by the Cambridge Platonists; but it is a weak link, and one that was even weaker in the case of later Shaftesburians like Joseph Addison. Alexander Pope wrote that

> All are parts of one stupendous whole,
> Whose body nature is, and God the soul.[121]

Here we might be reading an occult philosopher, but in fact we are not. By the late eighteenth century, a responsiveness to the sublimity of nature was so pervasive that it indicates nothing about its particular provenance. William Godwin remarked with admiration about Mary Wollstonecraft that 'When she walked amidst the wonders of nature, she was accustomed to converse with her God.'[122] Neither Godwin nor Wollstonecraft, of course, could be claimed for the occult tradition. Even when we can trace a direct descent from occult thought to Romanticism, there are often important differences. In the case of writers like Coleridge, for example, there was a clear attempt to rationalise occultism, to turn it into something like a 'philosophy' in the modern sense of the word. By the age of the Romantics, moreover, Nature was threatening to replace God as the object of mystical sensibility as the divinity it signified became incorporated into the sign itself. The essential attitude of the Romantics to nature is preserved in the twentieth century by the theologian Paul Tillich. Both 'man and nature belong together in their created glory, in their tragedy and in their salvation'. For Tillich, however, the emphasis is on how nature can save man rather than how man can save nature: 'Therefore commune with nature! Become reconciled with nature after your estrangement from it. Listen to nature in quietness and you will find its heart. It will sound forth the glory of its divine ground.'[123]

Among the English Romantics, it was William Blake who was most thoroughly rooted in traditional occultism. Blake's attitude to nature is the subject of some scholarly controversy. He once lamented that 'Natural Objects did & now do, deaden & obliterate Imagination in me.'[124] Such passages lend support to the view that Blake came to see nature as 'intrinsically evil'.[125] The problem with this interpretation is that nature had no independent status for Blake; therefore it could not have a moral status of its own. It is not necessary to agree with Stuart Curran that Blake was 'a Berkleyan'[126] to recognise that his outlook was fundamentally idealist; as Kathleen Raine observed, for Blake 'all natural phenomena have their existence in consciousness'.[127] This is why, in the 'Proverbs from Hell', he asserts that 'Where man is not nature is barren.'[128] Man's alienation from nature (which is what gives it the appearance of ontological independence) merely reflects a failure of imaginative vision:

> 'What', it will be Questioned, 'When the Sun rises, do you not see a round disk of fire somewhat like a Guinea?' Oh no, no, I see an Innumerable company of the Heavenly host crying 'Holy, Holy, Holy is the Lord God Almighty'. I question not my Corporeal or Vegetative Eye any more than I would question a Window concerning a Sight. I look thro' it & not with it.[129]

Blake saw a spiritual significance underlying the natural world (one which constitutes its ontological reality), but this significance is obscured by sensory perception:

> How do you know but ev'ry Bird that cuts the airy way,
> Is an immense world of delight, clos'd by your senses five?[130]

In contrast to the sensationalist psychology of Lockean empiricists, Blake regards the senses as limits to, rather than means of, perception.

J. G. Davies thought that for Blake 'the source of all evil was . . . the separateness of the individual soul from the rest of the universe – in other words, self-consciousness'.[131] In a sense this is true, but we then have to ask what are the roots of this self-consciousness. Blake belongs to the strand of occult thought that emphasises the epistemological aspects of the fall and redemption of nature. The natural world is not fallen in itself, but through a failure to see it correctly: 'If the doors of perception were cleansed, everything would appear as it is, infinite.'[132] Blake's project is

> To see a World in a Grain of Sand
> And a Heaven in a Wild Flower,
> Hold Infinity in the palm of your hand,
> And Eternity in an hour.[133]

Blake's Isaiah tells us that his 'senses discover'd the infinite in everything'.[134]

Blake takes to an extreme what has been called the 'perceptual miraculism' of the Romantics, the idea that the fallenness of the world is to be repaired 'through a fresh way of looking at it'.[135] For Blake, in order to see the world correctly it is necessary to have a 'double vision':

> For double the vision my eyes do see,
> And a double vision is always with me.

> With my inward Eye 'tis an old Man grey:
> With my outward a Thistle across my way.[136]

Double vision is not a passive process: it is equivalent to imagination, the faculty of divine creativity that, for Blake, is the core of our being. With single vision 'Some see Nature all Ridicule & Deformity, ... & Some Scarce see Nature at all. But to the Eyes of the Man of Imagination, Nature is Imagination itself.'[137] Double vision is a childlike characteristic, and it has been suggested that one of the purposes of the consciously naïve style of Blake's *Songs of Innocence* is to renew the reader's childlike apprehension of reality.[138] Describing one of his visions to Thomas Butts, Blake informed him that

> I remain'd as a Child;
> All I ever had known
> Before me bright shone.[139]

Those with double vision realise that 'Mental Things are alone Real; what is call'd Corporeal, Nobody knows of its Dwelling Place: it is Fallacy, & its Existence an Imposture.'[140] Blake told Henry Crabb Robinson that 'Everything is Atheism which assumes the reality of the natural and unspiritual world.'[141] The things of this world only truly exist in Eternity: 'the Oak dies as well as the Lettuce, but Its eternal Image & Individuality never dies, but renews by its seed ... There Exist in that Eternal World the Permanent Realities of Every Thing which we see reflected in this Vegetable Glass of Nature.' According to Blake, 'Eternity Exists, and All things in Eternity, Independent of Creation which was an act of Mercy.'[142]

Blake can be regarded as an occult thinker in the fullest sense; Samuel Taylor Coleridge, on the other hand, occupies a more ambiguous position. He disparaged Behmenism as 'a mere Pantheism', but he also recognised the need for theosophy 'despite all the contempt squandered on poor Jacob Behmen and [William] Law'.[143] He regarded Boehme as 'indeed a Visionary in two very different senses of the word': he was often deluded, '*ast tenet umbra Deum*' ('but the shadow contains God'). Boehme belonged 'in the highest rank of original Thinkers'.[144] The occult philosophy, however, had more appeal to Coleridge in the slightly rationalised form of German Idealism. German Romantic philosophy altered the emotional tenor of esoteric speculation, but it preserved its essential structure. This can be seen by comparing Boehme's theosophy with Schelling's philosophy.[145] For Boehme, the Fall was constituted by Adam turning his imagination from the Second Principle of the godhead into the Third Principle, that in which material existence is manifested. Adam thus foresook God's will for his own self-will. As a consequence man is himself 'half dead' and immersed in a merely natural world.[146] Schelling simply provides a more secularised account of the same idea. Humanity is no longer 'in its central position in relation to things', no longer stands above things, but 'has become a thing' because it 'wanted itself as a particularity, demanded its *own* being (*Seyn*), and thus became the *same* as things'.[147]

Coleridge's thought on nature as a divine signifier is identical to that found in the occult tradition. He tells us that

> 'Tis the sublime of man,
> Our noontide Majesty, to know ourselves
> Parts and proportions of one wondrous whole!
>   . . . But 'tis God
> Diffused through all, that doth make all one whole.[148]

God is 'by symbols only seen', and according to Coleridge 'all visible things' are 'steps, that upward to their Father's throne / Lead gradual'. God is 'Nature's essence, mind, and energy', and the things of nature are the 'True impress each of their creating Sire'.[149] Looking at the world of nature, Coleridge tells his baby son that

> so shalt thou see and hear
> The lovely shapes and sounds intelligible
> Of that eternal language, which thy God
> Utters, who from eternity doth teach
> Himself in all, and all things in himself.[150]

For Coleridge, the universe is the 'choral echo' of 'the great I AM'.[151] As Richard Holmes observes, Coleridge regarded the 'continuous living inter-change' between man and nature as the source of 'joy', a term which had something of a mystical significance for the poet.[152]

Like Blake, Coleridge had an epistemological rather than an ontological approach to the fall of nature. Humanity is alienated from the cosmos because of a failure to achieve the 'intuition of things which arises when we possess ourselves, as one with the whole'. Instead 'we think of ourselves as separated beings, and place nature in antithesis to the mind, as object to subject, thing to thought, death to life'.[153] By locating the problem in the separation of subject and object, Coleridge clearly indicates his indebtedness to German Idealism, but the basic structure of the idea derives from the inner–outer discourse of the occult mystical tradition. We are really 'Monads of the infinite mind', but we have fallen into an atomised existence. Coleridge, however, perceives the possibility of reintegration, of making

> The whole one Self! Self, that no alien knows!
> Self, far diffused as Fancy's wing can travel!
> Self, spreading still! Oblivious of its own,
> Yet all of all possessing! This is Faith!
> This is the Messiah's destined victory!

Man and cosmos merge into the godhead again, and the soul becomes 'self-annihilated' in 'exclusive consciousness of God'.[154]

In moving from Blake to Coleridge we are passing from a fairly traditional occultism to a modernised version of the same world-view. Some of this world-view can also be found in Wordsworth's attitude to nature. The belief that natural phenomena are 'The types and symbols of eternity' would not be out of place in the work of any occult philosopher. Similarly, Wordsworth tells us that God sends himself 'into the breathing world / Through Nature and through every kind of life'.[155] But we might suspect Wordsworth, as Blake apparently did,[156] of losing any real sense of the divine signified in an idolatrous objectification of the mundane signifier. Wordsworth's outlook harmonises with illuminism, but it is detached from its historical roots. Even in its rationalised form of Idealist philosophy, occultism had little appeal for him; he thought that 'Coleridge had been spoilt for a poet by going to Germany' and dabbling in metaphysics.[157] Wordsworth's nature mysticism, if such it was, was a relatively untutored response of his youthful disposition rather than part of a coherent esoteric theology. He became increasingly orthodox as he grew older, and some of this change in outlook can be discerned in the revisions he made to *The Prelude*. Though Nature had been a 'softening mirror of the moral world' in 1805, by 1850 it was merely a source of 'Apt illustrations' of this other dimension. In this respect, Wordsworth's personal development recapitulated the changes in eighteenth-century culture generally. By the end of the century the doctrine of cosmic correspondence had become diluted, forming a vague notion of 'divine analogy' drained of any inherent reality: 'Correspondences had become a phase of psychology, not of ontology.'[158] Traces of the occult philosophy can also be found among the American Transcendentalists, above all in the work of Amos Bronson Alcott. In 1835, Alcott wrote that man needs to be 'illuminated by a faith that perceiveth in all things and in all beings the same sustaining, upholding Life that quickeneth and filleth his own conscious being'. Like any occultist, he thought that 'Nothing can show itself in the exterior that has not a prior being and shaping within.' The external world is simply an expression of an inner spiritual reality: 'Matter is a revelation of Mind, the flesh of the Spirit, the world of God.'[159] Accordingly, man need only look within himself to discover the world: 'The knowledge of his own being includes, in its endless circuit, the alphabet of all else. It is a universe wherein all else is imaged.'[160] For Alcott, 'God, man, nature are a divine synthesis whose parts it is impiety to sunder.[161] In Alcott we also encounter a practical compassion towards his fellow creatures. He was a vegan, and he established a utopian community (Fruitlands) in which animals were not exploited even for purposes of draught.[162]

A responsiveness to the sublimity of nature permeated Western culture in the early nineteenth century. For Joseph von Eichendorff, 'A song is sleeping in all things'.[163] The natural world played a sanctifying role in life:

Da steht im Wald geschrieben
Ein stilles, ernstes Wort
Von rechtem Tun und Lieben,
Und was des Menschen Hort.[164]

(There is written in the wood a quiet, solemn word about right action and loving, and of what man's treasure is.) The world is a bridge to God 'over the stream of time'.[165] Not all the Romantics, however, shared this benign vision of nature. Balzac argued that 'the little we know of the laws of the visible world enables us to conceive of the immensity of higher spheres'. Nevertheless, he emphasised 'the immeasurable distances that separate the things of the earth from the things of heaven', and his spirituality involved an explicit disparagement of the mundane order, giving us a choice between 'heaven or the muck-heap'.[166]

A more sombre attitude towards nature can also be found in the poetry of Victor Hugo. It is clear that Hugo had inherited the panvitalism of the occult discourse on the natural world:

C'est que vents, ondes, flammes,
Arbres, roseaux, rochers, tout vit! Tout est pleine d'âmes.

(The winds, waves, flames, trees, streams, rocks, everything lives! Everything is full of souls.) For Hugo, no less than for other occultists and Romantics, the whole of nature speaks meaningfully:

Crois-tu que l'eau du fleuve et les arbres des bois,
S'ils n'avaient rien à dire, élèveraient la voix? . . .
Crois-tu que la nature énorme balbutie,
Et que Dieu se serait, dans son immensité,
Donné pour tout plaisir, pendant l'éternité,
D'entendre bégayer une sourde-muette?[167]

(Do you think that the water of the river and the trees of the woods, if they had nothing to say, would raise their voice? . . . Do you think that enormous nature mumbles, and that in his immensity God would give himself over for sheer pleasure, during eternity, to listening to the stammering of a deaf-mute?) According to Hugo, 'the plant wills, then it has a me, the universe wills, then it has a God'.[168] With Hugo, however, we encounter a more pessimistic attitude than in the writings of other Romantics. Nature is still decidedly fallen, and not at all redemptive:

Tout globe obscure gémit, toute terre est une bagne
Où la vie en pleurant, jusqu'au jour du réveil,
Vient écrouer l'esprit qui tombe du soleil.[169]

(Every obscure globe, every earth is a penal colony where life crying, until the day of awakening, comes to imprison the spirit which falls from the sky.) Like earlier occultists, Hugo believed that matter originated in evil, and that the gross body was a product of sin.[170] He tells us that 'Animals are nothing but the forms of our virtues and vices, wandering before our eyes, the visible phantoms of our souls.'[171] Hugo's attitude to nature is located within a belief in reincarnation:

> L'assassin pâlirait s'il voyait sa victime;
> C'est lui . . .
> >   Tout méchant
> Fait naître en expirant le monstre de sa vie,
> Qui le saisit.[172]

(The murderer would pale if he saw his victim: it's himself . . . Every evil-doer gives birth in expiring to the monster of his life, who seizes him.) Accordingly, Hugo regarded the natural world as a site of expiation and spiritual growth: 'The creation is a perpetual ascent, from the brute towards man, from man towards God.'[173] This pessimism about the natural world was not typical of Romanticism, and Hugo himself was not entirely devoid of a sense of the divinity within the cosmos:

> Vous habitez la seuil du monde châtiment.
> Mais vous n'êtes pas hors de Dieu complètement:
> Dieu, soleil dans l'azur, dans la cendre étincelle,
> N'est hors de rien; étant la fin universelle.

(You live on the threshold of the world of punishment. But you are not completely outside God: God, sun in the azure, spark in the cinder, is outside nothing, being the universal end.) Hugo tells us of God that

> L'éclair est son regard, autant que la rayon:
> Et tout, même le mal, est la création,
> Car le dedans du masque est encor la figure.[174]

(The lightning is his glance, no less than the ray: and everything, even evil, is the creation, for inside the mask is still the face.) In this assessment of evil Hugo recalls the Cabalist and Behmenist notion that it originates in a misbegotten impulse ultimately emanating from the divine being itself.

In some ways the Romantic rehabilitation of nature is illusory. When the Romantics saw the world, Maurice Bowra tells us, 'they seemed to be carried beyond it into a transcendental order of things'. Although Bowra thinks that they could do this only because 'they looked on the world around them with attentive and loving eyes',[175] this is clearly not to look at nature for itself, but only instrumentally, as a signifier of the divine. Much the same criticism could be made of occultist attitudes to nature. We might add that the mundane signifier sometimes seems not to point very far. As several critics have noted, there is a strongly solipsistic aspect to Wordsworth's worship of nature: 'The poet does not submit his individuality, passively and humbly, to the divine influx; rather it is his own individuality that appears to him deified.'[176] It is this, according to Gérard, that disqualifies Wordsworth from the title of mystic, but it is precisely this solipsistic attitude to nature that brings him close to occult mystical sensibilities. In this sense, a radical humanism appears to underlie both occultism and Romanticism. Romantic and occult discourses, however, tend to differ in a fundamental way. Romanticism, when it avoids degeneration into mere solipsism, removes man from the centre of the universe. The world is no longer responsive to his spirit: his spirit is (or should be) responsive to it. In this way, the occult philosophy and Romanticism develop a different concept of cosmic alienation. But this distinction is only relative, for already in esoteric thought there was a long tradition of the need for man to read the signs of nature correctly in order to achieve salvation.

Both the gnosis of the East and that of the West posit a transcendental self existing in 'immortality and freedom', but in the early modern Western tradition this transcendental self was to be realised through the practice of a this-worldly asceticism seeking an equally this-worldly fulfilment. That of the East, on the other hand, works through a radical detachment from the mundane order, a total renunciation of the world. These distinctive orientations are clearly not simply the product of the West's greater historical mastery over its material environment, since the divergence can be discerned long before Europe outstripped the Oriental cultures in economic development. In part the this-worldly outlook of Western gnostic religion is due to the fact that it was never the dominant discourse in European culture. Even in their spiritual quest, Europeans have been more inclined to turn their faces in the direction of the Land of Cockaigne than that of Nirvana. In their revulsion from a world of pain and illusion, Westerners have tended to seek the salvation of the empirical self of everyday life rather than its annihilation. Generally speaking, this salvation has been sought through a reconditioning of the world as well as a deconditioning of the self. It is this aspect of esotericism that led the occultists to play a complex role in the rise of modern science.

3   Science, magic and the occult

With the Fall, people had lost their dominion over nature, but not irretrievably. Like Faustus, the magician still could be 'Lord and commander of these elements'.[1] Shakespeare's Prospero boasted about his control over nature:

> I have bedimmed
> The noontide sun, called forth the mutinous winds,
> And 'twixt the green sea and the azured vault
> Set roaring war; to the dread rattling thunder
> Have I given fire, and rifted Jove's stout oak
> With his own bolt; the strong based promontory
> Have I made shake, and by the spurs plucked up
> The pine and cedar.[2]

Whether we consider Prospero's itemisation of his former achievements or Faustus's ambition to 'raise the wind, or rend the clouds',[3] the magician's claim to power is represented as performing the works of fallen nature. This, however, is to view magic from outside the occult tradition. It is true that some occultists seemed to share this negative attitude to magic. According to Pierre Poiret, human dominion over nature existed after the Fall only in the diabolic form of witchcraft.[4] Most occultists, however, would have agreed with Robert Turner that 'Magicke and Witchcraft are far differing Sciences.'[5] For an occultist, 'the science of Magic is not evil, for by the knowledge of it, evil may be eschewed and good followed'.[6] The word 'magician', according to Agrippa, 'doth not among learned men signify a sorceror, or one that is superstitious, or devilish; but a wise man, a priest, a prophet'.[7]

Mircea Eliade has observed that modern Western thought is dominated by the discovery 'that man is essentially a temporal and historical being'. Hence the preoccupation of Western thinkers with the factors conditioning existence. Eliade asserts that 'this problem of the "conditioning" of man . . . constitutes the central problem of Indian thought', but he adds that 'its corollory', the process of deconditioning, is 'rather neglected in the West'.[8] There is, however, a long tradition of meditation on the deconditioning process embodied in the Western gnostic tradition and its various occult descendants. The origins of this tradition are themselves to be found partly in Eastern thought,[9] and throughout its development it retained enough of a morphological similarity with its Eastern progenitor to be instantly recognisable as belonging to the same family of ideas. On the other hand, this family likeness has been attenuated by a process of miscegenation, and the Western preoccupation with this world surfaces even in its approach to non-conditioned being. The goal of the yogi's spiritual endeavour is a simple liberation from this world of illusion; the Western gnostic, at least in his later incarnations, seeks dominion over rather than release from the phenomenal world. Hence the different responses of East and West to magic. The yogi acquires various miraculous powers (*siddhis*) through his ascetic practices, but he must renounce these if he is to progress towards non-conditioned being: 'For as soon as the ascetic consents to make use of the magical forces gained by his disciplines, the possibility of acquiring new forces vanishes.' In Indian thought, 'all possession implies bondage to the thing possessed', and this is true of the *siddhis* as much as anything else.[10] For the Western occult mystic the magical powers conferred by his spiritual growth are welcomed for their utility rather than avoided as stumbling blocks.

The acquisition of magical power, however, depended on the renunciation of selfish ends. In medieval Hasidism, it was believed that the perfect Hasid had command over the elements 'as the true master of magical forces who can obtain everything precisely because he wants nothing for himself'.[11] This attitude survived into the nineteenth century; as the sage confesses in Balzac's *La Peau de chagrin*, 'I have had everything I wanted because I have learned to dispense with everything.'[12] Eliphas Lévi declared that 'Amorous, gluttonous, passionate, or idle magicians are impossible monstrosities . . . To will well, to will long, to will always, but never to lust after anything, such is the secret of power.'[13] It is true that works like Agrippa's *Three Books of Occult Philosophy* contain spells comparable to those of traditional magical handbooks like *The Book of Secrets* attributed to Albert the Great; and to this day works continue to be published promising magical ways of acquiring success in love or business. For the most part, however, the occult magician proposes a different end for himself than the working of love-magic or the acquisition of wealth. As Robert Turner observes, works like John Dee's *48 Claves Angelicae* were designed to be used 'to bring about great changes in the world and a new "state of perfection" in all things'.[14] Magic powers were gained by restoring the magician to the prelapsarian status of man as the complete image of his creator, thereby enabling him 'to participate in God's creative work'.[15] Magic is part of the redemptive process; through its use, man can redeem the creation from its bondage. Magi, according to Paracelsus, were 'natural saints', 'holy men in God who serve the forces of nature'.[16]

To restore man's prelapsarian dominion over nature was also a fundamental aspect of the Baconian scientific programme. The rise of modern science played an important role in the growth of the secular world-view. As William Shea argues, 'The Scientific Revolution consecrated a new method that was slowly to transform a civilization organized around Christianity into one centred on science.'[17] We might assume that this occurred by a simple process in which the scientific world-view grew by rejecting the religious one. This is the model of change posited by William Huffmann when he remarks that 'a new paradigm replaces the old by a process of total negation'.[18] Marx's representation of historical change, however, would seem to be more realistic: the new order grows in the womb of the old, and the conditions of one epoch actively develop those of the next. The modern, secularised world-view was nurtured by the religious conscious-ness of early modern Europe. This argument could be made in terms of orthodox Christianity. Robert Merton, for example, argued that Puritanism and Pietism played a role in the rise of modern science.[19] With Pietism, how-ever, we are coming close to the occult philosophy, and it is possible that early modern esotericism was of special importance in preparing the way for the Scientific Revolution. Frances Yates has argued that Renaissance Hermeticism is one of the contexts in which we can place the origins of modern science,[20] and similar arguments have been advanced by Charles Webster[21] and Allen G. Debus.[22]

Since its formulation, the 'Yates thesis' has been vigorously criticised. One criticism that has been made of it is that the notion of Hermeticism it employs is too vague. Charles Schmitt has minimised the importance of Hermeticism, stressing that 'It was Neoplatonism which served as a strong trunk onto which ideas derived from Hermetic, Orphic, Zoroastrian, Neopythagorean, Cabalistic and other sources could be drafted during the Renaissance, con-tinuing a tendency already begun in antiquity.'[23] It is certainly true that Yates lays too much emphasis on the Hermetic texts as such; and like Schmitt himself, she also exaggerates the importance of Neoplatonism, which was not necessarily the dominant ingredient in the very rich mix of early modern occultism. Other objections to Yates's thesis seem to be little more than an expression of an irrational faith in the inherently positivistic nature of the scientific enterprise. We tend to regard modern science as a system of knowl-edge dispelling superstition, a view which can be traced back to the propa-gandists of the New Philosophy themselves. Thomas Spratt, for example, wrote that experimental science had 'vanquish'd those wild inhabitants of the false worlds [fairies and apparitions], that used to astonish the minds of men'.[24] Despite such arguments, the boundaries of science and magic were far from being clearly drawn in early modern Europe. That science and the occult could easily coexist can be seen from the number of Oxford and Cambridge scholars who combined an interest in both in the late six-teenth and early seventeenth centuries.[25] Francis Bacon is hailed for his championing of the inductive method, which became programmatic for sub-sequent natural philosophers. Along with this method, however, Bacon also developed a highly speculative natural philosophy clearly indebted to the occult tradition. In fact, Bacon may have adopted the inductive method in an attempt to establish the validity of this philosophy.[26] Natural magic itself was professedly a system of natural causation, and even demonological handbooks could be regarded 'as contributions to scientific discourse'.[27] The occultists were fervent millenarians, and the widespread currency of millenarian expectations in the early modern period gave a special signifi-cance to the prophecy in Daniel 12:14 that there would be a revival of learn-ing in the last days, thus helping to constitute an ideology of scientific endeavour.[28] Millenarianism certainly underlay such groups as Johann Valentin Andreae's *Societas Christiana*, and possibly forms part of the back-ground to the growth of learned institutions like the Royal Society.[29] When men like Robert Boyle hoped that 'searchers into physical truths may cor-dially refer their attainments to the Glory of the Great Author of Nature, and to the Comfort of Mankind',[30] they were simply echoing a formula which had long been prefaced *ad nauseam* to most alchemical treatises. Boyle, the self-professed sceptical chemist, may not have been as averse to the alchemical tradition as was once assumed.[31] As Lotte Mulligan observes, 'If there is a problem about irreconcilable world views in seventeenth-century writers, the problem appears to be ours, not theirs.'[32]

Brian Vickers has argued that there was nothing new about Renaissance occultism, the implication being that if it was at the root of the Scientific Revolution this Revolution would have happened earlier. Vickers also alleges that the Neoplatonic and Hermetic texts were hostile to matter, and that occultists 'were never interested in matter for its own sake or in general terms'.[33] Neither of these arguments can withstand scrutiny. Even if we accept that there was nothing new in Renaissance occultism, it is still possible that it played an important role in the genesis of modern science. Ideas do not exist in isolation, and their significance depends as much on their context as their internal content. The context in which early modern occultism functioned certainly was new (unless we assume that the social, economic, political and intellectual conditions of Renaissance and Reformation Europe were identical to those of ancient Egypt). It is certainly possible that this new context activated latent elements of the occult philosophy that were favourable to the growth of modern science. It is not true, however, that there was nothing new about Renaissance occultism itself. The occult philosophy had changed in several ways, and was continuing to do so. Occultists, for example, were developing an increasingly positive attitude to the natural world, and this may have stimulated their desire to explore it. It is true that occultists 'were never interested in matter for its own sake', but Vickers is surely using the sort of underhand rhetorical device with which he charges Yates when he slips effortlessly into equating this with 'lack of interest in the physical world' *tout court*. This proposition can only be sustained by arbitrarily placing all scientists with known occult interests into the non-occult side of the balance. If, on the contrary, we recognise the esoteric enthusiasms of men like Newton, the clear empirical evidence is that occultists were interested in the physical world. Faivre notes that in the eighteenth century, the majority of illuminists 'occupied themselves with scientific works', citing Kirchberger, Eckartshausen, Novalis, Jung-Stilling and Saint-Martin as examples.[34] This is a judgement that could easily be applied to the seventeenth century, and, even if we exclude scientists from the balance, we only have to glance at the works of occultists with no developed scientific interests to know that the physical world preoccupied them.

It is still sometimes asserted that occult mysticism involved a repudiation of the New Philosophy. E. P. Thompson regarded 'Philadelphian and Behmenist thought . . . as a counter-Enlightenment impulse, as a reaction against the mechanistic philosophy of the time'.[35] It is not easy to afford hospitable accommodation within this view for men like George Cheyne, who was both a thoroughgoing mechanist and a Behmenist. Cheyne, for example, saw no difficulty in using Newtonian physics to bolster his belief in the gravitational pull of God on the soul.[36] Romantic illuminists were to develop a hostility to scientific mechanism, but this attitude should not be projected back onto early modern occultism. If the New Philosophy was inimical to religion, many of the mystics of early modern Europe were oblivious to the danger. William Law, who had been introduced to Behmenism by Cheyne, believed that 'the *true and infallible* Ground' of Newton's system 'was to be found in the *Teutonic Theosopher* [Jacob Boehme], in his *three* first *Properties of Eternal Nature*'; 'the illustrious Sir *Isaac* ploughed with *Behmen*'s Heifer'.[37] The Behmenist physician Francis Lee used Boyle's Law in his exposition of Genesis, and he hailed Leeuwenhoek's discovery of spermatozoa because he thought it gave support to the prophecy that 'the seed of the woman' would bruise the Serpent's head (Genesis 3:15).[38]

Enlightenment science, with its mysterious new forces of gravity and electricity, provided a fertile ground in which the seeds of occultism could grow.[39] On the other hand, the occultists themselves were at the forefront of investigating such 'occult fluids' as electricity, and illuminism and electrical science stimulated each other throughout the Enlightenment. The word 'electricity' itself was introduced into English in 1650 by the alchemist Jean-Baptist van Helmont. A century later the theosopher Prokop Davisch's experiments with electricity enabled him to anticipate Benjamin Franklin's invention of the lightning rod. By this time a number of 'electrical theologians' were incorporating electricity into their theosophical systems. Friedrich Oetinger identified electricity with the *anima mundi*, while Johann Fricker saw electrical bipolarity as a confirmation of Boehme's dialectical vision of reality. In Christopher Smart's praise of his cat in *Jubilate Agno* we can find the following lines:

For by stroking of him I have found out electricity.
For I perceived God's light about him both wax and fire.

> For the electrical fire is the spiritual substance which God sends from
> heaven to sustain the bodies of both man and beast.

Smart was insane, but there was nothing particularly eccentric about the electrical theology underlying this passage. If, as Erik Davis argues, 'the electro-
magnetic imaginary' is the technological matrix of modernity, its origins lie
partly in the endeavours of Enlightenment occultists.[40]

Discoveries like Albrecht von Haller's demonstration of the persistence of
movement in muscle-tissue after death encouraged a renewal of vitalist
understandings of matter.[41] Even among early modern materialists, matter
was not quite as dead and lifeless as it was to become. As Marx and Engels
observed, Bacon's materialism 'pullulates with inconsistencies imported
from theology'; in the thought of this 'first creator' of materialism, 'there
is an impulse, a vital spirit, a tension – or a "qual" to use a term of Jacob
Böhme's – of matter'.[42] John Toland, known to history as a materialist
and deist, also attributed a vital impulse to matter, under the influence
of Giordano Bruno.[43] Similarly the Baron d'Holbach, patron saint of
materialist atheists, could not conceive of matter without some sort of vital
principle, which he regarded as a necessary postulate to explain the fact of
life in a godless and exclusively material universe.[44] Materialism begins in
vitalism; the reign of matter was proclaimed by the all-embracing sovereignty
of life. In this respect, the world-views of the Enlightened and the Illuminated
overlapped.

One of the claims for the influence of early modern occultism on the rise
of modern science rests on the empiricism of groups like the Paracelsians.
If it is true that Hermetic texts like the *Asclepius* 'grudgingly permitted the
study of nature as a propaedeutic to piety',[45] this position evolved into
something like an imperative in the early modern period. Occultists were
at the forefront of the assault on the intellectual hegemony of Aristotle,
and they had nothing but contempt for Scholastic pedantry.[46] Esoteric
anti-Aristotelianism was often motivated by religious rather than scientific
considerations; as Thomas Vaughan argued, 'It is a terrible thing to praefer
Aristotel to *Aeolohim* and *condemn* the *Truth* of God, to *justifie* the *Opinions*
of *Man*.'[47] This attack on Aristotle nevertheless performed a valuable service
in liberating early modern thinkers from the tyranny of ancient dogma
posing as science. The emphasis on Nature as a second Scripture implied a
duty to study the world for theological insight. Paracelsus was certainly an
'empiricist' of sorts. He scorned mere book learning, advising doctors that
'The patients are your textbook, the sickbed is your study.'[48] He admitted
that his medical doctrines differed from those of the ancients, but claimed
that 'it is firmly based on experience, which is the mistress of all things,
and by which all arts should be proved'.[49] Heinrich Nolle observed that
'the Certainty and proof of the principles of all Arts, can by no other
meanes, be known and tryed but by practise, as *Paracelsus* doth rightly
say'. The physician must 'have a perfect experimentall knowledge by the

light of Nature'.[50] John Dee's supreme science or 'Archemastrie' was to be an 'Experimentall Science', although this empiricism included large servings of magic drawn from Roger Bacon and Avicenna.[51]

It is clear from the magical and mystical context of this empiricism that it is not quite the same thing as it is in modern science, and it is possible to exaggerate the Paracelsian commitment to empiricism. If the sixteenth century was the age of Vesalius and the 'anatomical renaissance', Paracelsus did not hold those who dissected corpses in high regard: 'After they have seen everything, they know less than before and into the bargain are soiled with the refuse and the cadaver.' According to the Swiss physician, it was impossible to learn anything of the nature of the living organism from its dead remains.[52] Sometimes Paracelsus's empiricism seems to be little more than a substitution of one set of authorities for another; rather than listen to the nonsense of the ancients, the physician 'must consult old women, gypsies, magicians, wayfarers, and all manner of peasant folk and random people, and learn from them'.[53] Such people may have been as wise in medical matters as Galenic physicians were foolish, and modern pharmaceutics is not averse to exploiting traditional medicine while disparaging it as quackery (the principle apparently being that what is profitable for pharmaceutical companies is science, and what is cheap and readily available is dangerous superstition). Even so, this is still reliance on intellectual authority rather than empirical testing. Occult empiricism shared the limitations of Roger Bacon's experimental science. The function of experiments was as much pedagogical as experimental in the modern sense, intended to demonstrate truths already accepted as valid. 'Experiment' meant simply experience rather than controlled tests of hypotheses, and the experience at the heart of the method might not be sensory at all: it could include inner illumination.[54] In a post-Lockean world, empiricism would seem to imply a passive theory of knowledge as dependent on the impressions made by objects on the senses. As we shall see in Chapter 6, the occult philosophers developed a thoroughly activist epistemology. Thomas Tryon, for example, asserted that the senses 'are the chief conveyors of what is presented before them, to the Influential Principles or Magic Powers of the Soul'. The five external senses are complemented by, and dependent on, five internal ones. Attaining knowledge is not merely a passive process based on external sense-perceptions. An object can be truly apprehended only through its 'signature', which points beyond the meaningless phenomenal appearance to its inner spiritual reality. The signatures of things are to be found not so much in the objects themselves as in human consciousness. Accordingly Tryon tells us that 'all true Understanding and knowledge begins at home'.[55]

It has been argued that the 'Pythagorean Platonism' of the occult entailed a '*quantitative* approach to the universe'. John Dee's 'Mathematical Preface' to Euclid's Geometry, for example, is said to envisage just such an approach.[56] Modern science is, of course, typically quantitative, and it is possible that we have here another contribution of the occult to the Scientific

Revolution. Dee's 'Mathematical Preface', however, also praises magic, and he recommended a quantitative aproach, not just because he was a mathematician, but also because he belonged to a tradition which saw a mystical significance in numbers. Dee's was a numerological science rather than a quantitative science in the modern sense.[57] This does not necessarily mean that it did not contribute to the rise of quantitative science. Early modern people were less inclined than we are to distinguish between mathematics and numerology, and it is possible that quantitative science was nurtured by the magical art of numbers. We have clear evidence of numerology entering into the mindset of men whose place in the history of modern science is unquestioned. One of the early Copernican treatises is Georg Joachim Rheticus's *Narratio Prima*, published in 1540, in which Rheticus gives a numerological explanation for the reduction of the number of planets from seven to six. According to the Pythagoreans, six is the first perfect number, and it is also the number of days that it took God to create the world; it is thus a fitting number to choose when deciding how many planets to create: 'the number six is honoured beyond all others in the sacred prophecies of God and by the Pythagoreans and other philosophers'.[58]

The occult philosophy may have played another role in the Copernican Revolution. Among the ancient authorities cited by Copernicus in support of his theory was Hermes Trismegistus.[59] Hermes has admittedly a very minor place in the *De Revolutionibus*; he is one of several authorities fleetingly referred to by Copernicus,[60] and they all appear only in order to supplement more strictly scientific arguments. It has been argued, however, that the mystical heliocentrism of Hermeticism prepared the way for the astronomical heliocentrism of Copernicus, and it is certainly true that the occult philosophers developed a high opinion of the sun. Not that astronomical heliocentrism was universally accepted by those who espoused a solar mysticism, at least before the later seventeenth century.[61] A combined mystical and astronomical heliocentrism, however, was clearly more consistent than a combination of geocentrism and solar mysticism. Whatever the impact of the occult philosophy on astronomy, in this sense we might agree with Nabil Matar that 'the victory of heliocentrism marked the consolidation of the hermetic tradition'.[62] In the late fifteenth century, Marsilio Ficino said that God had 'placed his tabernacle in the sun', and that he reigned in the middle of creation 'like the king in the middle of his city, the heart in the middle of the body, the sun in the middle of the planets'.[63] William Harvey was later to use this same comparison in his work on the circulation of the blood: sun, king and heart are equally central to their respective systems.[64] For Harvey's friend, Robert Fludd, this was no mere figure of speech. Man is a microcosm whose body, with its central heart, reflects the structure of the universe with its central sun; both reflect the God who had created them.[65] Solar mysticism seems to have achieved a popular currency in the seventeenth century. The Leveller, Richard Overton, developed a theology of God as 'true light'; the sun, which was 'the shadow of his brightness', was the present abode of Christ.[66] According to Walter Charleton, 'the visible Sun . . . is but a dark and contracted shadow' of 'the Invisible, Unperishable and Infinite Sun'.[67] There was a theory in Cambridge Platonist circles that white light was a pure spiritual substance pervading the universe.[68] Traditionally a distinction had been made between intellectual light (*lux*) and natural light (*lumen*). Writers like Thomas Aquinas treated the relationship between the two as being merely analogical, but in Neoplatonism *lumen* was conceived as proceeding from *lux* by a process of emanation.[69] A similar understanding of light can be found in the occult tradition. Thomas Vaughan believed that light 'is properly the life of everything'. In the cosmogonic process, it is light which impregnates the primal matter.[70] Vaughan thought that God is 'the *Metaphysicall, supercelestiall sun*'; the Son in the Trinity was its light, the Holy Ghost its heat, and the Father its source.[71] Vaughan was simply following Agrippa, who had written that the sun was 'amongst the other stars the image and statue of the great Prince, . . . the most exact image of God himself; whose essence resembles the Father, light the Son, heat the Holy Ghost'.[72] Thomas Tryon asserted that the

> wonderful Eye of Heaven the Sun, is the very Centre of Light of all the numberless number of Creatures, being the Foundation, and Well being of them all, who by its illuminating Beams, Communicates Light and Life to all the Host of Heaven and Earth, without which all would be a dark Chaos of Misery and Confusion.[73]

For George Cheyne, the sun's light 'is an *Image* of the *Light which enlightens every Man that comes into the World*; an *Emblem* of Him who came forth from the Father of *lights*; the *Light* and *Son* of the New *Jerusalem*, and of *Spiritual Nature*'.[74] Among the Romantics, Jung Stilling regarded the sun as 'the corporeal reflection' of Christ's magnificence.[75] For Coleridge, 'The natural sun is . . . a symbol of the spiritual.'[76] This solar and light mysticism is closely allied to fire symbolism. In one alchemical text we read 'that fire is the soul of everything, and that God himself is the fire and soul'.[77] William Law claimed that 'The Fire of the Soul, or that *spiritual Fire* which is the Soul itself, is kindled or enlightened by the Light of the *Sun*.'[78] There is a precise correspondence between the sun and its effects on the material world and the Son of God and his effects on the spiritual plane: 'the *natural Light* of this World is nothing else but the Power and Mystery of the *supernatural Light*, breaking forth, opening itself, according to its Omnipotence, in all Forms of Elementary Darkness which constitute this temporary World'.[79] In Behmenist thought, the sun represents the fourth property of Eternal Nature, the point at which 'the light and dark World do sever'. This is the pivotal point between the merely natural world, which is in itself dead, and the spiritual world, which is life eternal.[80]

Of the heroes of the Scientific Revolution before Newton, it is Johannes Kepler who shows the clearest signs of sharing a similar world-view to the occultists. Kepler rejected a numerological approach to the universe, but he did so in favour of an equally mystical geometrical approach, based on Pythagorean and Platonic thought.[81] Kepler believed that there were only six planets because God had constructed the universe by employing the five regular polyhedra (the cube, the tetrahedron, the dodecahedron, the icosahedron and the octahedron) each nesting in a series of concentric spheres. There is an empirical argument for this idea: the ratio of the radii of spheres containing the polyhedra in this order is roughly equivalent to the ratio of the radii of the planetary orbits, with the exception of Jupiter's.[82] But there is more involved here than a strict empiricism, and it is significant that Kepler referred to this aspect of his work as 'geometric Cabala'.[83] Kepler's method is arguably inductive insofar as he attempts to relate his theory to the empirical data, but it is hardly positivist; for him, what makes a theory adequate is not just that it provides an accurate mathematical description of phenomena, but that it also has a deeper mystical significance. We can see this by how his imagination works on the empirical evidence. Galileo had observed four moons orbiting Jupiter, and Kepler knew that the earth also had a moon in orbit around it. On this basis he constructed a theory that the planets of the solar system possessed satellites in a regular geometric sequence: one for Earth, two for Mars, four for Jupiter, and eight for Saturn.[84] Kepler's assumption was that the number and distribution of planetary satellites would be determined with mathematical precision. This was necessarily so, since the universe was the work of God, who would not create in an arbitrary way, but through eternal laws of harmony.

Kepler believed that the universe had been created in the image of God, 'For in the act of making, God played, arranging therein the adorable image of the Trinity.' At the centre of everything is the sun, which represents God the Father. The cosmos as a whole is a sphere, and its outer surface represents Christ. The space between the surface and the centre represents the Holy Ghost.[85] This aspect of Kepler's cosmology has left no lasting trace on modern astronomy, but it remains impossible to separate the mystical and scientific elements of his thought even in areas that were to become an accepted part of modern theories of the solar system. Copernicus, for example, remained committed to the belief that planetary motion was basically circular, since the circle is the most perfect shape.[86] It was Kepler who first realised that the planets move through elliptical rather than circular orbits. This was a major achievement in the history of astronomy, but in Kepler's account it had as much to do with a mystical way of viewing the universe as it does with modern, positive science. Kepler accepted that the circle was a perfect shape; it represented God. The straight line, on the other hand, is imperfect, representing mere creatures. Kepler regarded an ellipse as a combination of a circle and a straight line. In this way, the elliptical orbits of the planets represent a combination of perfection and imperfection. They inscribe in the heavens the story of how the creation is subjected to material necessity, incapable of reaching perfection, but yet constantly striving to become perfect.[87]

Kepler has been called the last great astronomer who was also an astrologer.[88] He rejected traditional astrology, but this was on the grounds of its imprecision rather than its invalidity, and he continued to believe that the planets exercised a 'temperamental influence' on the individual.[89] He is celebrated by modern astrologers for having discovered three new aspects to the heavens. Kepler was himself a horoscope-maker – apparently a successful one, since in 1624 he predicted Wallenstein's death ten years later.[90] Kepler's work culminated in his *Harmonices Mundi* of 1619, a book which in the history of astronomy is notable for having stated his third law of planetary motion, thus completing his contribution to modern science. It also developed Kepler's theory of the music of the spheres. Like many of his contemporaries, Kepler believed that the solar system was a musical concert; its harmonies could be heard from the position of the sun, the position of God the Father in Kepler's system. The music made by the planets was polyphonic. Saturn and Jupiter provided the bass, Mars was a tenor, Earth and Venus played the role of alto, and Mercury supplied the soprano.[91]

In Kepler's mind the cosmos was essentially a visible representation of God and his relationship to humanity; it was also a hymn of praise to its creator, the divine geometer. It is possible to separate this mystical cosmology from Kepler's contribution to modern science, but it would be totally anachronistic to do so. If we were able to ask Kepler what was his greatest achievement, his answer would probably be, not his three laws of planetary motion as such, but the way these laws contributed to our understanding of the world as a mystical expression of the divine being. Certainly for Romantic thinkers like Novalis, Kepler's achievement consisted in having created 'a spiritualized and moralized universe'.[92] Whether or not Kepler had particular occult sources for his work, he clearly thought about the world with the logic of the occult philosophy.

Similar remarks might be made about Isaac Newton. Until recently William Law's opinion that Newton 'ploughed with Behmen's Heiffer' was widely dismissed. Even George Cheyne, himself a rather credulous Behmenist Newtonian, doubted Law's claim, and Law consistently failed to provide the proof he claimed to have.[93] There is in fact a superficial resemblance between Newton's system and Boehme's: both construct the universe as pervaded by mysterious forces of attraction and repulsion.[94] What gives Law's claim some measure of plausibility is Newton's evident interest in alchemy. Newton wrote well over a million words on alchemy, and he corresponded with John Locke and Robert Boyle on the subject – which gives us the delightful picture of the founding fathers of the British Enlightenment dabbling in supposedly medieval superstition.[95] Close scrutiny of Newton's alchemical manuscripts has led some historians to recognise that the occult tradition had an important influence on the genesis of Newtonian science.[96] As Robert Westfall has argued, Newton became interested in alchemy because he was worried by what he regarded as the atheistical implications of the mechanical philosophy in its Cartesian form. He told John Craig that he thought Cartesianism 'was made on purpose to be the foundation of infidelity'.[97]

Newton's alchemical writings exist only in manuscript, which makes it easy to dismiss them as irrelevant to his science; this was the attitude of Thomas Pellett when he wrote on the manuscripts 'Not fit to be printed', an attitude shared by many later historians. It is also an attitude that many of Newton's contemporaries took to his published work, especially on the Continent. We are so familiar with Newton's theory of gravity that we sometimes forget how novel, even bizarre, it seemed in the late seventeenth century. Not for the first or last time in history, people with a down-to-earth, common-sensical world-view rejected a genuine scientific advance because it seemed like mystical stuff and nonsense. The problem with Newton's theory was that it was essentially one of forces acting at a distance rather than through direct contact. On purely mechanical assumptions, the notion that the universe coheres through a force of universal attraction is inherently implausible. As Westfall has argued, Newton was not working on purely mechanical assumptions. He had, ready to hand, a concept of force working at a distance: the concept of force to be found in alchemy.[98]

Apart from his theory of gravity, Newton is best known for his work in optics, and particularly his demonstration that white light can be broken up into a spectrum of colours. It is possible that Newton's famous experiment was devised to test a metaphysical and religious hypothesis rather than a purely physical one. Arthur Quinn has suggested that Newton was investigating an idea that had been discussed in Cambridge Platonist circles. It was believed that underlying the various different types of material substance in the universe there was also a single, pure, spiritual substance.[99] No one knew what this substance was, but white light had been suggested as a likely candidate. Newton's experiment showed that white light was itself composed of different colours, therefore it could not be the single, pure, spiritual substance. Newton's religious motivation does not lessen the scientific positivism of his empirical approach, but neither is it entirely irrelevant when assessing the culture of seventeenth-century science.

The most obvious contribution of the occult tradition to modern science is that made by alchemy to empirical chemistry.[100] Modern chemistry came into being when men like Andreas Libavius rejected the mysticism of alchemy,[101] but it nevertheless built on the achievements of this older tradition, and interacted with it 'through a dialectical process'.[102] At the very least, alchemy was important in developing modern laboratory equipment, and in encouraging close observation of chemical processes; it was, after all, alchemists who first identified such chemicals as alcohol, sulphuric acid, antimony and phosphorus.[103]

In the eighteenth century, esoteric thought and scientific endeavour tended to become separate in a way comforting to modern positivist sensibilities. Not that the victory of positivism in science was complete; Romantic scientists like Lorenz Oken continued to work within an unmistakably mystical framework. For Oken, science was the study of 'God's eternal transformations in the world', and 'natural philosophy is therefore in its highest principle Theosophy'.[104] With the nineteenth century, however, the relationship between the occult philosophy and science was shifting from the increasingly uncongenial realm of a mechanised physics to the more hospitable domain of biology, with its greater scope for cosmic organicism. The occult philosophy can be linked (albeit tenuously) to the great revolution in nineteenth-century biological science. Early in the eighteenth century Francis Lee had used Leeuwenhoek's discovery of spermatozoa to construct a seven-stage theory of the 'Vermicular Original of human Life'. This was not, as Serge Hutin supposed,[105] an early theory of evolution, since there is no question of the mutability of species.[106] G. F. Meier proposed the theory that animals ascend the scale of being over several lives: 'It is possible that animals representing the lowest class should be promoted through death into a second, from there into a third and finally, again through a transformation, they may become reasonable beings and spirits.'[107] This is clearly not a theory of evolution in the modern sense, but this idea of ascent through the scale of being could be wedded to later theories of the mutability of species to fix evolutionism within a cosmogonic and theogonic process: slowly and painfully, nature was becoming man, and man God. Some thinkers influenced by the occult philosophy, like Restif de la Bretonne and Charles Fourier, developed primitive evolutionary theories,[108] and were perhaps able to do so because the Pythagorean doctrine of the transmigration of souls made the boundaries between species less sacrosanct than in orthodox thought. This is not to claim that such thinkers had any influence on the modern theory of evolution, and evolutionary thought was reasonably common in the eighteenth century outside occult circles.[109] It does indicate that in many ways the occult philosophy, unlike some aspects of more orthodox religion, did not restrict the development of unconventional ideas. Insofar as there was a relationship of influence between occultism and biological science, however, it seems to have been the biologists who influenced the occultists: the theory of evolution offered a way of reformulating some of the basic ideas of the occult philosophy.

We can discern a faint shadow of occultism in the work of Arthur Russel Wallace, the co-discoverer of the theory of natural selection. Wallace dismissed 'Reincarnation and Theosophical Books' as irrational, but his own religious ideas clearly suggest an esoteric context.[110] As a young man, Wallace had been associated with an early nineteenth-century movement known as 'physical puritanism'.[111] It was a movement dedicated, among other things, to promoting health through a purely vegetable and water diet. The dominant figures in the movement were men like James Pierrepont

Greaves in England or Amos Bronson Alcott in America; their outlook was fundamentally occultist. In the 1860s Wallace turned increasingly to spiritualism, believing that a moral order could be guaranteed only if there was a life after death. Again this was a movement permeated by occultism.[112] In one way, Wallace was always more strictly 'Darwinian' than Darwin himself; whereas Darwin was willing to consider the possibility that factors other than natural selection might play a role in evolution, Wallace was firmly commited to natural selection as the sole evolutionary mechanism. On the other hand, Wallace undermined this austere Darwinian orthodoxy by developing a theory of evolution that was clearly providential and teleological in outlook. In 1869 Wallace wrote that 'an Overruling Intelligence has watched over the action of those laws [of natural selection] so directing variations and so determining the accumulation, as finally to produce an organization sufficiently perfect to admit of, and even to aid in, the indefinite advancement of our mental and moral nature'.[113] Wallace thought that the human body had ceased to evolve, since people were protected from the rigours of natural selection by their superior mental endowment and social capacity. This did not mean that people themselves were no longer evolving, but now it is only the human mind and society that continues to develop. This development of human mental and social capacities was the goal of the cosmos, and Wallace asserted that 'the whole *raison d'être* of the material universe . . . is to serve the grand purpose of developing human spirits in human bodies'.[114] Wallace's evolutionary thought simply takes the Idealist conception of history as the development of cosmic consciousness and roots it in biology. It is a modernisation and rationalisation of an idea that originated in occult thought.

Other nineteenth-century thinkers devoloped what Gershom Scholem has called a 'secularized mysticism' on the basis of evolutionary thought. The American Richard Maurice Bucke, for example, proposed the theory that the universe was gradually developing a 'cosmic consciousness' along Darwinian lines.[115] In England, the novelist and amateur scientist Samuel Butler propounded a similar theory. Butler thought that there was 'a single God-impregnate substance' in the universe, a substance which was 'the parent from which all living forms have sprung'. This was 'one spirit, and one form capable of such modification as its directing spirit shall think fit; one soul and one body, one God and one life'. It was in fact protoplasm, or 'the Known God', an aspect of 'the Unknown God' which was slowly evolving into a higher form. In this way, God was becoming conscious of himself in man: 'as man cannot live without God in the world, so neither can God live in this world without mankind'. Butler was a panpsychist, and he thought that we should 'see every atom in the universe as living and able to feel and remember, but in a humble way'. Like the occultists, he refused to make a radical distinction between mind and matter: 'Mind is not a thing, or if it be, we know nothing about it; it is a function of matter. Matter is not a thing or, if it be, we know nothing about it; it is a function of mind.'[116]

Sympathetic accounts of occult thinkers like Swedenborg are full of praise for their anticipations of later scientific discoveries.[117] Whatever the validity of this type of hagiographical writing, there are many examples that could be cited of people who combined high scientific achievements with a mystical outlook, nor are these merely anomalous figures from a 'transitional' past. Several eminent scientists in the nineteenth century were interested in spiritualism and psychical research. Some of these were admittedly physical reductionists in their approach: Sir William Crookes, for example, sought to explain telepathy in terms of X-rays. Others, like Oliver Lodge, expounded a more fully developed esoteric vision of the world; Lodge believed in the existence of an ethereal body free from imperfections, a doctrine which can be found throughout occult thought.[118] John W. Parsons was both a nuclear physicist and a Crowleyite occultist.[119] Parsons' science may not be directly indebted to his occultism, but another physicist, Wolfgang Pauli, developed an epistemology of scientific endeavour which, via Jungian psychology, is heavily indebted to the occult tradition. In a study of Kepler, Pauli argued that Jungian archetypes 'function as the sought for bridge between the sense perceptions and the ideas and are, accordingly, a necessary presupposition even for evolving a scientific theory. What is required is an approach which recognizes *both* sides of reality – the quantitative and the qualitative, the physical and the psychical – as compatible with each other, and can embrace them simultaneously.'[120]

Whatever the influence of occultism on modern science, these examples demonstrate that the rise of scientific positivism was not inherently inimical to a magico-mystical world-view. As O'Keefe has argued, 'there is no determinate or even predominate relation between magic and science. . . . Not only can magic both stimulate or depress science, and science both stimulate or depress magic, but all four trends are often present at once, though with different weights.'[121] Far from inevitably dispelling the dark clouds of 'superstition', science has often encouraged magical thought. Sometimes it has done this in a purely negative sense. In the late nineteenth century Gérard Encausse, a minor medical writer better known to the world as the occultist Papus, turned to esoteric thought because of his dissatisfaction with what he regarded as the desiccated truths of scientific materialism.[122] Occultists also demonstrated a remarkable capacity for cultural parasitism in their relations with positive science; repeatedly they have succeeded in co-opting new science, using it to validate the occult world-view. Cherry Gilchrist, for example, argues that such developments as quantum physics and chaos theory offer the possibility of *rapprochement* between modern science and the alchemical world-view: 'The old rigid boundaries between spirit and matter have crumbled.'[123] Fritjof Capra invites us to believe that there is a *Tao of Physics*, and James Lovelock's *Gaia* has entered the scriptural canon of the New Age alongside the work of people like the quantum physicist David Bohm.[124] This phenomenon is not as incomprehensible as those who are locked into a purely positivistic world-view might suppose. Arguing that magic 'works because people agree that it works', Daniel O'Keefe has observed that science can offer 'new language for patterning agreement'.[125] To demonstrate that a 'paranormal' experience has a 'normal' explanation is also to demonstrate that it is 'real' in terms of a given conventional world-view. The experience is thus licensed, a licence which (from a positivist point of view) is readily converted into licentious speculation by occultists. The boundary between what a culture chooses to call science or superstition is itself conventional. Newtonian physics is no more or less 'mystical' now than it was at the end of the seventeenth century; we have merely agreed not to regard it as such. As Sir Thomas Browne observed, 'at first a great part of Philosophy was Witchcraft, which being afterward derived to one another, proved but Philosophy, and was indeed no more but the honest effects of Nature'.[126] The same process can work in reverse. Despite its defiance of common sense, we may choose to regard quantum physics as positive science, but many people (including some quantum physicists) find no difficulty in seeing it as integral to a mystical world-view.

The question that needs investigating is not whether magic led to science, but what factors underlay the simultaneous sociogenesis of magical and scientific world-views. In Malinowski's theory, magic is a means of building confidence in uncertain situations.[127] More generally, O'Keefe has argued that magic arises when the 'paramount social-cognitive frame' or conventional world-view weakens or breaks down.[128] The attraction of Jungian psychology for Wolfgang Pauli or the appeal of the Upanishads for Erwin Schroedinger can be related to this theory: as Robert Westman observes, among early twentieth-century physicists 'The physical world lost touch with common sense.'[129] The quantum physicists were not only living through the breakdown of the conventional world-view, they were actively engaged in demolishing it. The same is true of the founding fathers of the Scientific Revolution; what, after all, is Kuhn's 'paradigm shift'[130] if not a breakdown of the common sense of a given community? We might postulate that scientists become peculiarly susceptible to mysticism precisely because they are scientists, tending to live their intellectual lives beyond the borders of conventional wisdom. Not that all scientists become mystics, but a surprising proportion of the most original and innovative of them have succumbed to the charms of mystical religion.

Whatever the historical relationship between science and magic, the two activities usually differ fundamentally in their orientation to the world. Science is completely alloplastic: it seeks to transform the world by acting on it as an external object. Until the development of quantum physics, Western science was premised on a radical disjunction between the subjective and objective order, a disjunction which devalued the objective world precisely by according it an epistemological primacy. Occultism also accepted that the subjective and objective orders were separated; this was the meaning of the fall of man and nature. For occultism, however, this divorce between object and subject is an urgent problem rather than an ineluctable fact. The occultist wants to reunite subject and object, and his attitude to the world is thoroughly autoplastic: he seeks to transform it by transforming himself. As Marcel Mauss observed, it is the magician's 'power over his own being' that constitutes 'the prime source of his strength'.[131] For men like Pico della Mirandola, 'subjective' magic, involving the spiritual illumination of the magician, would lead to 'transitive' magic, offering control over the external world.[132] This is why magic, even when it attempts to command the elements, is always a psychological system working through inner spiritual forces. It may involve elaborate rituals; it may even, as in alchemy, appear to be a primitive and misguided science. These external elements of magic are really no more than aids in concentrating the inner forces of the magician. Magic is an act of will. Balzac expressed the magician's outlook in one of his novels: 'The human will was a material force similar to steam-power . . . He who has learned the technique [of concentrating it] could modify as he pleased everything relating to mankind, even the absolute laws of nature.'[133]

The autoplasticism of the occult philosophy did not preclude the possibility of beneficent alloplastic intervention in the natural world. As we have seen, it was possible to be both an occultist and a scientist. It is historically inaccurate to argue that 'In order for modern science to come into being, the substance of the cosmos had first to be emptied of its sacred character and become profane.'[134] Increasingly, however, the scientific universe was desacralised. As Novalis complained, modern science 'reduced the infinite creative music of the universe to the monstrous clatter of a monstrous mill'.[135] It was perhaps in reaction to this that the Romantics regarded science and technology with suspicion. For the Romantics, man alone is fallen, and the badge of his fall is the 'civilisation' that distances him from a Nature which is still pregnant with the divine. The attempt to control and manipulate nature externally is seen as inherently perilous. This is the lesson of Mary Shelley's *Frankenstein* – although the science attacked by Shelley is not, as is often assumed, a positive one, but one inspired by Paracelsus and Agrippa.[136]

It has been argued that 'for modern, scientific man, the phenomenal world is primarily an "It"; for ancient – and also for primitive – man it is "Thou".'[137] Much of this I–Thou relationship with the natural world was preserved in occult thought. With this in mind, we might question Brian Vickers' characterisation of occultism and science as differing in that the latter has a 'disinterested' approach to natural phenomena while the former is only concerned with the transcendental reference of nature.[138] Not that occultism is ever disinterested, but it does display an ecological reverence; the world is a Thou to be treated with the same courtesy and respect as any other Thou. It would be naïve to believe that science, on the other hand, is or ever has been genuinely disinterested in its attitude to the world. Underlying the development of modern science is the Baconian programme of domination over nature, but this urge to dominate the world has been emptied of the moral content that was its precondition in the magical tradition. It is a fundamentally instrumental and utilitarian approach to our environment. Man is no longer the steward, but the master of nature. The world exists not merely to be wondered at and explored, and to be tended while it is used, but to be exploited – an exploitation that has no moral dimension because the world is an It. This is why the Romantics regarded humanity's growing technological mastery over nature with dismay, and they pointed out the reifying effects of this mastery on humanity itself, reducing as it did the industrial workers, like the world on which they worked, to the status of an instrument.[139] The Romantics generally shared Coleridge's antipathy to the mechanistic world-view: 'the philosophy of mechanism . . . in everything that is most worthy of the human Intellect strikes *Death*'.[140] It could not be otherwise, since mechanism perpetuated and strengthened the disjunction between object and subject that was at the root of human alienation from the cosmos. Blake's hostility to Bacon, Newton and Locke, the Urizenic demiurges of a dead material universe, is well known. It was to find an echo in the self-proclaimed 'last of the Romantics', William Butler Yeats: 'Descartes, Locke and Newton took away the world and gave us its excrement instead.'[141] In 'Fragments' – a title which recalls the ruptured nature of fallen humanity as much as the incompleteness of the poem – Yeats tells us that

> Locke sank into a swoon;
> The Garden died;
> God took the spinning-jenny
> Out of his side.[142]

Locke, the great empiricist playing the role of Adam, brings the Edenic world to death; and in compensation he is given not Eve, but an emblem of industrial triumph over nature.[143]

4　The body in occult thought

The myth of the Fall in occult thought symbolises an abrupt transition from unconditioned and non-contingent being into conditionality and contingency. If we read the fall of nature ontogenetically, it can be interpreted as representing the point at which the infant's all-encompassing narcissism is confronted with the uncomplying otherness of the world.[1] In psychological terms, we might characterise this myth as symbolic of the shock of weaning; such an interpretation would at least gain some support from the prominence of womb, breast and mother imagery in occult symbolism. This is a critical moment in the formation of full human consciousness, for in discovering that the world is 'other' the child also discovers that he or she is a 'self'. Self-hood is thus constituted not by its freedom, but by its contingency. It exists only in opposition to the Other, an otherness which limits and restrains. But this opposition is not a simple, clear-cut binary opposition. When (to borrow Winstanley's formulation) the world fell out of man, man also fell partly out of himself. The self confronts an invasive otherness which has taken hold of part of its own being: the body. On the one hand, the body is a precondition of 'the category of the person', inextricably bound up with our sense of ourselves.[2] Yet it is through the body that the otherness of the world invades our being. We experience the body both as an integral part of ourselves and as an object somehow 'out there'. The very language that we use to express our embodiment tends to reify it. Annie Mignard has argued that 'One does not *have* a body, one *is* a body.'[3] Perhaps so; but the awkwardness of this phrasing is surely more than grammatical. 'How', Helmut Schneider asks, 'can we ever be at unity with our body and with ourselves; how can we even *speak* about our body without removing ourselves from it, turning it into an external, thinglike object?'[4]

It is to the issue of embodiment as simultaneously subjectivity and objectivity that the occult discourse on somatic existence is addressed. We shall see in Chapter 6 how the occult mystics posit the existence of two selves, a transcendental self of freedom grounded in the godhead and an empirical self fettered to the world. To those who were touched by the occult philosophy it seemed clear that man also had two bodies, a material and a spiritual one: 'Within the human body is another body of approximately the same size and shape, but made of a subtler and less illusory material.'[5] The spiritual body, like the mystic's transcendental self, belonged to a world of authenticity and freedom. It was the body of our original creation, and it had literally become encrusted over by a grossly material body since the Fall. Thus, according to Cabalist teachings, the 'garments of skin' given to Adam and Eve at the Fall (Genesis 3:21) referred not to items of clothing, but to the Protoplasts' material bodies.[6] Through the material body man experienced himself as conditioned; at best as a special sort of object in a world of other objects.

This mystical physiology depends on a distinction between corporeal and material being. Even spirits, Samuel Pordage informs us, 'have bodies which are distinct from them, but not as our gross bodies, subject to our outward senses, but to our inward [ones]'.[7] 'As a fire must have substance if it is to burn', according to Jacob Boehme, 'so likewise the magical fire of the soul has flesh, blood and water.'[8] Similarly William Law stated that 'Every *creaturely* Spirit must have its *own Body*, and cannot be without it.'[9] George Cheyne also accepted this doctrine: 'all finite created *Spirits* have, and must have material Vehicles, of Purity and Fineness in Proportion to their natural and moral Powers conjunctly, not only to limit and direct their *Energy* and *Efficiency*, but to *commerciate* with other Animals, and inanimat[e] created Natures'.[10] Friedrich Oetinger also believed in the corporeality of spirit, and regarded corporeality as 'God's end' in creating the world.[11]

Discourses about the body have been at the heart of Christian religion since its earliest days. As Thomas Luxon argues, Paul wanted 'to privilege spirit as absolutely as he can over body, and to read one as an allegory of the other'.[12] The occult discourse on the body can be interpreted as an emphatic version of this Pauline allegorisation of the body, but the emphasis has the effect of eliding the distinction between body and spirit. Even God has a corporeal existence in much occult thought. This is a doctrine which is at least as old as Tertullian, who asked 'Who can deny that God is body, even though he is spirit? Spirit is also body of its own kind.'[13] The orthodox position was established by Augustine, however, who denied God's corporeality.[14] Against the medieval insistence on the incorporeality of God, several seventeenth-century writers re-endowed the divinity with bodily attributes. The learned, of course, did not indulge in the naïve anthropomorphism of the Muggletonians, whose God was like an old man, five foot tall.[15] Writers like Spinoza, Henry More and Newton did, however, conceive of God in terms of dimensionality and extension. This trend, as Amos Funkenstein suggests, was particularly strong among Protestants, and it represented a revival of the magical cosmos of ancient Stoicism.[16] Occultists tended to identify the body of God with nature or the cosmos. 'God is a spirit', according to Jacob Boehme, 'and so subtil as thought or will, and Nature is his Corporeal Essence, understand the Eternal Nature.'[17] 'This whole visible World', Thomas Tryon tells us, 'is nothing but the Great

Body of God.'[18] Cheyne asserted that 'the Supreme Spirit' was 'absolutely and entirely an infinitely pure *immaterial Spirit*, acting by its Power and Energy with equal Facility at all possible Distances'.[19] Nevertheless, he also suggested that '*universall Nature*, or the *created Universe*, may represent *GOD's Body*, or his Sensorium'.[20] These words recall a passage in Newton's *Opticks*, where he speaks of infinite space as God's 'Sensory', in which he 'sees the things themselves intimately, and thoroughly perceives them, and comprehends them wholly by their immediate presence to himself'.[21]

Christianity is a religion of the embodiment of God in the person of Jesus Christ. As one alchemist put it, it is 'the greatest mystery of Almighty God, and the highest and worthiest object of knowledge' that God 'should have expressed His nature in a concrete bodily form'.[22] The mystical ingestion of the body and blood of Christ is the central rite of Catholicism, and though many Protestants accord this rite a purely symbolic value, Christians are generally agreed that in some sense the Church itself constitutes the body of Christ. For some Christians, union with Christ effects a personal somatic transformation. In Interregnum England, William Franklin believed that 'his flesh was clean scrap't away, and his skin and bone hanged together: and his skin likewise very suddenly fell off from him, and that he had nothing left but the hair of his head, and of that not one hair was not diminished; and afterwards new flesh came as a young childe'.[23]

Christ is embodied mystically in bread and wine, or in the institution of the Church, or in the flesh and blood of the regenerate Christian; he also experienced a particular embodiment as Jesus of Nazareth. The Christian notion of Incarnation has often involved a slight contradiction: while orthodox thinkers are insistent that God did indeed clothe himself in human flesh, they also tend to emphasise what they regard as the 'purity' of Christ's body. This ambivalence can be seen in *The Glory of the World*:

> The soul and body of Christ and His divine nature were so inseparably joined together that they cannot be severed throughout all eternity. Nevertheless Christ had to die, and His soul had to be separated from His body, and once more joined to it on the same day, that His body might be glorified, and rendered as subtle as His soul and spirit.[24]

Valentin Weigel thought that Christ's true body came from the eternal Virgin, but it was necessary for him to assume a material body in the womb of Mary in order for him to be of any use to humanity.[25] William Blake was to question the assumption that Christ's body was in any way immune from the weaknesses customarily incident to the flesh:

> Or what was it which he took on
> That he might bring salvation?
> A Body subject to be Tempted,
> From neither pain nor grief Exempted?

> Or such a body as might not feel
> The passions that with Sinners deal?[26]

For Blake, the answer to this question was that Christ's flesh necessarily shared the frailty of the human body. For most occultists, however, Christ's body retained its purity and freedom from conditioning. Caspar Schwenckfeld accepted the reality of Christ's body, but he insisted that this was a purely spiritual embodiment.[27] Martines de Pasqually tells us that 'The body of Christ did not suffer any pain in the torments that were exercised upon him.'[28]

There is a superficial resemblance between the illuminists' concept of the corporeality of spirit and that of Lodowick Muggleton: 'No Spirit hath any being without a body.'[29] For the Muggletonians, however, this was a thoroughgoing reduction of spirit to matter. The doctrine of the corporeality of spirit is also given a materialist twist by some later occult writers. Charles Fourier, for example, insisted that 'souls are not separated from matter either before or after this life'.[30] In general, however, corporeality is distinguished from gross materiality in esoteric thought. This distinction between the corporeal and the material does not imply a dualist ontology. Coleridge, following Leibniz, thought that 'body and spirit ... may, without any absurdity, be supposed to be different modes or degrees in perfection of a common substratum'.[31] Similarly Herder asserted that 'We know of no spirit capable of operating without matter. What is more, we observe in matter so many powers of a spirit-like nature, that a complete *opposition* and *contradiction* of these admittedly different elements strikes me as at least unproven if not self-contradictory'.[32] Herder cited Joseph Priestley in support of this position,[33] but similar arguments had long been common currency in the Pietist circles in which he moved, and were a prominent part of occult thought. Body and spirit, according to one alchemical tract, must ultimately share an existential identity, since their union 'could not take place if the two had not been obtained from *one* thing; for an abiding union is possible only between things of the same nature'.[34] In the Behmenist tradition, the distinction between body and spirit is one between inner and outer. Boehme tells us that 'the internal continually labours or works itself forth to manifestation'. Thus 'The whole outward visible world is a signature, or figure of the inward world',[35] and 'each creature sets forth and manifests the internal form of its birth by its body'.[36] 'Everything that is outward in any Being is only *a Birth* of its own Spirit', William Law declared, 'For Body and Spirit are not two *independent Things*, but are necessary to each other, and only *inward* and *outward* Conditions of *one* and the *same Being*.'[37] This applies to both the gross and subtle bodies, since even before the Fall Adam and Eve possessed what were to become their material bodies, but these were '*concealed* and *covered* from *them* by their *paradisiacal* Glory'. What had changed is that '*another Sort* of Seeing, *another Sight of Things*, was opened in *Adam* after the Fall, than *that* which he had before it'.[38] A similar notion can be found in Michael Sendivogius's writings: 'The shadow of Nature upon our eyes is the body.'[39] The mutable body, according to Pernéty, belonged merely to the world of appearances: 'all individuals in the universe owed their existence only to a successive evolution of meta-morphoses that changed nothing at bottom, but only forms and figures'.[40] This is also Blake's doctrine in *The Marriage of Heaven and Hell*: 'Man has no Body distinct from his Soul; for that call'd Body is a portion of Soul discern'd by the five Senses, the chief inlets of the Soul in this age.'[41] The material body has an independent status on an epistemological rather than an ontological level.

As the outward expression of an inner reality the body was a signifier of meanings beyond itself. According to an early Cabalist work, the *Bahir*, the ten fingers represent the ten *sefiroth*.[42] The body as a whole is a repre-sentation of the Torah: the 248 positive commandments of the Pentateuch are reflected in the 248 members of man, and the 365 negative command-ments find their reflection in the body's 365 blood vessels.[43] Boehme thought that the T-shaped configuration of the coronal and sagittal sutures of the skull are a 'half Crosse in the Head', an anatomical sign pointing not only to the Crucifixion, but also to the loss of androgyny as a principle of mortal-ity: 'the Woman hath one half of the Crosse and the Man the other halfe, which you may see in the skull; . . . and therefore Christ must dye upon the Crosse, and destroy Death, on the Crosse'.[44] Fourier believed that the human body was 'a general table of the combined order', a symbolic sum-mary of the perfect society. The twelve ribs surmounted by the clavicle repre-sent the twelve fundamental human passions under the aegis of the thirteenth and supreme passion, 'harmonyism'. The 800 muscles of the body represent the 800 different personality types 'needed to make up a phalanx of attrac-tion' or perfect community.[45] In the eighteenth century the doctrine of somatic signatures bore fruit in the emergence of a new 'science', physiog-nomics. As Barbara Stafford remarks, 'What was new to eighteenth-century experience – as codes of polite behavior spread to broader and lower strata of society – was the frightening possibility that nothing stood behind decorum.' Physiognomics was a pragmatic response to the problem of penetrating beyond the masks of civility, with their latent threat of deception, to the underlying psychological reality.[46] But if it arose as a science in response to the disorienting effects of the civilising process, it also had an independent intellectual ancestry in the Paracelsian doctrine of signatures.[47] It can be no coincidence that the masters of Enlightenment physiognomics were men deeply versed in illuminism: Antoine-Joseph Pernéty, author of a *Discours sur la physiognomie* (1769), and Johann Caspar Lavater, who pub-lished his *Von der Physiognomik* in 1772. For men like Pernéty or Lavater, external differences in form were merely expressions of inner psychological or spiritual realities.[48] In earlier works in this tradition, like Thomas Hill's *Contemplation of Mankinde* (1571) or Jerome Cardan's *Metoposcopia* (1658), the forms of the human countenance were related not only to inner spiritual realities, but also to the planetary system. The correspondence between parts of the body and the planets or signs of the zodiac had long been a part of traditional astrology, forming the basis of 'iatromathematica' or astrological medicine as early as the Hippocratic writings. The body offered a variety of means for divination and the study of character: not only the analysis of lines on the forehead (metoposcopy) or hands (cheiromancy), but even the distribution of moles. All of these techniques were placed within an astrological explanatory framework. As always in occult thought, there is no sharp distinction between man and the cosmos.[49]

The belief in the existence of a spiritual body had not always been confined to heterodox thought. The idea of a subtle body has a biblical warrant, since Paul asserted that 'There is a natural body and there is a spiritual body' (1 Corinthians 15:44). Paul, however, is speaking about a resurrection body rather than one possessed before the Fall, and nothing he says implies that the spiritual body actually subsists in the natural one. In the ancient world, the idea of a spiritual body was a doctrine held by that great scourge of heretics, Irenaeus.[50] Lodovico Sinistrari, a Franciscan Consultor to the Inquisition in the late seventeenth century, believed that there were 'rational creatures having spirit and body', with 'a corporeity less gross, more subtile than man's'. These were the incubi and succubi, and their physical constitution had properties that we find ascribed to the prelapsarian body by occult mystics: they could walk through solid objects, and 'their body being less gross than the human frame, comprising fewer elements mixed together, and being therefore less composite, they would not so easily suffer from adverse influences, and would therefore be less liable to disease than man: their life would exceed his'.[51] Unlike the occult mystics, however, Sinistrari believed that there were also 'purely spiritual creatures, not partaking in any way of corporeal matter',[52] and he says nothing about the possibility of a prelapsarian spiritual body in humans. The concept of a spiritual body was developed in ancient Neoplatonism, where the subtle body is regarded as 'a quintessence or unitary element'.[53] The Neoplatonists believed that it was the 'medium between the soul and the gross body'.[54] It should be noted about the Neoplatonic conception of spirit that 'it invariably purports to be a corporeal entity'; and while 'In itself unshaped, it is capable of receiving the impression or pattern of any organized form.'[55] The tendency in early modern occult spiritualities is in fact to endow it with organic form.

The structure of occult mystical representations of the body was already fully developed in Paracelsian thought. Like the ancient Neoplatonists, Paracelsus believed that 'there are two bodies, an eternal and corporeal, enclosed in one';[56] the eternal body is variously referred to as 'spiritual', 'ethereal', 'sidereal' or 'astral'. Man's material body is composed of earth and water, and it is in itself dead; the sidereal body is formed from fire and air, and it is the living body. Adam's body had been created from the *limus terrae*, which was 'an extract from the firmament, of the universe of the stars,

and at the same time of all the elements'.[57] This theory provides the physiological basis of the doctrine of the microcosm: 'The fifth essence is extracted
from two bodies and has been combined in one body to form man. . . . Therefore man is the fifth essence, the microcosm, and the son of the whole world,
because he has been created as an extract of all creation by the hand of
God.'[58]

In Paracelsianism, both the elemental and sidereal bodies have a tripartite
structure. The material body is composed of Sulphur, Mercury and Salt, the
basic elements in Paracelsus's theory of matter. These are not identical to the
common substances with these names, but principles to be found in all substances, and whose qualities find their typical manifestation in ordinary
sulphur, salt and mercury. The sidereal body, on the other hand, is formed
from Feeling, Wisdom and Art.[59] As in Neoplatonism, the astral body was
identified with the world soul or *anima mundi*, but the Paracelsian world
soul differed from the Neoplatonic one in being a principle of differentiation,
providing form and function when conjoined to matter.[60] The ethereal body
was breathed into the terrestrial body by God, and Paracelsus informs us
that 'the two bodies are wedded, and both – that from God's breath and
that from the earth – are united as in marriage'. There is nevertheless a
natural antagonism between the terrestrial and ethereal bodies, since both
want different things.[61] Paracelsus tells us that 'Everything that comes
from the flesh is animal and follows an animal course; heaven has little influence on it. Only that which comes from the stars is specifically human in
us.'[62] Paracelsus's doctrine of the sidereal body appears to be rather confused and contradictory. He not only asserts that it was formed by divine
inspiration, he also says that it was the product of the Fall: 'Adam and
Eve acquired [it] in Paradise, through eating the apple; it was only by acquiring this body that man became completely human, with knowledge of good
and evil.'[63] In Paracelsian thought, therefore, the sidereal body has an
ambiguous moral status. It is because of this body rather than the terrestrial
one, for example, that man is able to eat and drink more than is necessary.[64]
In later occult thought these negative associations of the spiritual body are
abandoned.

Jacob Boehme asserted that 'the Body [is] an *Ens* of the Stars and
Elements; and also as to the internal ground an *Ens* of Heaven, *viz.* the
hidden World'.[65] Adam's body was originally composed of 'heavenly
flesh',[66] and the true Adamic image of God dwelled 'in one pure holy
element, whereof the four elements in the beginning of time are sprung'.[67]
'God the Father made Man; the beginning of whose Body . . . is the fifth
Essence.'[68] Samuel Pordage thought that the 'outward body cometh from
that womb: / That very LYMYS, whence this earth did come'.[69] Antoinette
Bourignon tells us that the matter out of which the prelapsarian body was
made was the 'Quintessence of all Natural things'.[70]

One of the fullest accounts of the spiritual body is to be found in the works
of the eighteenth-century physician George Cheyne.[71] He thought that the

particles composing the primitive body were in the form of 'the three most simple Figures, . . . *viz. Spheres, Cubes* and *equilateral triangular Prisms*'.[72] Originally the human body had been composed of 'elements of a *celestial* and *spiritual* Nature (so to speak) infinitely more subtile and refin'd than the Matter of *Light*, more elastick than the finest æther'.[73] The terms of this comparison are not fortuitous, and both ether and light play an important role in Cheyne's physiology. As Anita Guerrini notes, Newton's reformulation of the notion of a pervasive ether gave Cheyne 'sanction for the introduction of spirit into his natural philosophy'.[74] Cheyne routinely refers to the original creation body as ethereal, but the role of ether in human physiology is not confined to the paradisaical state. Cheyne tells us that muscular activity

> and the other abstruse Appearances in the Animal and Vegetable King-
> doms, particularly *Vegetation, Elasticity, Cohesion,* the Emission,
> Reflexions and Refractions of *Light, Attraction* in the greater and
> lesser Bodies, and all other secret and internal Actions of the Parts of
> Matter upon one another, are . . . owing to an infinitely subtil elastick
> Fluid, or Spirit . . . distended thro' this whole *System.* . . . And by this
> *æther, Spirit,* or most subtile Fluid, the Parts of Bodies are driven
> forcibly together, and their mutual attractive Virtue arises, and the
> other beforemention'd Appearances are produc'd.[75]

Ether is therefore a cohesive and animating principle in the gross material body. It is also the medium through which light, the other of Cheyne's 'two Kinds of most active Fluids', works.

Light, according to Cheyne, is a 'material Substance' composed of very fine, rapidly moving particles.[76] It 'actuates and enlivens the whole material *System* of Bodies here below, without which they would languish, deaden, chill, and be motionless, and this seems to be the active *energetick* Principle (together with that other [ether])'.[77] The source of light is the sun, whose emissions are material particles. Since these are absorbed by bodies on earth, 'it is evident that the Quality of Heat and Light in the *Sun* does daily decrease'.[78] One context in which to understand the role of light in Cheyne's physiology is the solar mysticism which characterised much occult thought.[79]

The spiritual body is the link between the soul and the material body. The alchemist Thomas Norton asserted that 'the subtle, pure, and immortal soul can never dwell with the gross body, except the [vital, natural and animal] spirits act as media between them'. The spirit 'joins the body and soul together by partaking of the nature of both'.[80] As Agrippa noted, if body and soul were to be united, there is 'need of a more excellent medium, viz. such a one that may be as it were no body, but as it were a soul, or as it were no soul, but as it were a body'. The soul is in fact 'joined by competent means to this gross body'. It is first 'involved in a celestial and aerial body', through which it becomes 'infused into the middle part of the heart . . . and from thence it is diffused through all the parts of the body'. This mediating substance is 'the Spirit of the World, viz. that which we call the quintessence'.[81] The fourteenth-century alchemist John Dastin attempted some sort of obstetric precision on this subject by following traditional teaching on the animation of the child in the womb:

> Indeed, when the fetus has been conceived in the woman's womb, within a period of forty days all its members are formed and it receives from the four elements and the woman's whole body a single fine, pure, noble vapor similar to nature in a celestial way which is called spirit. As soon as that spirit is formed, the soul descends quickly at God's command to the infant's body by means of the great fineness of the spirit.[82]

Basil Valentine thought that matter itself was produced by the union of soul with spirit:

> A celestial influence descends from above, by the decree and ordinance of God, and mingles with the astral properties. When this union has taken place, the two bring forth a third, namely, an earth-like substance, which is the principle of our seed, of its first source, so that it can show an ancestry, and from which three the elements, such as water, air and earth, take their origin.[83]

Cheyne, characteristically giving a modern scientific gloss to the doctrine of spirit as the medium between body and soul, asserted that they were joined through the ether: 'this intermediate material Substance, may make the Cement between the human Soul and Body, and may be the Instrument or *Medium* of all its Actions and Functions, where material Organs are not manifest'.[84] Body and soul are thus linked by spirit, which pervades the body. It should be noted, however, that early modern occult writers represent spirit not simply as an amorphous substance, but as something which itself takes organic form.

The prelapsarian body, according to Antoinette Bourignon, was 'incomprehensibly more beautiful and more perfect' than our present bodies. It was

> clear, subtile, agile, and transparent; its Skin like *Muscovy* Glass; its Flesh like Crystal; its Veins like Streams of Rubies; its Waters like Diamonds; its Nerves like the Hyacinth; the Substance of the Fruits its Aliments, that of all good Odours its Excrements, all its parts within and without, its Bones, Muscles, Sinews, Bowels, all so bright, fram'd with such Art, that all the Beauties of the Universe were nothing to the least part of it.[85]

Jacob Boehme asserted that at first Adam had been created as 'a totally bright clear Cristalline *Image*'.[86] Boehme informs us that Adam's body could 'go through Earth and Stone, uninterrupted by anything'.[87] According to Saint-Georges de Marsais, Adam's prelapsarian body was 'glorious, transparent, clear and very beautiful'. The angels still had bodies 'composed of the most subtle matter in the universe, so subtle that it is perceived as spiritual in relation to our elementary bodies'.[88] In the seventeenth century, Michael Sendivogius wrote that the prelapsarian body was made of 'the elements of paradise', which were 'most pure and incorruptible heavenly essences'. This was why the body before the Fall had not been subject to the law of decomposition and death.[89] Thomas Vaughan thought that, since in his prelapsarian perfection the '*Mental part* of *Man* was united to *God per Contactum Essentialem*, . . . the sensitive *Faculties* were scarce at all imployed, the *spirituall* prevailing over them in him, as they do over the spirituall now in us'.[90] Speaking of the prelapsarian body, Bourignon asserted that 'all Nature obey'd it. If he [Adam] design'd to go on the Waters, they supported him; if to the Center of the Earth, it yielded to him; if through the Air, it was a Chariot to him.'[91] According to the Chevalier Ramsay, man had at first possessed 'a luminous, heavenly, ethereal body', which served the soul 'as a vehicle to fly through the air, rise to the stars and wander over all the regions of immensity'.[92] Speculation about the primordial perfection of the body continued into the nineteenth century. Charles Fourier, for example, believed that 'the primitive height of the human race was $72^2/_3$ inches'.[93] This was once an idea to be found in more orthodox circles. In 1594 the Puritan John Dove wrote that man 'is of lower stature, less strength, shorter life than at first he was'.[94]

It is clear that the subtle body represents freedom from the normal constraints of material existence. In mythologies throughout the world this 'perfection of a primordial, non-conditioned state' is frequently symbolised by the idea of the original androgyny of humanity.[95] It is not surprising, therefore, to find that androgyny was a characteristic that early modern mystics ascribed to the prelapsarian body.[96] The Chevalier Ramsay tells us that Adam 'contained in himself the two sexes, or both the principles of fecundity'.[97] In Behmenist circles it was generally believed that procreation was at first intended to be effected through the imagination, or magically;[98] Adam originally 'loved and impregnated himself, through the *Imagination*'.[99] Thus Edward Taylor tells us that Adam was able to reproduce asexually because his 'pure Body' was no more 'obstructive to his Magical Will' than light is to glass.[100] Martines de Pasqually believed that Adam was intended to reproduce 'with purely spiritual essences'.[101] Bourignon, on the other hand, endowed the androgynous Adam with reproductive organs:

> there was in his belly a vessel where little eggs were born, and another vessel full of liquid which rendered the eggs fertile. And when man

warmed himself in the love of his God, the desire that he was in that there should be other creatures than him to praise, to love, and to adore this great majesty, spilled [the liquid] through the fire of God's love on one or more of these eggs with inconceivable delights; and this fertilised egg passed some time afterwards from this canal, outside the man, in the form of an egg, and came, a little afterwards, to hatch a perfect man.[102]

Whether or not he agreed with this vision of oviparous prelapsarian reproduction, George Cheyne accepted that '*originally*, there must have been no Difference of the Sexes, because at *last*, in their restor'd and recover'd State, there will be none'. Like William Law and the Bourignonists, he thought that 'the Female was but a *secondary* Intention', created to buttress Adam's 'falling edifice'.[103]

Between the Fall and the Resurrection, human beings are encumbered with a gross material body, whose 'monstrous Form or Shape indeed is not God, nor of his Essence, or Substance'.[104] Boehme tells us that 'the outer body is from the outer world, from the four elements and the stars, and this external dominion rules the outer life'.[105] Edward Taylor thought that since the Fall man's body has become 'subjected to the Astral Evil Influences, and to the divided Properties of the Elements'.[106] With Adam's lapse from grace, according to Sendivogius, 'The pure elements of his creation were gradually mingled and infected with the corruptible elements of the outer world, and thus his body became more and more gross, and liable through its grossness to natural decay and death.'[107] Thomas Bromley thought that the body we now have is merely a 'false covering' which the spirit 'wrapped itself in, through the Fall, instead of that naked Innocency in which there was no uncomeliness'.[108] Man, according to Cheyne, 'is a diminutive Angel, shut up in a Flesh Prison or Vehicle'.[109] Ramsay informs us that through sin the ethereal body 'was contracted, imprisoned and buried in a living sepulchre, a coarse covering, which does not continue one moment the same, and is something merely accidental to our substance'.[110] It was Eve's succumbing to temptation, Boehme asserted, that had 'introduced an Evil malignant venome and poyson into Man into the science or root of his body'.[111] Bourignon leaves us in no doubt as to the deleterious consequences of the material encrustation of Adam's body:

all its Humours and Parts being disordered, his glorious Body becomes filthy, dark, and deform'd in every part of it, contracts that gross Crust of Corruption which we now carry about with us, and which has seized on every the least part of it within and without. . . .The Senses also become gross, dull, feeble, could discern nothing but the outside of things, and the whole Body became full of disorder within, subject to all the Impressions of all the Creatures, and at last to Dissolution and Death.[112]

According to Edward Taylor, some of the physiological consequences of the Fall are particular to specific groups of people: Tartars are born blind, like cats and dogs, while Africans are black 'like their Evil Natures'.[113] Francis Lee thought that God's curse on Eve (Genesis 3:16) had produced 'a Change in the Woman's Body, as that the Execution thereof must necessarily follow in the Course of Nature'; so 'the Labour in bringing of Children forth, is not from the Conformation of their Parts in the State of Innocence; but is from a subsequent Mutation of them upon the divine Sentence'.[114] It was also with the Fall that Adam acquired his '*bestiall form* and shape of Masculine Members'.[115] Edward Taylor regarded these 'Bestiall Genitals' as a 'Monstrous, Filthy, Brutish Deformity'.[116] Similarly Cheyne thought that 'all the Difference of the *Sexes* lies in the different *Configuration* of the superinduc'd Crust or Shell laid over the primitive *ætherial* Body, which in both is probably pretty near the same Figure, Size and Materials, originally'.[117]

Despite his mystical physiology, Cheyne describes the fallen body in completely mechanistic terms:

> An *animal* Body is nothing but a *Compages* or Contexture of Pipes, an hydraulic *Machin[e]*, fill'd with a Liquor of such a Nature as was transfus'd into it by its *Parents*, or is changed into it by the *Nature* of the *Food* it is nourish'd with, and is ever afterwards good, bad, or indifferent, as these two sources have sent it forth.

Cheyne tells us that the body is formed of solids and fluids, but the physician can only work effectively with the latter. In this 'It is *Diet* alone . . . which is the sole *universal Remedy*.' Since the body is an hydraulic machine, ensuring the proper flow of the fluids is of fundamental importance for the maintenance of health. This depends primarily on the viscosity of the fluids themselves and the size of the channels through which they are to flow.[118] Gout, for example, is caused by 'narrower and more stiff' capillaries than those of a healthy person. This results from 'the Abundance of Tartarous, Urinous, or other Salts, introduc'd into the Blood by the Food', which 'necessarily form Obstructions, and give Pain, when, by the Force of the Circulation, they are thrust through narrower and stiffer small Vessels'. To remedy this, the small vessels or capillaries can be widened by exercise, but 'Moderation in eating and drinking' is also required in order to reduce the level of salts in the blood. We should be particularly cautious with regard to fish, meat, wines and spirits.[119]

It is sometimes supposed that Cheyne's combination of mysticism and mechanism poses a paradox. Although G. S. Rousseau has argued that we need to take Cheyne's religion seriously if we are to understand his true place in eighteenth-century culture, he nevertheless speaks of 'conflicting aspirations: iatromedicine on the one hand and mystical religion on the other'. Rousseau resolves this apparent paradox by positing a shift from mechanism to animism in Cheyne's intellectual development.[120] Similarly, Robert Schofield talks of Cheyne's 'progress from kinematic mechanism toward vitalistic materialism'.[121] Cheyne in fact remained a mechanist throughout his life, and this did not present a paradox. Mystical writers were perfectly capable of using a mechanistic framework in their discourse on the fallen body without having to abandon their customary modes of thought. Mungo Murray approved Pierre Poiret's clock analogy to explain man's individual life expectancy:

> In the moment of his formation the spirit of the world & of the Stars enters into him[,] fashions his mac[h]in[e] & makes his springs & chain strong or weak[,] long or short, and at his birth the same is more or less wound up when by respiration he incorporat[e]s abundantly into his blood the same spirit of effluvias of the stars & elements.[122]

Murray shows no embarrassment at all in mixing his occult effluvias with mechanism. Cheyne himself was never a mere mechanical reductionist: '*MECHANISM* takes place and operates by itself only, on dead *Matter*; but is actuated and govern'd in its Operations, by animated living Bodies or *spiritual* Substances.'[123]

For anyone thinking within the occult tradition, both physiology and psychology are really aspects of cosmology and theology; mind and body are illusions, epiphenomena of a single substance. When that substance is morally diseased, it approximates to 'body', and the morally healthier it is, the closer to 'mind' (or rather, spirit) it becomes. Because the health of this substance is morally determined, it has been thoroughly diseased since the Fall. Hence the seeming paradox that writers like George Cheyne or Thomas Tryon,[124] whose religious views could be read as primarily 'idealist' in tendency, developed a physiological discourse overwhelmingly 'material-ist' in appearance. The occult philosophers were prepared to adopt the trappings of the mechanical philosophy, but they were nevertheless to retain and emphasise the essentially moral problematic of traditional discourses on the flesh and spirit. If the derogation of human dignity supposedly implicit in the concept of *l'homme machin* was problematic to those who adhered to a one-body theory of human nature, it was precisely what was required by the mystics' dualistic physiology. The fallen body was lodged in the realm of the conditioned and the contingent; conceptualising it in terms of mechanism gave perfect expression to this view.

The body can be seen as a reification and objectification of what is properly personal and subjective. As in much traditional theology, therefore, there was a tendency in occult mysticism to represent the flesh and the spirit as antagonistic. In the Hermetic writings we read that 'Unless you first hate your body, my child, you cannot love yourself'; man must choose between the 'corporeal and incorporeal'.[125] For Valentin Weigel, the soul itself has no need for regeneration, since it is the divine spark in man.[126] Boehme tells us that 'when we speak of Heaven, we speak of our native Country, which the enlightened Soul can well see, though indeed such Things are hidden from the Body'.[127] The body tended to lead the soul astray. Robert Fludd believed that the performance of geomantic rites 'emanated from the very soul'; any errors were therefore due to the 'incongruous mutations of the body'.[128] According to Roger Crabb, 'it is the grossness of the flesh / that makes the soul to smart'.[129] It was the growth of Henry Vaughan's 'forward flesh' that checked 'the health and heat' of God's spirit in him.[130] According to Vaughan, the body is a veil separating man from God:

> This veil, I say, is all the cloke
> And cloud which shadows thee from me.[131]

The body is 'impure, rebellious clay',[132] the soul's coffin and a 'quickened mass of sin'.[133] In one of his poems, Vaughan regarded a dead infant as blessed in that its soul 'Flew home unstained by his new kin', the body.[134] Vaughan's brother, Thomas, believed that 'The Soul of Man whiles she is in the *Body*, is like a *Candle* shut up in a dark Lanthorn, or a Fire that is almost stifl'd for want of Aire.'[135] William Blake regarded the body as a fetter:

> Thou, Mother of my Mortal part,
> With cruelty didst mould my Heart,
> And with false self-deceiving tears
> Didst bind my Nostrils, Eyes & Ears:
> Didst close my Tongue in senseless clay,
> And me to Mortal Life betray.[136]

Blake thought that 'The Natural Body is an Obstruction to the Soul or Spiritual Body'.[137] Similar attitudes continued to be expressed into the nineteenth century. For Balzac, bodies were 'but a mode of detaining' the soul: 'if bodies were themselves living things, they would be a cause; they would not die'.[138] According to Victor Hugo, 'Man has a body which is at once his burden and his temptation.'[139] Helena Blavatsky thought that the 'spiritual self' was 'the divine spark in man', and as such it was omniscient. It was, however, incapable of manifesting 'its knowledge owing to the impediments of matter'.[140]

Despite this disparagement of the material body, which the occultists shared with their wider culture, esoteric discourses on the body also have a more positive element. Novalis could write that 'There is only one temple in the world, and that is the human body. Nothing is more sacred than that noble form.'[141] This positive attitude can be seen in the notion of the organic corporeality of spirit, and the denial of any absolute ontological distinction between flesh and spirit. The occult philosophers did not seek a life without personal, organic manifestation, but conceived of existence as essentially embodied. Even in terms of the gross body, the goal of the occult mystics was the subordination of the flesh rather than its annihilation. Although there is a strongly ascetic impulse in occult thought, there is also a deep respect for the body. Leone Ebreo, a sixteenth-century Jewish Neoplatonist-Cabalist, interpreted the myth of Adam and Eve as an allegory of mind and matter. The Protoplast had been created as an androgyne, his male aspect representing intellect and his female aspect being 'body and matter'. Body should be subordinate to intellect, but it also has its own legitimate needs. This is why God separated Adam's two genders by creating Eve; only by granting the female somatic principle a relative independence from the male intellective principle could its interests be guaranteed a fair hearing.[142] Similarly, in one alchemical tract we are told that the union of body and soul is comparable to 'the wedlock of a bride and bridegroom'. In this union it is important 'that the wife does not rule the husband', but it is equally important 'that the husband does not abuse his authority over the wife'.[143] The body might even be seen to work positive spiritual effects. William Law believed that 'the supernatural Light stream[s] forth its Blessings into the World, through the *Materiality* of the Sun'.[144] Law argued that 'the reason why, even the most Profligate Persons do not *fully know*, and perceive their Souls to be in this miserable State, *a dark Root of self-tormenting Fire*, is this, because the Soul, though thus fallen, was still *united to the Blood* of an human Body, and therefore the sweet and *cheering Light* of the Sun, could reach the Soul'.[145]

A rough indication of how positive or negative was the attitude to the body can be seen in attitudes to sexuality. Generally speaking, the occult philosophers disparaged the pleasures of the flesh, and we can detect a pathological distaste for sexuality in much of their writings. There was also a counter tradition that celebrated sexuality, seeing it as playing a sacramental role in human life. The Jewish Cabalist tradition is an example of this approach; so too are the Ranters of Interregnum England.[146] In the nineteenth century, when the Saint-Simonians took to mysticism under the leadership of Barthélémy-Prosper Enfantin, they began to talk about 'the rehabilitation of the flesh', a principle which underlay the growing advocacy of free love in the movement. By the early twentieth century, Karl Kellner was introducing a Westernised Tantrism in his Ordo Templi Orientis, and Tantric sexual mysticism has become firmly established in contemporary New Age movements.[147]

It would be difficult to argue that the occultists developed a positive attitude to the body on the basis of their sexual philosophy alone. Twentieth-century occultism does appear to be generally positive in its attitude to sexuality, although sometimes (as in the case of Aleister Crowley)[148] this might be regarded as being as pathological as the obsessive celibatarianism of earlier occult thinkers. Firmer evidence of the growing respect for the body in esoteric circles can be found in their medical discourse. As we shall see in the next chapter, if occult thinkers derogated the material body, they also conceived the project of its physical salvation.

5 The body in health and death

Early modern occult spirituality was closely associated with medicine, and many of the writers whose works we have been examining were either professional physicians or lay practitioners of the healing arts. The occult philosophy shaped sixteenth- and seventeenth-century medicine through the doctrine of signatures, which was not just a piece of metaphysical speculation, but also had a practical medical application. In his *Botonologia*, Robert Turner observed that 'God hath imprinted on Plants, Herbs, and Flowers, as it were in Hieroglyphicks, the very Signature of their Vertues.'[1] The form of a plant indicated its medical properties by its similarity to either the afflicted organ or the disease to be cured. Walnuts, for example, are good for the brain, and kidney beans for kidneys. In its medical form, the doctrine of signatures was of widespread currency, forming the background to such herbalist works as Nicholas Culpeper's *English Physitian*, a book which is still in print in a variety of editions, mostly under the name of *Culpeper's Complete Herbal*. Culpeper's medicine was also based on astrology: 'he that would know the reason of the operation of the Herbs, must look up as high as the Stars, astrologically'.[2]

Astrology, a science closely related to (although far from identical with) the occult philosophy, provided an important 'system of preventative and explanatory physic' throughout the sixteenth and seventeenth centuries.[3] If astrology itself was to decline as an element of learned medicine after the seventeenth century, some of its assumptions were to enjoy a revival in late eighteenth-century mesmerism. Franz Anton Mesmer taught that the universe was permeated by a subtle fluid which was the medium of the 'mutual influence between the celestial bodies, the earth and animate bodies'.[4] Sickness was due to the obstruction of the flow of this cosmic fluid, and health could be restored by its magnetic manipulation.[5] Mesmer's notion of animal magnetism was simply a reformulation of traditional ideas concerning the occult forces permeating the universe. Already in 1603 Christopher Heydon had argued that the influence of the heavenly bodies on the human body was similar to that of a lodestone on iron, and in the seventeenth century esotericists like Rudolf Gockel, Athanasius Kircher and Jean-Baptist van Helmont were already employing magnetic therapies.[6] Mesmer's disciple, the Marquis of Puységur, was soon to add a mysterious new occult force to animal magnetism proper, one that can still be found today both in some forms of psychiatric practice and in popular entertainment: hypnotism. In fact hypnotism had long been part of the magician's art, under the name of 'fascination'.[7]

The occult philosophy continued to play a role in medical practice in the nineteenth century. Schelling's *Naturphilosophie*, a barely rationalised form of Behmenism, was widely influential on nineteenth-century German medicine. One of Schelling's medical followers, Dietrich Kieser, argued that health was a balance of negative and positive qualities. Disease occurred when this balance was upset by the arousal of the negative principle – a medicalisation of Behmenist theodicy. The influence of Schelling's system in German medicine was apparently not always to the good; Justus von Liebig, at least, regarded it as 'the black death of our century'.[8]

Of the occult philosophers it was Paracelsus who played the most important role in the development of modern medicine, and his achievements in this field are due precisely to those aspects of his thought that appear 'irrational' or 'superstitious'. Charles Webster has argued that his 'sympathetic approach . . . to popular magic . . . suggested a manner in which secularization could be pursued without insensitivity to the prevailing cosmic order'.[9] In espousing magic, as far as Paracelsus himself was concerned, he was also championing a purely natural as opposed to a miraculous explanatory and curative framework.[10] Believing that disease was a magical phenomenon was a step towards ousting direct divine or diabolic intervention from its etiology, a move towards constructing it in purely natural terms. Because they regarded disease as natural in this sense, Paracelsus and his followers developed something of an empirical approach to medical science. The Swiss physician declared that 'only he who receives his experience from nature is a physician, and not he who writes, speaks, and acts with his head and ratiocinations aimed against nature and her ways'.[11] Paracelsus also moved medicine away from a humoral system of generalised somatic imbalances to one dealing with specific organic dysfunctions: disease, for Paracelsus, was a phenomenon localised in particular organs. Paracelsus understood this novel concept in a far from modern way. He represented the body as if it were a society of organs, each governed by its own 'archeus', and these archei act 'more or less like internal alchemists'.[12] It was in this way that Paracelsus made one of his major contributions to medical science, by formulating 'the first modern theory of metabolism', involving 'a functional conception of physiology'. This aspect of Paracelsian thought is related to his understanding of man as a microcosm.[13] Just as we understand the organic whole of the cosmos in terms of functional differentiation, so we should understand the human body in similar terms. In itself, this idea has more appeal to the practitioners of modern conventional medicine than it does to those who favour a more holistic approach. Our own tradition of alternative medicine, however, can also be traced back to Paracelsus. From the 1790s Samuel Hahnemann began developing a revised Paracelsianism, partly under the influence of Jacob Boehme.[14] The form of medicine established by Hahnemann in his *Organon der rationellen Heilkunde* – homeopathy – is increasingly popular, if still controversial.[15]

In some occult thought, the medical practitioner becomes a sort of priest of the body. Paracelsus called the physician 'a god of the Little World [i.e. man], appointed as God's deputy'; God himself was 'the oldest physician'.[16] The first law of the Rosicrucian fraternity was 'That none of them should practise any other thing than to cure the sick, and that *gratis*'.[17] The securing of health and long life was one of the traditional goals of alchemy; this, after all, is the purpose of the elixir of life. The notion of such an elixir was first developed in Chinese alchemy, which was preoccupied with the search for longevity rather than gold-making. It was imported into the West by Arab traders after the eighth century, and was to be increasingly common in early modern European alchemy.[18] The elixir in Western alchemy functions primarily as allegory; 'the great and glorious medicine for all passion, pain, and sorrow' is none other than Christ.[19] This does not preclude a more literal interpretation of this miraculous substance. One alchemical writer informs us that God has 'bestowed upon us an earthly antitype [of the Medicine of the Soul, Christ], or the Medicine of the Body, by means of which wretched man may, even in this world, secure himself against all bodily distempers, put to flight anxiety and care, and refresh and comfort his heart in the hour of trouble'.[20] Another tract tells us that in all ages 'God-enlightened men . . . endeavoured laboriously and fervently to discover whether Nature contained anything that would preserve our earthly body from decay and death, and maintain it in perpetual health and vigour.' The author admits that nothing can prevent death, since God had imposed this penalty on man at the Fall, but a secret remedy had been revealed to Adam and bequeathed to the Patriarchs, whereby humans could at least prolong their lives.[21] Helvetius (Johann Friedrich Schweitzer) affirmed that 'even now the Medicine is prepared which . . . has the virtue to bestow that which all the gold in the world cannot buy, *viz*. health.'[22] An eighteenth-century tract tells us that the 'great Treasure' of the alchemists 'healeth all manner of Diseases in Human Bodies, even renewing Youth and prolonging Life'.[23] Some alchemists were believed to have achieved exceptional longevity. A rumour was circulating in the 1730s that Eugenius Philalethes (who published his tracts in the 1650s) 'was yet alive . . . and above a hundred years old'.[24] Eugenius Philalethes was the pseudonym of Thomas Vaughan, who died in 1666, aged 44.

Health and long life were to be achieved by helping Nature to do her own work, in accordance with the principle that *natura naturam curat*. Paracelsus insisted on the body's capacity to heal itself by virtue of its own inherent balsam, which he called 'mummia': 'Flesh possesses an inner balsam which heals, and every limb has its own cure in it.'[25] The natural curative properties of the body were transferable, and they could even survive death; this, for Paracelsus, explained the ability of saints' corpses to effect cures.[26] Here the body is evaluated positively. In contrast to this is Michael Maier's theory of the somatic etiology of mental disorders: 'in many cases the causes of mental maladies appeared to be material, and to consist in an excess or defect of the bile, or of some other bodily substance'.[27] In the struggle for health the body can be perceived as either the perpetrator or the victim of disease.

Despite Maier's somatism, there was a genuine awareness in occult thought of the psychogenetic etiology of much physical illness. Paracelsus argued that 'There are two kinds of disease, one material affecting the body, the other immaterial in the spirit', but 'when the spirit suffers, so does the body, for it manifests itself in the body'.[28] Agrippa noted that 'it is a common opinion of the magicians, that unless the mind and spirit be in good case, the body cannot be in good health'.[29] Robert Fludd believed that it was necessary to cure the mind and spirit of the patient before the physical disease.[30] Heinrich Nolle attributed bodily illness to the debilitating effects of sin on the soul, which becomes 'impotent and unfit to govern the body'; as a consequence, 'the bodily faculties are profusely wasted and abused'.[31]

This position is taken to an extreme by some occult thinkers. As Kathleen Raine observed of William Blake's thought, the diseases of the body are caused by those of the soul: 'The only disease is spiritual disease, the only death spiritual death.'[32] According to William Law, 'Wrath [i.e. sickness] . . . can have no *Existence* or *Manner* of working in the Body, but what it has directly from Spirit.'[33] For Oberlin, 'no illness could have a material cause'.[34] In the nineteenth century, Mary Baker Eddy was to base the Christian Science movement on this principle.[35] This is a dangerous position, but it would be hard to contradict Herder's belief in the psychogenetic etiology of many bodily disorders: 'When, one day, the same systematic study that is now devoted to the cure of physical diseases will be applied to disorders of the mind, it will be found that many of the former are in fact attributable to the latter.'[36] The occultists may have performed a valuable service to medicine in preserving the idea of the psychogenetic origins of bodily disorders in the eighteenth century, counteracting the naïve somatism of the period. Even George Cheyne, who is often regarded as espousing a fully somatic etiology of disease, believed in psychosomatic occurrences:

It is well-known to Physicians what wonderful Effects, the *Passions*, excited by lucky or unlucky Accidents, (which are justly reckon'd *Intellectual* or *Spiritual* Operations) have on the Pulse, Circulation, Perspiration, and Secretions, and the other Animal Functions, in *Nervous* Cases especially, even to the restoreing from Death, and destroying Life, as innumerable Instances demonstrate.

Cheyne cited the case of Colonel Townshend, who 'cou'd *die* or *expire* when he pleas'd, and yet by an *Effort*, or some how, he could come to Life again'.[37] Cheyne's curative regime was not purely physical; for the most serious cases of mental disturbance, he knew 'no other remedy but to drown all other Passions in that Spiritual One of the Love of God'.[38]

Occult thought on the spiritual origins of disease was located in a moral discourse. The conscience, according to the mesmerist Nicolas Bergasse, is 'a true organ', the nerves of which unite it 'to all the points of the universe'. The other organs are dependent on the conscience, and 'If in a sick being the organ of the conscience suffers, the perfect re-establishment of the ordinary organs is impossible; and thus you arrive at this primary and luminous idea, that it is necessary to be good to be absolutely healthy'.[39] Physicians had long believed that 'Diseases and Death are marks of Divine justice in the punishment of sin',[40] and much occult thought on health can be understood as medical theodicy. The occult position, however, went beyond a merely forensic notion of the origins of disease: illness had a redemptive function. There was nothing new about Christian Morgenstern's belief that 'Every disease has its special meaning, for every disease is a purification, one only needs to find out from what.'[41] Among the Romantics, Novalis represented disease even more positively: 'Our sicknesses are all phenomena of a heightened sensation that is seeking to pass over into higher powers.'[42] On the point of death, Balzac's Séraphîta suffers a great deal of pain; 'Such pain', she observes, 'makes me glad; it is indispensible to escape from life.'[43] In the sixteenth century, Paracelsus wrote that

> God has sent us some diseases as a punishment, as a warning, as a sign by which we know that all our affairs are nought, that our knowledge rests upon no firm foundation, and that the truth is not known to us, but that we are inadequate and fragmentary in all ways, and that no ability and knowledge is ours.

'Every disease', he adds, 'is a kind of purgatory', and those diseases sent by God as a chastisement were incurable until the appointed period of chastisement was complete.[44] Disease, according to Heinrich Nolle, is 'an expiatory penance' to be borne patiently by 'every child of God (in imitation of his blessed Son)'.[45] This is the basis of Henry Vaughan's paradox, that 'Sickness is wholesome.'[46] For Lady Conway, herself a victim of repeated bouts of migraine, physical suffering had a spiritual function:

> every Pain and Torment excites or stirs up an Operating Spirit and Life in every thing which suffers: . . . because through Pain, and the enduring thereof, every kind of Crassitude or grossness in Spirit or Body contracted is attenuated and so the Spirit captivated is set at Liberty, and made more Spiritual, and consequently more Active and Operative, through suffering.[47]

Cheyne shared this medical theodicy, telling us that 'PAIN, *Punishment*, and *Suffering*' are 'a natural, necessary, and (as it were) a *mechanical* Mean of Expiation, Purification and Perfection, to all sentient and intelligent Beings, in this present State of Existence.'[48] Origen believed that the body was a punishment for the soul's sin in its premundane state,[49] a line of thought with which Cheyne was in full agreement. The body itself is represented as a sickness inflicted by God in order to fulfil his redemptive plan. God, Cheyne tells us,

> contrived this wonderful Expedient, viz. to tye down, sopite [to lull to sleep] and restrain the Acts and Exertion of the Natural Powers, of laps'd, *sentient* and *intelligent* Beings, for a determin'd Space of Time, by Chains and Fetters made of the *Elements* of this ruinous Globe, in order to punish and purify them, and so to vindicate his *Sovereignty*, to repair the Indignity done to his *Purity*, to warn and deter other Orders of his standing *Hierarchies*, and at the same Time, by lessening the Strength and Activity of the Natural Powers in their full Vigour, to allow Freedom and Uninterruption from them, for the Restoration and Advancement of the Moral Powers.[50]

Cheyne advised Richardson that 'you must go through your State of Purification, in Body as well as Soul, before you can enter on the Land of Promise'. Like Nolle, Cheyne believed that being ill was an imitation of Christ, who 'was made perfect by Suffering [and] became dead to every Thing but infant Love and Beauty'.[51]

There is an apparent contradiction between a belief in the redemptive value of sickness and the physician's commitment to the elimination of disease. Side by side with the idea that the sufferings of the body have a soteriological function, we can also find another medical theology in occult thought. Paracelsus argued that disease affects the material body, and it is the physician's task to cure it in order to free the spiritual body from encumbrance: 'Medicine acts upon the house by purging it, so that the spiritual body may be able to perfect its actions therein, like civet in a pure and uncontaminated casket.'[52] For Cheyne in the eighteenth century, no less than for Paracelsus in the sixteenth, the body's well-being was to be sought not simply for its own sake, but also in order to facilitate spiritual growth. It was clear to Cheyne that 'the lighter and thinner (while sweet and healthy) the *Crust* and *Plaister* from this *elementary System*, that is laid over this *Creation Body*, the more the Natural Powers of the Spirit will be at liberty to exert their Functions, and acquire the Moral ones'; hence the importance of sound diet.[53]

Samuel Butler ridiculed the Hermeticists for undertaking 'to teach any Kind of mysterious Learning in the World by Way of Diet'.[54] Certainly occultists were capable of strange dietry whimsies in their search for enlightenment; an eighteenth-century French illuminist, Duchanteau-Touzay, is said to have died after spending forty days imbibing only his own urine in hope of obtaining the Philosophers' Stone.[55] There was also a less fanciful dietry discourse in occult thought. Diet, according to Marsilio Ficino, was one of the means through which it was possible to make the human spirit more celestial, bringing it into harmony with the *spiritus mundi*.[56] Paracelsus thought that man shared the properties of the macrocosm because 'All he eats out of the Great World becomes a part of him, and he maintains himself by that which he is made of.'[57] Sendivogius wrote that the dominion of the elemental world over man's body was furthered by the ingestion of 'perishable substances'. This was a cumulative process: 'The continued use of corruptible substances rendered their [Adam's descendants'] bodies more and more gross – and human life was soon shortened to a very brief span.'[58] Cheyne also thought that 'the spiritual Nature . . . is crusting over more densely the primitive *celestial* Body by Nutrition, and the animal Functions with a gross *leprous* Plaister'.[59] Diet had obvious implications for the health of the body. Paracelsus wrote that 'all diseases can be traced to a coagulation of undigested matter in the bowels'.[60] Man 'has death in him, and through nourishment he must hold it at bay'.[61] Cheyne was even more emphatic on the importance of sound diet for maintaining health, clearly having the Paracelsians in mind when he castigated 'The *Alchymists*, or more conceited and whimsical sort of Chymists' for their reliance on drugs at the expense of diet.[62]

'In the first ages of the world', according to John Gerard, plants 'were the ordinary meate of men.'[63] The idea that prelapsarian humanity had been vegetarian was widespread in the early modern period, and some authorities thought that people remained so until God specifically sanctioned meat-eating after the Flood.[64] Edward Taylor believed that one of the unfortunate effects of the Fall was that people now eat the same sort of food as animals, and like animals they kill to acquire it. American Indians carried this dietry degeneracy further than most, and Taylor informs us that they not only eat raw meat and unclean animals like serpents, but some of them are also cannibals.[65] Boehme tells us that before the Fall, Adam lived on a diet of 'Paradisiacal Fruit', and he 'needed no teeth for that'.[66] 'Upon the Tree of Life he only fed', asserted Samuel Pordage, this being one of the reasons his relations with the animals were so harmonious.[67] For Antoinette Bourignon, the aliment which nourished the prelapsarian body was 'the Substance of the Fruits'.[68] Cheyne also believed in the vegetarian fare of prelapsarian man: '*Milk* and *Honey* were the Complexion of the *Land of Promise*, and *Vegetables* the *Diet* of the Paradisiacal State.'[69]

Given these beliefs, it is not surprising to find vegetarianism in the occult milieu. In the nineteenth century, Auguste Gleizes believed that fruits were 'the envelopes under which the good spirits of the earth live and make themselves visible'; it was the animals who were the forbidden fruit.[70] According to Helena Blavatsky, meat should be avoided since 'when the flesh of animals is assimilated by man as food, it imparts to him, physiologically, some of the characteristics of the animal it came from'. There was a hierarchy of risk in consuming animals: mammals were most dangerous, followed by birds; fish offered the least risk.[71] Although Rudolf Steiner was a vegetarian, he was not dogmatic about it: 'It is better to eat meat than to *think* meat.'[72]

Already in the 1640s vegetarianism had established itself in the English sectarian milieu; some people believed that ''Tis unlawful to fight at all, or to kill any man, yea to kill any of the creatures for our use, as a chicken, or on any other occasion.' Thomas Edwards recorded a Familist bricklayer who thought that it was wrong to kill 'any creature that had life because it came from God'.[73] Such attitudes were particularly common among occultists. In the late eighteenth century Ralph Mather found 'abstinence from animal foods' being practised by several 'persons in whose Minds the Light of God has Arisen, or is graciously Rising'.[74] Mather belonged to a circle of Behmenist-inspired pietists, and the vegetarian tradition among the Behmenists dates back at least as far as the 1650s. It was in 1653 that Roger Crab, a Behmenist whom Christopher Hill regards as the original Mad Hatter,[75] retired to 'a small Roode of ground' near Uxbridge, adopting a diet of 'Corne, Bread, and Bran, Hearbs, Roots, Dock-leaves, Mallowes, and grasse'.[76] Crab's vegetarianism stemmed from the belief that 'the eating of flesh is an absolute enemy to pure nature'. It was meat-eating that had led to the Fall: 'if naturall *Adam* had kept to his single naturall fruits of God's appointment, namely fruits and hearbs, we had not been corrupted'. According to Crab, '*Mars* being the god of War, is the governour of these destroyers [meat-eaters]: and while he can get flesh to feed on, he will encrease his desires to destroy flesh, till they are full of corruption.'[77]

At the beginning of the eighteenth century there was allegedly a sect of 'Tryonists' in London, who were 'such as forbid eating Flesh, Fish, or anything that is killed, as contrary to Scripture'.[78] Whether or not such a sect existed, Thomas Tryon himself was certainly a vegetarian. A Behmenist who, like Crab, had once been a hatter, Tryon believed that people were 'digging their *Graves* with their own *Teeth*'.[79] Food, we are told, 'is the Substance of each Mans Body and Spirit'.[80] An unnatural diet was evidently soporific, since animals are less inclined to sleep than humans: 'The principal cause why the creatures are not so drowned in this drowsy Death, is, they have not broken God's Law, but live more intire, and according to their Original, their Meats and Drinks being more suitable to their Original Natures.'[81] Tryon recommended

> a *spare, thin, clean Diet*, and no *Flesh*, for Temperance and Cleanness in quantity and quality of Meats and Drinks not only make People Healthful, but Ready, Vivacious, and Quick in the discharge of all the Actions necessary to Life, and conserves the Mind in Serenity, Acuteness and Vigour, and all the Offices of the Body in a due Tone, Strength and Agility.[82]

We should 'remember that all Beasts are not only endued with senses equal with Man, but also with all kinds of Passions as Love, Hate, Wrath, and the like, which their Flesh and Blood is not freed from'.[83] Tryon asserts that 'every sort and particular [food] hath its own Complexion, and its whole Business and Inclination is to advance that Property which is strongest in it'.[84] Meat should be avoided for the sake of moral health as much as physical, since flesh and fish 'generate in the Body . . . the *Diseases*, and promote the *Passions* the Creature was subject unto in its Life'.[85]

We are reminded that 'the Groaning of those Creatures that suffer Pain, never fail[s] to procure Misery to the Actors thereof'. If animals are to be eaten at all, they should be such as have been killed by 'a Wound which may cause the free Evacuation of the original Properties of *Saturn* and *Mars*'.[86] Most fish and fowl, however, are killed by suffocation, 'whereby the pure Spirits and sweet Vertues (by the Agony of the poor Creatures at the departure of their dear Lives) are fixt or overcome'.[87] This passage points to a humanitarian reason for avoiding meat, 'for killing and eating the Flesh and Blood of Beasts, cannot be accounted human, for men have no Example in all the Creation, but only the cruel, fierce, savage Beast of the Desart, in which Creatures fierceness and wrath have the Ascendant'.[88] Both animals and humans are part of God's family, 'For all the Beasts of the Field are in one Sense our Brethren, and the Great Creator of all Beings hath ordained the same Way and Method for their Generation, decay and Corruption, as he hath to Man; there being no difference in the Grand Point.'[89] 'God's Creatures', we are told, 'bear the Image of their Creator in a great Measure as well as ourselves.'[90] Tryon therefore extended the Golden Rule to encompass the animal kingdom: 'to do to all God's Creatures as we would be done unto' is one of the principles 'of true Religion'.[91]

Tryon admitted that God had sanctioned meat-eating, but insisted that this was a product of the Fall, arising out of Boehme's First Principle, that of wrath.[92] He called on the sad example of 'our first Parents' to witness to the power of food to sink us 'into the deepest Misery and Depravity', since 'whosoever doth Eat and drink without the Eye of Wisdom, and distinguishing of God and Nature in themselves, must of necessity eat the Forbidden Fruit'.[93] Like Crab, Tryon ascribed the Fall to a gastronomic cause:

> for so soon as Mankind Tasted Blood, together with the Flesh, it presently awakened and rouzed up all the dark, morose, unclean Spirits, and dark Properties of the fallen Magia, and Incorporated with, and strengthened their Similies, which did quickly prepare him to do the like by his own kind, (*viz.*) To kill and Slaughter, and to have no more Mercy nor Compassion, than he had of the Beasts, being both done from the same Principle of Violence.[94]

According to Tryon, 'there is no way [for man] to reinvest and obtain his first Condition of Unity, and the Understanding of himself and the Signatures of his own Composition; but Temperance, Cleanness, and to abandon all Violence and Oppression, both to Man and Beast'.[95]

Tryon's belief that 'the most hopeful means' of effecting a cure for the mad 'would be to keep them with a Clean Spare Diet'[96] was to be a theme adopted by another dietary philosopher, George Cheyne. As with Tryon, there is a humanitarian aspect to Cheyne's thought on diet. He could see no difference in reason or equity 'between feeding on *human Flesh*, and feeding on brute animal Flesh, except *Custom* and *Exampl[e]*'.[97] Also like Tryon, Cheyne was concerned with recommending 'that plain Diet which is most agreeable to the Purity and Simplicity of uncorrupted *Nature*, and unconquer'd *Reason*'.[98] Unlike Tryon, however, he was not a strict vegetarian. Cheyne did not propose to set up his 'Opinions or Ideas in Opposition to those of *holy Writ*', and it was from the Bible that 'the Patent for *animal* Food is deriv'd'. Meat, moreover, is the most suitable food for producing 'the firmest hardest human Flesh, and warmest strongest Blood'.[99] '*Milk, Fruits, Seeds and Vegetables*' are nutritionally inadequate because 'they have lost their Vigour, Energy, and Balsam since the Deluge'.[100] It is only when '*animal Food* will no longer do' that we 'are to try what *Milk* and *Seeds* can do to ease our Pains'. It is true that God's 'first Intention for Man had Been Vegetables', but such a diet is suitable only 'in a paradisiacal state, or on a better unspoil'd Planet'.[101] The teeth, liver, pancreas and other organs are all evidently designed for meat-eating, and 'It is certain that by our Make . . . we are now fitted as for Vegetables, so for animal Food.'[102]

Cheyne's thought on meat-eating was not simply a carnivore's charter. There is an element of snobbery in his attitude and, as Akihito Suzuki observes, 'Cheyne's medical discourse [w]as a symbolic politics of the cultural hegemony of the elite over the plebs.'[103] A vegetarian diet 'will never be required or be necessary or fit for the *governed*, but the *governing*, never for those whose Excellence lies in their *Limbs*, but for those whose Superiority lies in their *Heads* and thinking *Faculties*'.[104] Although he does not express his thought on diet within a strictly Behmenist framework, it is nevertheless as firmly located within a spiritual discourse as Tryon's. He tells us that meat-eating 'never was *intended*, but only *permitted*, as a *Curse* or Punishment, and a *Cure* for a *Malady*'. The malady is a spiritual rather than a physical one, and eating meat is a remedy precisely because of its deleterious effects on the body. It allows people to '*feel* and experience the natural and necessary Effects of their own Lusts and Concupiscence, by painful and cruel Distempers', so producing such a 'dislike of *inordinate Lusts* and Enjoyments, that might make them think, ponder, and return to *Order, Love of Virtue*, and its *Source* and *Original*'. It also helps 'To sink and contract the *natural Powers* of the Soul . . . into a *Level* with the decayed and lapsed *moral Ones*', giving the latter an opportunity to recover. God in fact gave people permission to eat meat in order 'To shorten the Duration of their natural Lives, that *Sin, Misery*, and *Rebellion* might not increase infinitely'.[105]

In the nineteenth century, occult thought on diet culminated in 'physical puritanism'. One of the more notable expressions of this movement was the utopian community of Fruitlands, established by the American educationist Amos Bronson Alcott in 1843. The daily routine at Fruitlands was simple and austere. Rising at dawn, the Fruitlanders would bathe in cold water, which Alcott fondly believed would guarantee 'cheerfulness'. They would then enjoy a music lesson before breakfast. The occupational routine in the community was determined by 'the spirit's dictates' rather than economic exigencies, which made work varied but rather inefficient. The Fruitlanders wore light clothing, since Alcott thought that this would ensure sexual 'purity'. They assuaged their thirst with water: tea, coffee, alcohol and milk were all prohibited. Alcott's community was strictly vegetarian, and the Fruitlanders avoided any exploitation of the brute creation. Wool was regarded as proper clothing for sheep, not humans, and animal muscle was not co-opted even for purposes of draught.[106]

At the same time as the Fruitlands experiment took place, a similar community was established in England by the followers of Alcott's friend and fellow educationist, James Pierrepont Greaves. This Surrey community, known as Concordium, was also dedicated to vegetarianism:

> Their food is simple and wholesome, and free from slaughter and bloodshedding. Their table is never polluted by the mangled limbs of the innocent animal – the flesh and blood of animals constitute no part of their simple fare; they therefore escape the innumerable filthy necessities of those who indulge their vitiated appetites in such unseemly aliment, as well as avoid many diseases to which the flesh-eater is subject.[107]

The Concordists declined to take advantage of the full range of gastronomic delights that even a vegetarian diet affords. Thomas Frost describes them as living on 'raw carrots and cold water . . . when the snow lay thick upon the ground'.[108] According to George Hollyoake, salt, sugar and tea were all forbidden at Concordium. When his wife visited the community she asked for some salt to season her breakfast of raw cabbage; the Concordists obligingly provided her with some, hidden under a plate to prevent this decadent substance becoming a general temptation.[109] There seem to have been three motives underlying Concordist vegetarianism: concern for animal welfare, the belief that meat-eating was detrimental to health, and a desire to avoid 'the innumerable filthy necessities' of the carnivore. This last consideration referred to the belief that eating meat excites the sexual appetite: for the Concordists, a healthy mind in a healthy body required celibacy.

Physical puritanism was an attempt to recover the perfection of Paradise by regenerating both body and soul. Regaining the original purity of the body had long been one of the goals of alchemy. For this to be achieved, body and spirit 'must be changed, the one into the other', so that 'the body leavens the spirit, and transmutes it into one body, and the spirit leavens the body, and transmutes it into one spirit'.[110] This is, of course, a *coincidentia oppositorum*, reducing a false duality to its original unity. At the end of the process 'the Soul and the Spirit are combined with their Body . . . into a fixed and indissoluble Essence'.[111] In this way, 'the body loses all its grossness, and becomes new and pure'.[112] It is 'When bodies become spirits, and spirits bodies' that the 'work is finished; for then that which rises upward [man] and that which descends downward [God] become *one* body.'[113] According to Agrippa, the number seven, the number of body and soul combined, 'doth signify a certain fulness of sacred mysteries'. [114] In *The Book of Lambspring* we learn that there are two fish (soul and spirit) swimming in a sea (the body); we are advised to cook the fish

> in their own water;
> Then they also will become a vast sea,
> The vastness of which no man can describe.[115]

This vast sea might be God, in which case Lambspring is representing our ultimate fate as incorporation into the body of God.

Annihilationism, the doctrine that at death the soul is simply reabsorbed into the godhead, was common among occult-minded spiritualists in Interregnum England. Richard Coppin taught that 'the body is of the earth, and to the earth it must return again, . . . but the spirit, that is the soul, returns to whence it came'.[116] This recalls the Paracelsian doctrine that the physical body returns to its elemental matrix, the astral body to the sidereal spirit, and the soul to the godhead.[117] Thomas Vaughan also thought that 'the *Earthly parts*, as we see by experience, return to the *Earth*, the *Coelestiall* to a superior heavenly *Limbus*, and the Spirit to God that gave it'. He did, however, accept that 'the *Astral Man* hovers sometimes about the *Dormatories* of the Dead', but these ghosts survived no longer than 'the Circuit of One year, for when the Body begins fully to corrupt, the Spirit returnes to his Originall Element'.[118] According to Gerrard Winstanley, the soul is like a bucket of water taken out of the sea (God); at death it will be 'poured into the sea again, and becomes one with the sea'.[119]

George Foster combined a belief in annihilationism for the regenerate with the idea of the reincarnation of the unredeemed: when the spirit 'comes out of one man where I the God of gods doe not rule, it goes into another wicked man, and there acts the same things which it did at first'.[120] Given the Pythagorean impulse underlying the occult philosophy, it is not surprising to find this belief in reincarnation elsewhere among the mystics. The idea of the transmigration of souls was one of the teachings of the Jewish Cabala.[121] According to some Cabalists, every soul is allowed three lives to achieve its spiritual destiny; if the soul is so weak that three lives are insufficient for this purpose, it is strengthened by being united to another soul.[122]

The doctrine of reincarnation was not necessarily tied to the notion of expiation and eventual release. Kirchberger believed that 'the most holy men are obliged to appear again in this world in the form of the commonest men'.[123] This is reminiscent of the Buddhist ideal that the enlightened voluntarily forego nirvana and re-enter the world of illusion in order to work for the release of their fellow beings. Although the concept of reincarnation in Western occultism has a Pythagorean provenance, since the nineteenth century it has been increasingly reformulated in terms of Eastern religious thought, most notably in the work of Helena Blavatsky and the Theosophical Society.[124]

William Blake may also have 'believed in the Platonic doctrine of reincarnation', if Kathleen Raine is to be believed, and it is true that he 'at no time believed in the resurrection of the mortal body'.[125] Blake tells us that 'in Paradise they have no Corporeal & Mortal Body'.[126] Blake sometimes seems to suggest another possibility, that postmortem embodiment will be in the form of the cosmic man, Albion. This is a common enough notion: it is found in the Adam Kadmon of the Cabala, in Swedenborg's Homo Maximus and, in a slightly secularised form, in Herder's concept of *Humanität*.[127] A similar thought may underlie an obscure passage in one of Peter Sterry's sermons:

> When the body of a Saint crumbles and scatters into the Dust; Every Dust lies gather'd up into the Bosome of some Holy Angel. There all the single Dusts are comprehended in one Form of a glorious Body. In this Form the Angel brings them forth at the call of Christ: This is the resurrection of the Body.[128]

It is not clear from this passage whether Sterry envisages a collective or a personal postmortem embodiment. This, however, is not necessarily of any great importance. The idea of collective embodiment as the cosmic man did not preclude that of personal embodiment, as long as each individual is conceived as simply a part of a greater organic whole.

Despite the currency of annihilationism and the belief in the reconstitution of the cosmic man, there was a strong tendency among occult mystics to represent the afterlife in thoroughly anthropocentric terms. The seminal figure in this respect was Emanuel Swedenborg, whose ideas on the afterlife dominated nineteenth-century conceptions. A list of those who were attracted by Swedenborg's thought reads something like the Western literary canon: they include Coleridge, Carlyle, Tennyson and the Brownings in England; Emerson, Thoreau and Henry James Sr in America; and Goethe, Schelling, Heine, Balzac, Hugo and Strindberg on the Continent.[129] Swedenborg saw the afterlife more as a continuation than a negation of this life. Death would involve no radical change in either personality or life-style: the deceased 'knows no otherwise than that he is still in the natural world: for he has a similar body, a similar face, similar speech, and similar senses'.[130]

Swedenborg was prone to visit the deceased in heaven, which he describes in thoroughly earthly terms. In Swedenborg's afterlife we will find families, schools, gardens, sensual enjoyments, all the trappings of our mundane experience made perfect. Swedenborg thought that life after death would be a continuous progress in spiritual delights, taking place through three heavenly spheres. The first of these, the natural sphere, was barely distinguishable from this life, and in the second, or spiritual sphere, life would be like a more idealised form of earthly existence. Human beings would achieve their full spiritual perfection in the third, or celestial, sphere; life in this sphere was compared to that of Africans.[131]

This comparison of the celestial sphere with African societies may be indebted to the idealisation of the noble savage by Rousseau and his followers. There had been a tendency in European culture to see the lifestyle of primitive peoples as representing admirable simplicity ever since Montaigne wrote his essay on cannibals.[132] The noble savage, however, was usually American rather than African, and European perceptions of black people were overwhelmingly negative.[133] In associating the celestial sphere with Africa, Swedenborg may have been thinking about another common European stereotype: the idea that blacks were more sexual than whites.[134] Generally this was part of a racist ideology, a way of representing blacks as closer to animals than whites. For Swedenborg, however, this would have had a positive appeal, since his vision of the afterlife was highly sexualised.

According to Swedenborg, 'the mutual and reciprocal love of the sex remains with human beings after death'.[135] We are told that 'marriage love is the very plane into which the Divine flows'.[136] This being so, marriage is necessary to heavenly existence, and Swedenborg tends to treat it as synonymous with heaven itself. If people have contracted unions with unsuitable partners on earth, these will be dissolved to permit new unions to be formed. Those who have no partner in this life will find one in the next.[137] People who prefer to be celibate will be allowed to remain so, but they will be consigned to a 'side of heaven' to prevent their perversion contaminating others.[138] Marriage in heaven will involve an ever closer union between man and wife, so much so that they will appear to others as one angel rather than two.[139] It would also be egalitarian, since 'The love of dominion of one over the other takes away marriage love and its heavenly delights.'[140] According to Swedenborg, heavenly marriage would be no merely ethereal union of souls; it would include sexual intercourse, the delights of which would be heightened, since 'angelic perception and sensation are much more exquisite than human perception and sensation'.[141]

Swedenborg's vision of heaven is not just about sex, but it was this aspect of his thought which had the greatest appeal for the Romantics. In a good deal of Romantic writing and art, there is a fusion of sexual and spiritual love, and entry into eternal bliss is represented in terms of the reunion of true lovers.[142] Nor was this simply an artistic conceit: it was the promise of reunion with his dead fiancée that drew Friedrich Schelling to Swedenborg's works. Swedenborgian notions quickly entered the mainstream of nineteenth-century culture. Charles Kingsley thought that his feelings for his wife Fanny, including his sexual desire, were an integral part of his personality; if his immortality was to mean anything, these feelings must also survive death.[143] Similarly, in Anne Brontë's *The Tenant of Wildfell Hall*, Gilbert Markham finds little consolation in the prospect of meeting Helen Graham as 'a disembodied spirit, with a frame perfect and glorious, but not like this'. Gilbert tells her that 'if I am to be so changed that I shall cease to adore you with my whole heart and soul, and love you beyond every other creature, I shall not be myself'.[144] We might contrast this with the orthodox Augustinian view, that any relationships in heaven will be homogenous and secondary: there will be no special loved ones, and the saints will love each other only in order to love God the better.[145] Gilbert Markham's attitude is one that would have surely struck an earlier generation as thoroughly blasphemous, but Brontë presents it as wholly right and proper.

An important feature of Swedenborg's work is that it involved substantial contact with the dead: he knew so much about heaven because he frequently visited the place. This happy contact between the living and the dead is itself something new in European culture. There had always been a popular belief in ghosts, but they were something to be feared and avoided. From the eighteenth century, however, we increasingly encounter people who actively sought the company of the dead. Already in the late seventeenth century Jane Lead, who anticipated several aspects of Swedenborg's thought,[146] was fond of talking with one of her deceased friends.[147] At the end of the eighteenth century, Cagliostro enjoyed socialising with the dead; he recalled that on one occasion he dined with Voltaire's spirit, which must have embarrassed the great sceptic.[148] Oberlin kept a wall-map of the other world, on which he could chart his journeys.[149] William Blake also consorted with the dead, believing that 'our deceased friends are more really with us than when they were apparent to our mortal part'; he claimed that his unique method of relief-etching was devised by his dead brother, Robert.[150] Victor Hugo also contacted the dead, and Shakespeare occasionally dictated poems to him (in French, of course, since death had liberated him from the imperfections of his native tongue).[151]

In 1787 the Société Exigetique et Philanthropique of Stockholm held what might be regarded as the first organised seances, in an attempt to facilitate contact with the dead by using someone in a hypnotic trance; henceforth there was to be a firm connection between mesmerism and spiritualism.[152] Contacting the dead with the aid of a medium became something of a craze, especially after Katherine and Margaret Fox demonstrated their mediumistic talents in America in 1848. Another American, Daniel Dunglas Home, brought the craze to Europe in 1855, becoming, in his own words, 'Medium to the Crowned Heads of Europe'.[153] Not all occultists accepted the validity of this craze. According to Helena Blavatsky, the supposed 'materialisations' of spirits at seances were 'usually the astral body or "double" of the medium or someone present'.[154] Blavatsky herself, however, had once acted as a medium, and her later scepticism was perhaps more a matter of business rivalry than esoteric theology. An interest in mediums and the spirits of the dead continued to be a prominent concern of occult thinkers in the twentieth century, the best known example being W. B. Yeats.[155]

Occultist thought on the afterlife harmonised with the concept of the spiritual body. The fourteenth-century alchemist Petrus Bonus of Ferrara asserted that after the resurrection 'The body will become wholly transfigured, incorruptible, and almost unbelievably subtilized, and it will penetrate all solids.'[156] In the fifteenth century, Marsilio Ficino argued that the soul 'needs its own body made everlasting'; this would be 'a temperate, immortal, celestial body'.[157] Henry Vaughan thought that the body would rise again 'Like some spruce bride, . . . clothed with shining light'; in one of his poems the soul reassures the body that 'Thou only fall'st to be refined again.'[158] Jane Lead rejected the notion of a disembodied regenerate spirit: 'though it be Born a pure Spirit, yet it must not be naked, and without a Body'. The resurrection body would be 'a pure and fine Robe made up of Diaphonous Matter, from one Eternal and Unmixed Element'.[159]

In its resurrection, the body would enjoy the freedom from conditionality of its prelapsarian counterpart. According to Basil Valentine, 'the bodies of angels, . . . not being alloyed with sin or impurity, are injured by no extreme of heat or cold. When man shall have been glorified, his body will become like the angelic body in this respect.'[160] Jacob Boehme assures us that 'the good power of the mortal body shall come again, and ever stay or live, in a beautiful, transparent, crystalline, material property, in spiritual flesh and blood'.[161] Lavater thought that the resurrection body could become bigger or smaller at will.[162] The face of the resurrected individual would be 'renewed according to *the Image of Him who created it*, not having spot or wrinkle or any such thing, but . . . holy and without blemish'.[163] The nineteenth-century French spiritualist Allan Kardec thought that the spirits of the dead inhabited the other planets of the solar system. The purest live on Jupiter, and Kardec describes the Jupiterian body just as other occultists described the spiritual body: 'The conformation of the body is somewhat similar to bodies of this world, but less material, less dense and with a lower specific gravity. While we crawl painfully over the Earth, the inhabitant of Jupiter transports himself from one place to another by floating over the surface almost without fatigue, like a bird or fish.'[164]

The doctrine of a bodily resurrection was perfectly orthodox, although the emphasis on the beatific vision in mainstream theology tended to relegate it to the periphery of thought on the afterlife. There was some disagreement about whether the resurrection body would be physical or spiritual. The apostles John and Paul, Origen and the Eastern Church generally tended to the view that the resurrection would be purely spiritual. The Nicene creed was ambiguous on the question, but the synoptic Gospels, the Apostles' and Athanasian creeds, Tertullian and the Western Church in general were inclined to a belief in physical resurrection.[165] Calvin thought that the natural and spiritual bodies differed in quality rather than substance, and this difference was due to distinct vivifying principles; the natural body is quickened by animation, but the spiritual body will be quickened by inspiration.[166] After the Reformation, thnetopsychist mortalists (who believed that body and soul would be reconstituted at the Last Judgment) like Overton, Hobbes and Milton developed an emphatically materialist representation of the resurrection body.[167]

In contrast to orthodox thinkers, the occultists tended to neglect the beatific vision in their discourse on the afterlife, being preoccupied with the idea of a somatic immortality. They emphasised that postmortem embodiment would be purely spiritual, but they were equally emphatic that it would be *embodiment*, and they went into detail as to its nature. The occult mystical representation of the spiritual body clearly represents a yearning to be released from an existence that was conditioned and contingent. The mystic wanted to return to a reality that transcends our mundane experience, but he wanted to return *in person*.

Not that early modern occult spirituality was entirely free from the desire for a simple absorption into the divine being; annihilationism was precisely that. Yet there was another trend in occult thought, one seeking to preserve human personality in the union with God. It has been argued (perhaps with some exaggeration) that this was the distinctive contribution of Behmenism to the Western mystical tradition.[168] Occultism was often characterised by what Denis Saurat called an 'optimistic materialism', leading it to reject an other-worldly afterlife in favour of a vision of postmortem existence as involving an 'expansion of personality'.[169] A nineteenth-century spiritualist received the reassuring message from the spirit world that 'You will never lose your identity. If god designed to absorb all souls into himself, there would have been no necessity at first to give off from himself distinct identical germs, possessing all the characteristics of independence.'[170] Accompanied, as esoteric thought on the afterlife is, by a medical discourse seeking the rehabilitation of the mortal body, it expresses less an otherworldly orientation than a renewed commitment to this world. To borrow Yeats's terminology, the Western mystical tradition that we are dealing with begins with the transcendentalising 'primary' path of Platonism; it ends, as Yeats did himself, in an immanentalising 'antithetical path', based on 'a dynamic and substantializing force as distinguished from the eastern quiescent and supersensualizing state of the soul – a movement downwards upon life, not upwards out of life'.[171] Even in their rejection of life as they find it, occult mystics announce a profound reluctance to forgo the familiar world of everyday experience. Their renunciation of the world is no more than a strategic retreat; ultimately, they seek to capture the mundane order for themselves.

6 The mind in occult thought

One of the minor puzzles of intellectual history is the relationship between Agrippa's *De occulta philosophia* and his *De incertitudine et vanitate scientarum*. In the latter work Agrippa seemed to renounce all human learning, including the magical sciences: 'Al[l] Sciences are nothing els[e], but the ordinaunces and opinions of men, so noysome as profitable, so pestilent as [w]hol[e]some, so ill as good, in no part perfecte, but doubtfull and full of errour and contention.'[1] This book was composed in 1526, some sixteen years after Agrippa wrote his *De occulta philosophia*. We might suppose that by this time Agrippa had come to see the futility of magical studies. Why, then, did he choose to publish *De occulta philosophia* only in 1531, the year after he put *De incertitudine* to the press? Why, also, did later occultists not understand the *De incertitudine* as a repudiation of the occult philosophy? Thomas Vaughan, for example, cites the work approvingly in his *Anthroposophia theomagica*.[2] Frances Yates suggests that *De incertitudine* was intended to forestall the charge of heresy that Agrippa's magical textbook might provoke.[3] It is also possible to understand *De incertitudine* as satirical, but another reading of both works together suggests that they may not be incompatible at all: both denigrate reason in favour of revelation.[4] Agrippa's scepticism and his occultism might even be regarded as complementary, if we locate them in the epistemological tradition that distinguishes between reason (*Vernunft*) and understanding (*Verstand*).

Already in the Middle Ages a distinction had been made between discursive reason (*ratio*) and *intellectus*, meaning 'intuition or creative insight or imagination'.[5] In its modern form, this distinction can be traced back to nominalism, the philosophical outlook which had dominated German universities since their foundation in the fourteenth century. The nominalists made a radical separation between reason and faith. This established a degree of intellectual autonomy for inquisitive minds: if faith did not depend on reason, reason could not threaten faith; it therefore could be left safely to go its own way. But while nominalism thus attempted to protect reason from ecclesiastical interference, it did not devalue faith, and nominalist fideism nurtured German mysticism as much as it promoted academic curiosity. Luther, who had undergone a nominalist training at Erfurt, continued this tradition by distinguishing reason *ante fidem* and *post fidem*. Neither were particularly merit-worthy; if reason unseasoned by grace had a demonic flavour, even the reason of a true Christian was strictly subordinate to faith.[6] Writers like Schwenckfeld, Weigel and Boehme extended Reformation solefideism from the realm of soteriology to that of epistemology; all true knowledge depended on divine grace rather than human effort.[7] A similar position had already been reached by Jewish mystics. The Cabalists distinguished the 'Luminous Mirror' of the soul, the faculty of prophetic knowledge, from its 'Non-Luminous Mirror', the faculty of ordinary knowledge.[8] According to Isaac ibn Latif, the intellect can reach no further than the back of the divine being, whose face is only revealed 'in supra-intellectual ecstasy'.[9]

In the mystical tradition, as C. J. Barker observed, 'the organon of divine knowledge is not the head'.[10] Although he sometimes used the word 'reason' in a positive, Neoplatonised sense, Johann Reuchlin had no time for mere logic-chopping. He tells us that theology 'is not susceptible of treatment by those gossips and talebearers, syllogisms, for it is not, properly speaking, a science of the immediate world'. The obscurity of divine matters is 'penetrable by neither sense nor rational thinking'.[11] Paracelsus identified magic with faith, and he declared that 'magic is a great secret wisdom, just as reason is a great public folly'.[12] Jacob Boehme constantly disparaged 'the *works* of Reason' as inferior to those of faith.[13] According to Walter Charleton, 'We must quit the dark Lanthorne of Reason.' Having done so,

> the minde shall have all her knowledge full, entire, abstracted, in one single act; not successive, not extorted, by oblique violence of premises, not erroneous, controvertible, or dubious; she shall no longer groan under the perplexity of framing Demonstrations, by wresting, deducing, inferring one thing from another.[14]

For William Blake, the imagination was the divine spark at the heart of human existence, but 'the Reasoning Spectre / Stands between the Vegetative Man & his Immortal Imagination'.[15] The illuminists repeatedly stressed the need for direct divine inspiration in order to gain spiritual knowledge, a train of thought which was transformed in Romantic notions of poetic inspiration.[16] This epistemology was also related to an emotionalist ethic in which the quality of knowledge was evaluated in terms of its moral function. Saint-Georges de Marsais wrote that 'it is from the heart, where God has his abode, that he darts his rays on the intellect that he illuminates'. For Dutoit-Membrini, man 'always has enough light (and he never has enough love), and even always has too much of it, when love does not keep it company'.[17]

The distinction between discursive reason and intuitive understanding, and the epistemological primacy of the latter, became an integral part of German Romantic thought. For writers like Friedrich Schlegel, 'rationally thinking reason' (*vernünftig denkende Vernunft*) was inimical to 'the beautiful confusion of the fantasy'.[18] F. H. Jacobi stressed the limits of reason in achieving a knowledge of God as a person; what was necessary was feeling, intuition, or the power of faith.[19] Systems of reason resemble a game of solitaire; they are self-referential systems of knowledge, which is to say, not systems of knowledge at all.[20] So great was the denigration of reason in the German philosophical community that Hume's scepticism and purely pragmatic fideism was interpreted as a defence of faith against reason.[21] Herder complained about the 'philosophy of mechanized thinking' which dominated his century, warning that 'Reason, too carelessly, too uselessly diffused, may well weaken desires, instincts and vital activity.' He asserted that 'our lives are far more enriched with love and joy caused by the feelings of the heart rather than by the profound deliberations of reason'.[22] F. W. J. Schelling believed that understanding 'deserves *first* place, reason the second', since our 'demand that everything should be *made* comprehensible to reason' implies 'that reason is not that which *originally comprehends*'. Reason 'is precisely that which holds together, that which limits, whilst understanding is that which widens, progresses, is active'. The two faculties, however, stand in a dialectical relationship to one another, which makes reason necessary to understanding: 'understanding only raises itself to the concept of the positive *via* reason's contradiction of understanding'.[23]

The occult philosophers developed the activist epistemology which was already implicit in Neoplatonic thought. In the fourth century, Synesius wrote that 'hearing and sight are not senses, but organs of sense, servants of the common [sense], as it were doorkeepers, who notify their mistress of the sense object outside, whereby the out-turned organs of sense have their doors knocked upon'.[24] Sensation here is not a function of the sensory organs themselves, but of the percipient intellect (the common sense). The basic assumptions of occult epistemology are also present in the writings of Albert the Great, whence they found their way, via Master Eckhart, into the German mystical tradition. Following Augustine, Albert taught that there are two parts of the intellect, active and passive. The passive intellect can function only because it is illuminated by the active intellect, which is itself illuminated by the divine intellect. Ultimately, all knowledge is an act of God.[25] The same structure of thought can be found in Agrippa's treatise on occult philosophy. God illuminates man's mind, which then illuminates his reason. From reason the light passes on to imagination, which further illuminates the celestial vehicle of the soul (the spiritual body). This finally sheds its light on the elemental body, 'in which the light is made manifestly visible to the eye'.[26]

For Paracelsus, knowledge is an active interaction between the object known and its equivalent in man. He distinguished three types of knowledge: *experimentum*, empirical knowledge in the simple sense; *scientia*, which is a property of the object whereby it is knowable; and *experientia*, an intuitive understanding of the *scientia*.[27] Paracelsian epistemology, with its emphasis on the similarity of the subject and object of knowing as a precondition for knowledge, obviously depends on the theory of the microcosm. This was also the starting point for Valentin Weigel, who developed what has been called a 'Paracelsian Augustinianism'. For Weigel, knowledge of the world is active and subjective, coming from the knowing subject rather than the known object. There is also an intellectual knowledge which is passive and objective. This is the knowledge of the spirit, which knows its object directly; it comes from within, through knowledge of the self.[28] The occult theory of knowledge permeated the Pietist spirituality that formed the background of much German academic life, and it became indirectly one of the major intellectual roots of Kant's epistemology.[29]

Paracelsus's theory of knowledge is parallel to a basic principle of his medicine: just as like cures like, so only like can know like. This is a principle with theological implications. Man, according to Valentin Weigel, is in himself incapable of knowing God; our knowledge of God is in fact only God's knowledge of himself.[30] This was also a doctrine accepted by Jacob Bauthumley in Interregnum England: 'For if I say that I see thee, it is nothing but thy seeing of thy selfe; for there is nothing in me capable of seeing thee but thy selfe.'[31] The human encounter with the divine can only take place if the divine actually dwells in human beings in the first place. For Thomas Vaughan, man must be transfigured by divine illumination as a precondition of spiritual knowledge: 'A Flash or Tincture of this [divine light] must come, or he can no more discern things spiritually, then he can distinguish Colours naturally without the light of the Sun.'[32] This was also the basis of the inner light theology of Quakerism: 'Christ Jesus is the Way, who hath lighted every Man and Woman that cometh into the World. . . . this Light is not at a distance from you, but it shineth in your hearts.'[33]

In our discussion of occult epistemology we have already seen something of the illuminists' views on the structure of the mind: it is part of a hierarchy extending from God downwards through man to the sensory world. Thomas Vaughan expounded an anthropology (derived from Agrippa) based on man as microcosm and microtheos:

As the great World consists of Three parts, the *Elemental*, the *Coelestiall* and the *Spiritual* above all which God himselfe is seated in that Infinite inaccessable *Light*, which streames from his *Nature*; Even so man hath in him his Earthly Elemental parts, together with the *Coelestial*, & *Angelical natures* in the *Center* of all which moves, and shines the *Divine Spirit*.

At the top of this hierarchy is the *mens* or *intelligentia abscondita*, which 'is that Spirit which God himself breathed into Man, and by which Man is united again to God'. Beneath this is the angelical self, which

> adheres sometimes to the *Mens* or *superior portion* of the *Soul*, and then it is filled with the *Divine Light*, but most commonly it descends into the *æthereall inferior portion* . . . where it is altered by the *Coelestiall Influences*, and diversely distracted with irregular *Affections* and passions of the *sensuall Nature*.

It is the '*Coelestiall, æthereall part* of man', identified with the *anima mundi*, which 'is that whereby we move, see, feel, taste, and smell, and have a commerce with all *materiall Objects* whatsoever'. The celestial man is the medium through which 'the Influences of the *Divine Nature* are conveyed . . . to the more material part of the Creature'. It is also through this 'æthereall nature' that 'Man is made subject to the Influence of the Stars, and is partly dispos'd of by the Coelestial harmony'.[34]

The objective of the regenerative process in occult thought is for human consciousness to ascend from the elemental realm through the celestial and spiritual in order finally to apprehend the divine being. Johann Reuchlin described the process in terms of an ascent through the ten *sefiroth* of the Cabala, from Malkhut, representing the phenomenal world, to Kether, the 'mind' which is the first manifestation of the ineffable godhead. The ascent occurs in three stages. In the first of these, called 'animal', the soul takes over from the body; in the next stage, known as 'man', reason supercedes the soul; finally, in the stage called 'God', mind replaces reason.[35]

According to Barbara Stafford, 'Neoplatonism stressed self-fashioning. It was from within, from the inner faculties, that the rehabilitated soul regenerated itself, not through the sensible world or the coupling of bodies.'[36] This is broadly true of the occult philosophy as a whole. In the process of self-fashioning, the illuminists had a powerful tool at their disposal: the imagination. The concept of imagination has generally carried negative associations in Western culture. In Jewish thought the imagination (*yetser*) was associated with the Fall, since it lay at the heart of Adam's hubristic desire to become godlike.[37] While Hebraic thought was preoccupied with the moral status of the imagination, Hellenic philosophy explored its epistemological and ontological status. Plato regarded the imagination as the lowest of man's mental faculties, ontologically deficient and epistemologically insecure. True reality resided in a transcendent world of Ideas, of which the phenomenal world was merely a reflection or copy. The imagination was at a second remove from reality, being an imitation of a world that was itself an imitation.[38] This suspicion of imagination was inherited by the Neoplatonists. Plotinus, for example, asserted that 'we cannot apprehend intelligible entities with the imagination, but only with the faculty of contemplation'.[39]

Aristotle abandoned Plato's realm of transcendent Ideas and derived all knowledge from sensory experience. His account of imagination is more positive than Plato's, regarding it as playing a necessary role in cognition, since all thought involves the use of images. The imagination mediated between sensation and reason, but it remained a primarily mimetic faculty which is properly subordinate to reason in its operation.[40] The Aristotelian privileging of sensation enjoyed a marked revival in the seventeenth and eighteenth centuries with the rise of mechanistic accounts of the mind, but the new empiricist psychology of the Enlightenment was no more favourable to the faculty of imagination than earlier rationalist accounts. According to the psychology of Locke and his followers, all ideas are really replications of images originally derived from sensation. If the replication is faithful to the data supplied by the senses, the result is 'memory'; to the extent that the replication involves a reordering of the original data, the result is 'fancy' or 'imagination'.[41] This psychology involves the assumption that all ideation, including imagination, is dependent on the senses; it has no ontological status of its own, and indeed its ontological status is inherently problematic. It follows from this that all ideation, and especially imagination, is a degradation of the pristine form of knowledge given by sensory experience. As Thomas Hobbes expressed it, imagination 'is nothing but *decaying sense*'.[42] It may have its legitimate place in the economy of the human mind, but that place is necessarily subordinate to that of sensory experience.

Empiricist sensationalism is premised on a radical disjunction between consciousness and the world, between what the occult thinkers referred to as 'inner' and 'outer' aspects of reality, or what later philosophers termed 'subject' and 'object'. This assumption does not obtain in the occult philosophy. Far from there being an ontological gulf between subject and object, the two are inseparably bound together, as a simple consequence of the doctrine of microcosmic correspondence. As we have seen, this doctrine entails an epistemology in which it is sensory experience which is dependent on the percipient subject. Given this point of view, the idea that imagination is 'decaying sense' is meaningless; if anything, it is sense which is decaying imagination. Far from being epistemologically deficient, according to esoteric thinkers, imagination was a superior mode of knowledge. Paracelsus, for example, wrote that 'He who is born in imagination discovers the latent forces of Nature. . . . Because Man does not imagine perfectly at all times, arts and sciences are uncertain, though in fact they are certain and, obtained by means of imagination, can give true results.'[43]

Despite the general derogation of imagination in Western culture, the high regard that the occult mystics had for this faculty had a long ancestry. There were already suggestions of a special spiritual function of the imagination in Plato's writings, and these were more fully developed in Neoplatonic thought.[44] The Platonic Ideas may be located in a purely transcendent realm, or they may be given 'a secondary location within the human mind itself'.[45] In the latter case the mind has a more direct access to the Ideas than by way of their reflection in the phenomenal world. This opens the possibility that the images formed by the imagination are not a mimesis of the world of sensory experience; they may be immediate reflections of the transcendent Ideas themselves. The imagination thus becomes a faculty for perceiving the Ideas in visionary ecstasy.

Not that early modern occultists were unaware that the imagination had acquired a somewhat less flattering reputation among the multitude. Francis Okeley observed that 'we are apt erroneously to consider [imagination] as only an *airy*, *idle*, and *impotent Faculty* of the human Mind, dealing in Fiction, and roving in Fancy or Idea, without producing any powerful or permanent Effects'.[46] This is because imagination is confused with fantasy, which is its fallen counterpart. As Francis Lee conceded, the imagination 'in its lapsed, depraved state is filled with innumerable broken images, very inadequate and preposterous'.[47] In its fallen state the imagination is reduced to fantasy, which, as Paracelsus declared, 'is not imagination, but a fool's cornerstone'.[48] In Carl Jung's words, the imagination is not synonymous with 'phantasia', but 'is the real and literal power to create images'.[49]

As Jung observed, in Paracelsian thought '*imaginatio* is the active power of the *astrum* (star) or *corpus coeleste sive supercoeleste*, that is, of the higher man within'.[50] The imagination, a faculty of the astral spirit located in the heart, is the medium through which knowledge of nature is achieved; it is also a faculty through which man can gain control over the external world.[51] Since the Fall, according to Mungo Murray, the imagination has become 'enslav'd to ye irregularities of ye passions, senses & all external objects'.[52] Even in the fallen world, however, the imagination could still exert its power. Paracelsus thought that 'It is not the curse or blessing that works, but the idea. The imagination produces the effect.'[53] Imagination, given a cosmic dimension, was incorporated into Paracelsus's theory of disease. The powers of the human imagination were such that it might poison the heavens and consequently cause epidemics.[54] Nolle informs us that an '*imaginative faith*' was 'infused and planted' in man by God at the creation. A patient's imagination was often more effective than 'either remedy, or the Physician' in curing disease: 'Our faith that it will be so, makes us imagine so: imagination excites a Star, that Star (by conjunction with Imagination) gives the effect or perfect operation.' Nolle believed that the soul working through the imagination could affect 'health or sicknesse, and that not onely in her own body, but Extraneously, or in other bodies'.[55] This idea can also be found in the writings of Agrippa, who informs us that imagination can not only 'change the proper [i.e. one's own] body with sensible transmutation', it can also affect other people's state of health: 'the soul being strongly elevated, and inflamed with a strong imagination, sends forth health and sickness, not only in its proper body, but also in other bodies'. It is because of the possibility of contamination by other people's imaginations that Agrippa thinks we should avoid the company of evil people and seek that of the good.[56] Similarly, Jacob Boehme believed that babies were susceptible to the imaginative imprint of the characters of those around them, which is why it was important to have godly witnesses at baptisms.[57]

In occult thought, imagination is a creative faculty in the fullest sense of the term: 'it *creates* and *substantiates* as it goes, and all things are possible to it'.[58] In fact, it was originally a *procreative* faculty, since it was through his imagination that the prelapsarian Adam had been intended to reproduce. Boehme tells us that Adam 'loved and impregnated himself through the *Imagination*; and so also was his propagation'.[59] Francis Lee believed that Adam had given birth to Eve 'as Images are used to be formed by us in our Dreams'.[60] Even after the Fall, according to Paracelsus, something of this procreative function remains. Man, we are told, has no 'embedded seed'; his seed is created by desire, which Paracelsus perceptively recognises as a function of imagination.[61]

The role of imagination in foetal development had been a commonplace of Western embryology since the time of Hippocrates and Pliny.[62] According to Franciscus Junius, it was man's superior 'mental agility' that led to a greater degree of morphological variation in humans than in other animals.[63] Paracelsus thought that an expectant mother's imagination had a decisive impact on foetal development: 'The imagination of a pregnant woman is so strong that it can influence the seed and change the fruit in the womb in many directions, so that its nature is thereby deeply and solidly shaped and forged.' It is the parents' imagination that endows the foetus with reason, and it also 'makes the child's reason turn to higher or lower things'.[64] According to Heinrich Nolle, pregnant women 'by force of an inflamed or exalted imagination, . . . impress into the very child, the perfect form and figure of it'.[65] In the eighteenth century, Lavater incorporated the embryo-logical function of the imagination into his theory of physiognomy:

> When the imagination is powerfully agitated by desire, love, or hatred, a single instant is sufficient for it to create or annihilate, to enlarge or contract, to form giants or dwarfs, to determine beauty and ugliness: it impregnates the organic foetus, with a germ of growth or dimunition, of wisdom or folly, of proportion or disproportion.[66]

Occult thought on the role of imagination in foetal development sometimes seems designed to test one's credulity to the full. Jean-Baptist van Helmont, for example, thought that if the mother's imagination imprinted a cherry-like birth-mark on her foetus, this would be 'a certaine *reall production*, which buds, blossomes, and ripens in its due season'.[67] The theory that the mother's imagination helps form the foetus was being challenged in the eighteenth century by sceptics like James Auguste Blondel, who published his *The Power of the Mother's Imagination over the Foetus* in 1729. If the learned élite were ultimately to abandon the belief in the embryological function of the imagination, the notion was nevertheless to survive in both popular and occult discourses until our own times.

Occult cosmogonies are basically procreationist;[68] given esoteric thought on the role of imagination in reproduction, we might expect to find it playing a leading part in the creation of the world. The association of the imagination with the creation is an ancient one. In Hebrew, for example, the words for both concepts derive from the same root (*ysr*).[69] The Hermetic writings suggest that the phenomenal world is the product of divine imagination: 'Coming to be is nothing but imagination.'[70] George Cheyne believed that the particulars in the world 'cou'd come from nothing else but from their original *Ideas* and *architypal Patterns*, in the *divine Mind* or *Imagination*'.[71] Cheyne's terminology points to a Neoplatonic source for his thought, but his specifying the imagination as the divine creative faculty probably stems more from the Behmenist tradition. In Behmenist cosmogony, the process of creation begins when God looks into the Virgin Sophia or divine Wisdom, who 'is a Looking-Glass of the Deity, wherein the Spirit of God seeth it self'. The Virgin Sophia is God's 'Looking-Glass of all Substances, in which all things have been seen from Eternity, whatsoever there should or *could* be'.[72] This 'Virgin-like *Matrix*' is 'the substantiality of God, . . . apprehended in the Imagination, of[,] from or by the Spirit of the *Abyss* of Eternity'.[73] When God looks into the mirror of the Virgin Sophia, he sees the structure of his own being: the seven fountain-spirits which will become the structure of the world. This is not simply a matter of the passive perception of a reflection; it is more an active projection of an image, or an imaginative impregnation of the Virgin, who 'generateth no Image, but receiveth the Image'.[74] The world is thus simply an 'out-birth or express Image' of God, conceived in the Virgin Sophia.[75] A later Behmenist, Thomas Tryon, also depicted the creation as the imaginative work of God through 'the *Magie* or *Generating Wheel* of the seven *Forms* of *Nature*'. Tryon added that, since 'the Soul of Man . . . is a compleat Image of its Creator', it too is fundamentally imaginative: 'never hath any man ceased from *Imaginations* one quarter of an hour in his whole Life, or indeed one moment'.[76]

Occult writers give different accounts of the place of imagination in the economy of the soul. Agrippa, with his Renaissance humanist background, favours what might be called an intellectualist theory compatible with Neoplatonism. He divides the soul into mind, reason and imagination, and tells us that 'the mind illuminates reason, reason floweth into the imagination'. These divisions of the soul clearly correspond to Agrippa's 'threefold world', the intellectual, celestial and elementary.[77] The imagination can be understood as performing an executive function in the elementary world on behalf of reason and mind. Paracelsus, on the other hand, stands at the head of a vigorous native German tradition which can be categorised as voluntarist. He divides the soul into will and imagination, with imagination dependent on the will.[78] As with Agrippa, however, cosmology parallels psychology. The will corresponds to the Mysterium Magnum, and the imagination has affinities with the Yliaster. The first of these is 'the uncreated centre of the world from which everything develops', while the Yliaster is 'the first concrete materialisation' of the Mysterium Magnum.[79]

The occultists were not alone in believing in the power of the imagination. In 1784 a French Royal Commission on mesmerism attributed successful mesmeric therapy to imagination rather than animal magnetism; ironically, it was the mesmerists who adopted a materialist stance by placing their faith in what could be construed as a material substance.[80] What distinguishes the occult discourse on imagination is the belief that it was a magical faculty.[81] According to Francesco Cattani di Diacetto, 'a strongly emotional disposition of the imagination' was of fundamental importance to 'the diligent capturer of planetary light'.[82] Francis Bacon accepted that imagination had a magical power when strengthened by faith.[83] In the nineteenth century, Eliphas Lévi explained the efficacy of magic in terms of the imagination working through the Astral Light or Universal Agent permeating the cosmos: 'By its intervention we heal diseases, modify the seasons, warn off death from the living and raise the dead to life, because it is the imagination which exalts the will and gives it power over the Universal Agent.'[84] W. B. Yeats held a similar theory of magic: 'The central principle of all the Magic of power is that everything we formulate in the imagination, if we formulate it strongly enough, realises itself in the circumstances of life, acting either through our own souls, or through the spirits of nature.'[85]

Of the efficacy of the imagination the occultists had no doubt. In Thomas Vaughan's opinion, it was through the '*Idolum*' or astral self as 'the seat of the Imagination' that ghosts occurred, since 'it retaines after Death an Impresse of those passions, and Affections, to which it was subject in the body'.[86] Thomas Tryon believed that 'all Material and Immaterial [things] were and are brought into Manifestation first by Imagination, Desire and Motion'.[87] Francis Okeley tells us that 'our *Imaginations* . . . are the greatest Realities we have, and are the true *Formers* and *Raisers* of all that is real and solid in us. All *outward Power* that we exercise in the Things about us, is but a *Shadow* in *Comparison* of that *inward Power*, which resides in our *Will, Imagination*, and *Desires*.'[88]

The efficacy of the imagination can be explained either cosmologically or theologically. Agrippa believed that imagination functions as a magical faculty because of its ability to draw on the power of the stars: 'For our mind can through imaginations, or reason by a kind of imitation, be so conformed to any star, as suddenly to be filled with the virtues of that star, as if it were a proper receptacle of the influence thereof.'[89] Similarly, it is clear from Paracelsus's discussion of the role of imagination in foetal development that he saw it as working through a correspondence between the 'inner firmament' and 'outer' one.[90] In both Agrippa and Paracelsus, the efficacy of the imagination depends on the fact that man is a microcosm, a little image of the world. For Francis Okeley on the other hand, imagination 'is an *Out-birth* of the *Divine Magia* or *Imagination*'.[91] Here the efficacy of the imagination depends on the fact that man is a microtheos. These two approaches, of course, should not be seen as mutually exclusive.

One of the more important functions of the imagination is to act as the human organ of perception with regard to the divine. According to the Cambridge Platonist, John Smith, 'visionary experience is as real as sense perception', and it 'is perceived by the imagination'.[92] For Francis Lee, when the imagination is 'in its restored and pure state', it 'becomes a bright mirror, to reflect the immaculate and entire image of God'. In this way, 'the spirit of the soul, as in a glass, may be said to behold God, and the Divine world'.[93] Similarly, Eliphas Lévi assures us that 'Imagination is in effect the soul's eye; therein forms are outlined and preserved; thereby we behold the reflections of the invisible world; it is the glass of visions and the apparatus of magical life.'[94]

The imagination played a central role in William Blake's thought. Blake tells us that 'The Imagination is . . . the Human Existence itself.'[95] It is 'a Representation of what Eternally Exists, Really & Unchangeably',[96] and 'our Imaginations' are 'those Worlds of Eternity in which we shall live forever in Jesus our Lord'.[97] Nature, according to Blake, 'has no Outline, but Imagination has. Nature has no Tune, but Imagination has. Nature has no Supernatural & dissolves: Imagination is Eternity.'[98] Occultists taught that 'Imagination is the star in man, the celestial or supercelestial body.'[99] This was an idea that Blake appropriated: the imagination is 'the Human eternal body in Every Man',[100] and 'the Divine Body of the Lord Jesus, blessed forever'.[101] For Blake the imagination was not at all a form of fantasy, but a superior way of knowing: 'What is it that sets Homer, Virgil & Milton in so high a rank of Art? Is it not because they are addressed to the Imagination, which is Spiritual sensation, & but mediately to the Understanding or Reason?'[102] W. B. Yeats was in full agreement with this attitude: 'the imagination has some way of lighting on truths that reason has not'.[103]

The imagination played an important role in the thought of many other Romantics.[104] J. G. Fichte regarded it as being 'the very possibility of our consciousness, our life and our being'.[105] According to Novalis, 'the whole world is only a sensibly perceptible imaginative force which has assumed the shape of a mechanism'.[106] For Franz Schubert, imagination was 'the supreme jewel of mankind'.[107] Wordsworth thought that 'Fancy is given to quicken and beguile the temporal part of our Nature, Imagination to incite and support the eternal.'[108] Among the English Romantics, apart from Blake, it was perhaps Coleridge who developed occult thought on imagination most thoroughly.[109] Coleridge tells us that 'Imagination is possibly in man a lesser degree of the creative power of God.'[110] He distinguished between the 'primary' and 'secondary' imagination. The first of these is 'the living power and prime agent of all human perception', being 'a repetition in the finite mind of the eternal act of creation in the infinite I AM'. The secondary imagination, that of the poet, differs from the primary imagination 'only in degree and the mode of its operation'. It too 'is essentially *vital*, even as all objects (as objects) are essentially fixed and dead'.[111] Imagination was a fecundating faculty in the world, since without it 'all the products of the mere reflective faculty partook of death, and were as the rattling twigs and sprays in winter into which a sap was yet to be propelled'.[112]

Richard Kearney has noted that the modern validation of the imagination was prefigured in theosophical and mystical writings, but he argues that these works were of little historical importance since 'such writings were largely confined to marginalized hermetic cults'.[113] Such a judgement can be excused only by ignorance. The writers who were responsible for the Romantic rehabilitation of the imagination were deeply versed in mystical (and especially Behmenist) writings: Blake, Coleridge, Schlegel, Tieck, Novalis, Schelling are all pertinent examples. It is true that there were non-occult sources for Romantic thought about the imagination. Even some of these, however, lead back ultimately to esoteric thought. In both England and Germany, for example, Romantic thought was influenced by the Shaftesburian tradition, which itself was grounded in Neoplatonism. The aestheticising of the moral order in Shaftesburian writers like George Turnbull and James Fordyce entailed the demotion of reason as the 'major human faculty' in favour of the imagination. As Turnbull argued, 'It is imagination therefore that renders us capable of social intercourse and commerce, even about moral ideas.'[114] Whatever the importance of this Shaftesburian tradition, it remains the case that virtually every important aspect of Romantic thought on the imagination was anticipated by the occult philosophers, and (with a few exceptions) the Romantics themselves were far from diffident in proclaiming their admiration for esoteric thinkers. This being the case, there can be no grounds for denying that the occult philosophy was the major source of Romantic thought on the topic.

The 'spiritual reformers' of the sixteenth and seventeenth centuries regarded heaven and hell as inner states rather than 'terminal places', and their eschatology prioritised spiritual experience in the present over an historical millennium.[115] This was an attitude shared by many occultists, whose project was to achieve a transformation of their mundane lives as much as to prepare for postmortem bliss. It has been suggested that 'alchemy might be called the art of the transmutation of the soul'. As a spiritual art, the object of the alchemical process is to reduce the soul to its 'original state, as yet unconditioned by impressions and passions'. Once this has been achieved, the alchemist 'crystallizes it anew in a nobler form'.[116] This is a dangerous process, and the alchemists are constantly warning of the perils of their art. 'I could give some instances of men who set about this matter with great levity', one writer informs us, 'and were heavily punished by meeting (some of them) with fatal accidents in their laboratories' ('laboratory' in spiritual alchemy is a code-word for body or mind). We are admonished to 'Haste slowly – for it is of the greatest importance that the influence of the fire should be brought to bear gradually and gently.' This is because 'If thou strivest unduly to shorten the time thou wilt produce an abortion. Many persons have, through their ignorance, or self-opinionated haste, obtained a Nihilixir instead of the hoped for Elixir.'[117] Another alchemist lamented the downfall of his over-precipitous colleagues in similar terms: 'Where they should have distilled with gentle heat they sublime over a fierce fire, and reduce their substance to ashes, instead of developing its inherent principles by vitalizing warmth.'[118] 'Too powerful a fire', warns a third alchemist, 'prevents a true union of the substances' (i.e. God and man).[119]

William James observed that in religious discourses there is often a sense of 'heterogeneous personality' or 'the divided self': 'There are two lives, the natural and the spiritual, and we must lose one before we can participate in the other.'[120] The occultists occupied a relatively extreme position in this regard, believing that there are two radically different selves, the empirical self of everyday life, and a transcendent self grounded in the divine being. This 'conviction that the familiar phenomenal *ego* is not the real I' is a standard feature of mystical discourses; from this principle, it follows that 'The chief object of man is the quest for his own self and right knowledge about it.'[121] Novalis asserted that 'The highest goal of development is to gain control of one's transcendental self, to become equal to the ego of the ego.'[122] According to Helena Blavatsky, 'Esoteric philosophy teaches the existence of two *Egos* in man, the mortal or *personal*, and the higher, the divine or *impersonal*, calling the former "personality" and the latter "individuality".' The aim of members of the Theosophical Society was 'to bring their *Divine Self* to guide their every thought and action, every day and at every moment of their lives'.[123]

According to Victor Hugo, the difference between the eternal self and the self as it is experienced in everyday life was comparable to that between waking and sleeping: 'The self (*moi*) who continues after waking is the self who is anterior and exterior to the dream. The self who continues after death is the self who is anterior and exterior to life.'[124] The illuminists' position is expressed in an eighteenth-century *Livre des initiés*:

> Man: an assemblage of a me who is me, and a me who is not me. The me who is me exists in its atmosphere; it can extend itself, etc., and it exists everywhere where it extends. The me who is me is happy when it raises itself towards the divinity, and disengages itself from the me who is not me. This me who is me will never perish. The me who is not me serves as a prison for the me who is me. This prison is only a gross bark which will be destroyed.[125]

The thought here can be traced back to the ancient Gnostic belief that the soul is part of the divine being trapped in matter. This Gnostic concept survived in a modified form in the view of Master Eckhardt and the Rhenish mystics that at the heart of our being is 'a little spark' of the godhead.[126] It was also expressed by later occultists, such as Victor Hugo: there is 'in every human soul . . . a primitive spark, a divine element, incorruptible in this world, immortal in the next'.[127]

The two selves are antithetical, the empirical self impeding the proper development of the transcendent self. The mystics therefore identified the 'self-will' of their everyday existence as their great enemy. 'There is no other way to blessedness than to lose one's self-will', Hans Denck tells us, in words that are echoed throughout mystical literature.[128] The occultists believed that a radical renunciation or emptying of the empirical self was necessary to enable the transcendent self to flourish in the soul. The necessary state of resignation is sometimes symbolised in Behmenist writings by virginity:

> For the Virgin life is not attained till the Will of the soul is brought through death to be passive as to will, to desire and act nothing but what the Essential essence of love wills, moves, and acts thorow it; for until then the soul cannot be a pure Virgin, nor live without all desire, lust and imagination, which must all cease, before the life of God can come to be all in all.[129]

The soul is to be modelled on the divine Wisdom, which is 'pacific, quiet, not rigid for its own right, moderate, obsequious, persuasabl[e], yielding'.[130] The mystics seek to restore their humanity to its original status as the image of God, and 'the unchangeable Nature of God' is itself 'a meer passive nothing'.[131] If the soul is to ascend to God, according to Jane Lead, it must die three types of death, to its animal, rational and sensitive lives; in short, it must die to all that binds it to its everyday conscious experience.[132] William Blake asks God to 'Annihilate the Selfhood in me: be thou all my life!' For Blake, 'In Selfhood we are nothing.'[133] Eliphas Lévi expressed a similar sense of the vacuity of human existence and the fullness of the divine being: God is 'the only I', and Lévi exclaims, 'Oh God, not being thou, I suffer from continuing to exist.'[134]

The mystical objective of conforming the human will to that of God should not be confused with simple obedience to an externally imposed code of conduct. The divine will must be internalised and become identical with the human will, implying a degree of mundane sanctification that would seem impossible to a Calvinist. Despite their language of radical negation, the mystics are not merely engaged in a project of self-annihilation.[135] They aspire to the state of transcendence described by Tennyson, in which 'the loss of personality (if so it were)' seemed 'no nebulous ecstasy, but the only true life'.[136] If the empirical self is to be cast down, it is in order to exalt the transcendent self. In McGregor Mather's words,

> The whole aim and object of the [Cabala's] teaching is to bring man to a knowledge of his higher self, to purify himself, to develop all qualities and powers of the being, that he may ultimately regain union with the Divine Man latent in himself, that Adam Qadmon, whom God hath made in his own Image.[137]

The goal of the process is not to undo God's handiwork in the creation by absorption into the godhead, but to restore man to Paradise. It is, however, a Paradise found within. The mystic's death to selfhood opens up a realm which transcends normal consciousness; its basic premise is the interiority of the true self.

The selfhood of everyday life is constituted by its contingency; although it may be experienced as subjectivity, it in fact belongs to the realm of objectivity. True subjectivity can be found only in God, 'the being of all beings' who announced himself to Moses as 'I Am That I Am' (Exodus 3:14). As Eckhardt expressed it, 'The word *Sum* can be spoken by no creature but God only: for it becomes the creature to testify of itself *Non Sum*.'[138] To be authentic, subjectivity must be grounded in God; to become truly himself man must be restored to his status as the image (i.e. imaginative projection) of God. For the Christian occultist, this restoration is effected through Christ: 'With him', as Novalis puts it, 'I have become truly human.'[139] This means much the same thing as another expression of Novalis's: the realisation that 'We *are* God.'[140]

7 Occultism and analytical psychology

The discovery that alchemy was an art of the transmutation of souls rather than metals is generally attributed to the nineteenth-century American writer, Ethan Allen Hitchcock. His understanding of alchemy might be described more properly as ethical rather than psychological, since it is based almost entirely on the identification of the Philosophers' Stone with a good conscience.[1] Nor were Hitchcock's views particularly original; they were anticipated in the seventeenth century by Patrick Scot in his *The Tillage of Light* (1623). For Scot, alchemy was simply an allegory of the process of acquiring wisdom. Most occultists, however, would have agreed with Robert Fludd's repudiation of Scot: the transmutation of souls rather than metals was the philosopher's true goal, but the alchemical process was nevertheless a metallurgical reality.[2]

It was not until the twentieth century that more strictly psychological interpretations of alchemy were developed.[3] That such interpretations should occur is perhaps not surprising, if we accept the view that psychoanalysis is itself a secularisation of occultism.[4] Daniel O'Keefe, for example, has observed that 'Freudian psychoanalysis had the social effect of reviving magical curing.'[5] The connection between occult thought and modern psychology is clearest on the wilder fringes of psychoanalysis. Although he attempts to present his ideas in terms of a modern scientific discourse, Wilhelm Reich showed a clear affinity with occult thought. In his later work, Reich postulated the existence of a primordial cosmic energy, 'orgone'. His therapeutic technique, involving 'orgone irradiation' in an 'orgone energy accumulator', seems to be little more than a modernised version of the mesmeric tub.[6]

Several less eccentric psychoanalytical writers have taken an interest in alchemy, arguing that it performs certain psychological functions. The seminal work in Freudian accounts of alchemy was *Probleme der Mystik und ihrer Symbolik,* by the Austrian psychoanalyst and Freemason, Herbert Silberer. He begins his account by analysing a parable in *The Golden Tract,* noting its dream-like qualities. There are sudden changes in scene; objects appear and vanish for no apparent reason; knowledge is achieved without the mediation of perception, or there is a strange uncertainty and lack of knowledge; sudden, unexpected obstacles are encountered; and the whole narrative has a 'peculiar logic' of its own. Silberer proceeds to give the parable a psychoanalytic gloss. Obstacles, for example, represent conflicts of will, and a mill in the story signifies the vagina or womb, since 'to grind' means to have sexual intercourse.[7] A similar psychoanalytical account of alchemy has been expounded by Johann Fabricius, who regards this aspect of the art as an accidental by-product of the attempt to transmute metals: 'through the indirect way of projection and free association the alchemists came to activate the unconscious which allied itself to their work in the form of visionary or hallucinatory experience'.[8]

It is possible that Freud's own work may be rooted in occultism, more specifically in the Jewish Cabala, if we accept David Bakan's argument that 'Freud consciously or unconsciously secularized the Jewish mystical tradition.'[9] In a letter to Jung, Freud spoke of 'the specifically Jewish character of my mysticism', a strange phrase for a man who also described himself as 'a completely godless Jew'.[10] Freud seems to have had at least some knowledge of the Cabala; the Cabalist scholar Chaim Bloch recalled visiting him and discovering that his library included several German books on the Cabala and a French translation of the *Zohar*.[11] Freud's closest associate in the period 1887–1902, the period when he was formulating his distinctive ideas, was Wilhelm Fliess, a writer who seems to have a connection with the occult tradition.[12] Fliess was the author of *Die Beziehungen zwischen Nase und Weiblichen Geschlechtsorganon* (1897), a work devoted to a supposed relationship between menstruation and the turbinate scrolls of the nose. Much of Fliess's account is numerology barely disguised as science. There are two major periodic cycles in animals and plants, a male one of 23 days and a female one of 28, and important events in people's lives are explicable in multiples of these. Goethe, for example, died on the 30,156th day of his life, 'when the 1,077th feminine menstruation had exhausted the last bit of his wonderful organization'.[13] This is Fliess, not Freud, but it does establish a possible esoteric context for the development of psychoanalysis. After 1902, Fliess was replaced by another occult-minded colleague as Freud's closest associate, Carl Jung. Though always himself an avowed sceptic, Freud nevertheless seems to have been unconsciously attracted to occultists.

There are, in fact, several parallels between psychoanalysis and Cabalism. The Cabala is supposed to be transmitted from master to pupil, 'orally to one person at a time', just as the psychoanalyst is initiated into his profession by being analysed himself.[14] The medieval Cabalist Abulafia developed a method of understanding the mystical meaning of the Bible which he called 'jumping and skipping'; in essence, it is a form of free association, a standard psychoanalytic technique.[15] Dream interpretation is important in both the Cabala and psychoanalysis.[16] Freud's concept of our basic bisexuality might be read as a biologising of the Cabalist notion of primordial androgyny.[17] It is certainly true that 'Freud's use of the idiom of sexuality as the basic one for the expression of all the deeper and more profound problems of mankind is entirely in the spirit of the Kabbala.'[18]

Bakan's argument is interesting, but ultimately conjectural. The evidence is entirely circumstantial, and there is no overt suggestion of Cabalist influence in any of Freud's writings. It seems unlikely that Freud drew on the Cabala consciously, but he may nevertheless have been influenced indirectly or unconsciously by the occult philosophy. In fact, given that occult mentalities permeated Germanic culture, at least in the rationalised form of Idealism, this would seem to be a probability.

Medieval psychology employed a model in which mental processes were considered as occurring on the surface of the mind. Emotions were 'seen as inherent in aspects of reality' rather than phenomena arising from within the individual.[19] Insofar as they had any reference beyond themselves, the superficial workings of the mind were represented as the product of extrinsic factors – the body, or the stars, or the Devil – rather than as events emerging from inner psychic depths. As its name implies, melancholy was caused by 'black choler', either in a specific organ, or 'pervading the entire body through the veins'.[20] Hysteria was the product of a barren womb, which explained why it was commonest among virgins and widows. Starved of nourishment by the male seed, the womb was liable to produce venomous fumes which infected the brain.[21] Even erotic obsession with a particular person, diagnosed as 'heroic love', had a purely physiological basis. When the vital spirits became overheated, they could dry out the anterior ventricle of the brain, the seat of memory, leading to a fixation of the image of the beloved.[22] If not the body, then the stars could be held responsible for mental disturbances, and astrologers like Richard Napier or Simon Forman were able to build thriving psychiatric practices.[23] Madness could also be explained by demonic possession, and in the late sixteenth century Protestants and Catholics, keen to demonstrate the superiority of their own faith, competed in exorcising devils from the persons of the insane.[24] Astrological and demonological explanations of mental phenomena began to decline in the late seventeenth century,[25] but somatic discourses continued to flourish. Both physicians and patients were eager to construct mental disease as 'incorporated in the body', and attention was simply shifted to the nervous system as the cause of mental aberration.[26] By the nineteenth century, biologism was firmly entrenched in scientific discourses.[27]

The mystical world-view was fundamentally antithetical to somatic psychology. The inner–outer ontology of occultism tended to reduce body to a function of mind, and the importance given to the imagination furthered this tendency to psychologise somatic disturbances. The mystics, moreover, believed that there were regions of the soul inaccessible to everyday human consciousness. In the early modern period, however, those aspects of mental or spiritual life beyond conscious experience were not represented as a realm below the surface of consciousness, but above it. Interiority meant superiority, not inferiority. The unconscious mind was a hierarchy leading upwards, ultimately connecting man to the source of all being, God himself. Not that illuminism was devoid of a darker vision of our unconscious life. Pietism encouraged people to examine themselves closely, laying particular stress on the hidden motives underlying their actions.[28] The Behmenist idea that there was a wrathful Dark Principle, which was a structural element of all being, endowed the depths of the soul with a pathological core. This Principle resembles Arthur Schopenhauer's concept of the Will as the problematic substratum of all existence. Schopenhauer admired Boehme, but even if there was no direct influence in this respect, it is certain that he drew inspiration from Eastern mystical thought. Schopenhauer's concept of the Will is highly sexualised, and it has been suggested that it was an important source for the Freudian notion of the libido.[29]

The notion of an unconscious mind was explored by several nineteenth-century writers, especially in Germany. Carl Gustav Carus, for example, equated the human unconscious with the consciousness of God,[30] an idea which points both backwards to the esoteric tradition and forwards to Jungian thought. Nineteenth-century esotericists regarded dreams as a means of access to levels of mental or spiritual activity beyond consciousness long before Freud's work in this area; this was a topic which much interested Oberlin, who was an important influence on one of Schelling's followers, Gotthilf Heinrich Schubert. Schubert himself is supposed to have anticipated Freud in his *Die Symbolik des Traumes* (1814).[31] Freud is in fact dismissive of Schubert's understanding of dreams as 'a liberation of the spirit from the power of eternal nature, a freeing of the soul from the bonds of the senses'. According to Freud, all attempts to 'represent dreams as an elevation of mental life to a higher level seem to us now to be scarcely intelligible'. He was content to leave such fancies to 'mystics and pietists'.[32] The father of psychoanalysis had an altogether darker vision of the truths revealed in dreaming, but he and Schubert are united in seeing dreams, properly understood, as potentially emancipatory. For Schubert, this is an emancipation into the unconscious; for Freud, an emancipation from it. Freud, like Hamann, regarded dreaming as 'a journey to the Inferno of self-knowledge'.[33]

Among English explorers of the unconscious, F. W. H. Myers's thought was clearly influenced by the occult tradition. He believed that human beings participated in four parallel realms: the physical, the cosmic ether, 'the world of spiritual life' and the World Soul.[34] Myers distinguished between a supraliminal mind which dealt with the external, physical world, and a subliminal mind, encompassing the unconscious elements of our mental existence. According to Myers, 'we should now see the subliminal self no longer as a mere chain of eddies or backwaters, in some way excluded from the mainstream of man's being, but rather as itself the central and potent current, the most truly identifiable with the man himself'.[35] At the heart of Myers's thought is a belief that is also the core of the occult philosophy: 'That which lies at the root of each of us lies at the root of the

Cosmos too. Our struggle is the struggle of the Universe; and the very God-head finds fulfillment through our upward striving souls.'[36] There is no evidence that Myers had any influence on Freud; his understanding of our unconscious life, like Schubert's, was far too optimistic for Freud's outlook. Myers was, however, one of the inspirations for Carl Jung's psychology.

Jung had a lifelong interest in religion, especially the esoteric mystical tradition. His doctoral thesis was dedicated to the 'Psychology and Pathology of So-Called Occult Phenomena' (1902), and many of his later works are psychological analyses – or perhaps better, expositions – of Gnosticism and alchemy. Jung regarded the alchemists as having come close 'to our most recent discoveries concerning the psychology of the unconscious';[37] which is to say, they had anticipated Jung's own theories. The Swiss psychologist admired 'Jacob Boehme's philosophic and poetic stammerings' as the product of a 'primordial vision',[38] and there are strong parallels between Behmenist and Jungian thought on gender.[39] As Jung himself recognised, his fundamental understanding of the nature of the divine being was the same as Boehme's: 'The visionary genius of Jacob Boehme recognised the paradoxical nature of the God-image.'[40] According to Boehme, God contains both a dark side and a light one, a wrathful First Principle and a loving Second Principle. Similarly, Jung understood that God 'is kind and terrible', that the simultaneous 'light and darkness of God' were ineluctable facts.[41] This does not, as John Gruchy supposes, make Jung 'a latter-day Manichaean, or a Hindu, but certainly not a Christian', distancing him from the Judaeo-Christian tradition of the West.[42] On the contrary, it places him firmly within a flourishing, though heterodox and often neglected, strand of this tradition. Jung had a heightened sense of the sublimity of nature,[43] and in this he is a typical example of the mysticism with which we are dealing, a mysticism that focuses at the same time on the innermost self and the external world. Such is the extent of Jung's engagement with occult thought that his analytical psychology can be regarded as a reformed occultism in the strictest sense.

Jung stressed the reality of the psyche: what happens in the mind is every bit as real as any external event. He pointed out that Kant had postulated the objective existence of a material world which is inaccessible as such to our consciousness. Jung himself postulated the existence of an objective psychic or spiritual world, which was equally inaccessible as such to consciousness: 'We know as little of a Supreme Being as of Matter. But there is as little doubt of the existence of a Supreme Being as there is of Matter.'[44] While he agreed with Freud that the mind was divided into a conscious and an unconscious, the two men differed in their evaluation of the relationship between them. Freud thought that the unconscious mind was formed exclusively by the repression of elements from consciousness, but Jung argued that the unconscious mind was historically prior to consciousness,[45] and whereas Freud tended to regard the unconscious as inherently pathological, Jung thought that it performed positive psychic functions. The mind, according to Jung, was constituted basically from psychic energy, which he called 'libido', using the word in a broader way than Freud's narrowly sexualised concept. The libido flows between two poles, or opposites. In its progression, it is concerned with satisfying conscious needs, or with adaptation to the external world. In its regression, the libido is concerned with unconscious needs, or with adaptation to the inner psychic reality. Both progression and regression are healthy and necessary; they constitute an 'enantiodromia', a conversion of the opposites into each other – the *coincidentia oppositorum* of occult thought. If this process is blocked, the libido becomes concentrated in the unconscious, whence it ultimately breaks forth as neurosis or psychosis.[46]

Jungian psychology is based on the theory that there are four functions in the psyche, which Jung called thinking, feeling, sensation and intuition. These are expressed in occult symbolism: the significance placed on the four elements, for example, or Blake's four Zoas.[47] Sensation, Jung tells us, 'establishes what is actually given, thinking enables us to recognize its meaning, feeling tells us its value, and finally intuition points to the possibilities of the whence and whither that lie within the immediate facts'.[48] These functions are commonly in imbalance. One of the functions is generally dominant and fully conscious; this 'differentiated function' is assisted in the conscious mind by an 'auxiliary function'. Below the surface of consciousness is an 'undifferentiated function' and its auxiliary. The psychic conflict between the two auxiliary functions is not as severe as that between the differentiated and undifferentiated functions, and for this reason the unconscious auxiliary is often promoted to the conscious mind.[49] Given this distribution of the functions between the conscious and unconscious minds, it is not difficult to see why, although in both alchemy and the unconscious there are distinct leanings to quaternity, symbolising psychic wholeness, 'there is always a vacillation between three and four'.[50] As a text cited by Jung puts it, 'All things do live in three, But in four they merry be.'[51]

The psyche is therefore fragmented into two halves, conscious and unconscious. The four functions tend to be distributed differently in the two sexes; the thinking function, for example, is often the dominant one in men, while intuition frequently appears as a differentiated function in women. Because of this different distribution of the functions in the sexes, the conscious and unconscious halves of the mind each have a specific gender. The male conscious mind is itself male, but the unconscious in men is inhabited by the repressed feminine elements of the psyche, and the most repressed function is represented by what Jung called the anima. Conversely, women repress the male aspects of the psyche, which become the animus.[52] These are not simply abstract structures, but are commonly personified; the Virgin Mary, the fairy-tale princess, the witch and the hag are all archetypal representations of the anima. According to Jung, this division of the psyche into gendered halves is symbolised in alchemy by the primordial androgyne.

The objective of Jung's psychology is to reintegrate the fragmented personality by the assimilation or 'mutual interpretation of conscious and unconscious contents' of the psyche.[53] This is known as the individuation process, and it finds symbolic expression in alchemy in the perfect balance of the four elements (representing the four functions of the psyche), or in the Philosophers' Stone (representing the fully individuated person).[54] It is also symbolised in the sacred marriage of the sun and moon (the conscious mind and anima, or the male and female aspects of the psyche).[55] Jung tells us that 'It is the moral task of alchemy to bring the feminine, maternal background of the psyche, seething with passions, into harmony with the principles of the spirit.'[56] Although it has become an integral part of what has been called 'the feminism of yin and yang',[57] Jung's psychology tends to be androcentric; in this he is the authentic heir of spiritual alchemy. Both appear to be more concerned with the regeneration or individuation process in men, who are regarded as needing to be more in touch with their intuitive functions. As in esoteric thought, there is a tendency in Jungian psychology to be suspicious of a hubristic rationalism. Like the occultists, Jungians have a high regard for the imagination. According to one of Jung's followers, the imagination is 'the waking method of looking into the unconscious, as dream is the method used in sleep'.[58] Fantasy, Jung tells us, is 'the maternally creative side of the masculine spirit'.[59]

Jung argued that the symbols of alchemy can be found both in mythologies throughout the world and in the dreams of our contemporaries who have never encountered the alchemical art. They are not idiosyncratic products of particular minds, but have a universal resonance. They are in fact 'archetypes', images produced by what Jung called the 'collective unconscious', which he defined as 'a common substratum [of psyches] transcending all differences in culture and consciousness'.[60] The collective unconscious is distinct from the personal unconscious, and it has an objective existence of its own. As its name implies, the collective unconscious is transpersonal, something that we share. This can be regarded as a restatement of the Idealist concept of a universal Spirit or Mind (*Geist*) as the fundamental reality. The collective unconscious links us together, and Jung tells us that 'In some way or other we are part of an all-embracing psychic life, of a single "greatest man" to quote Swedenborg.' He describes the collective unconscious as 'a collective human being combining the characteristics of both sexes, transcending youth and age, birth and death'.[61] The collective unconscious corresponds to the primordial cosmic man of occult thought, Adam Kadmon. The cosmic man unites individual human beings to God; similarly, at its deepest level, the collective unconscious links man to God.

A fundamental archetype of the collective unconscious is the Self, which is distinct from the ego. The ego refers to the conscious mind, but the self represents our whole being. The Self is the 'objective phenomenon of which the ego is the subject'.[62] It is symbolised in various forms, Christ and the

Buddha being two of the most important;[63] the Self is 'the archetype of the God-Image'.[64] Marie-Louise von Franz tells us that the Self is 'the regulating centre that brings about a constant extension and maturing of the personality'. In order for 'this creatively active aspect of the psychic nucleus' to function, however, the ego must rid itself 'of all purposive and wishful aims' and arrive at 'a deeper, more basic form of existence'.[65] Similarly, Jung informs us that the individuation process culminates in 'a consciousness that is detached from the world'.[66] The affinity of the Jungian Self and ego with the transcendent and empirical selves of mystical discourse is obvious, as is the prescription of an attitude of radical resignation (*Gelassenheit*) towards the world.

Modern psychological interpretations of alchemy are interesting in themselves, and they may throw some light on the motivation behind the alchemical art. There are, however, limitations to the usefulness of applying modern psychologies to our understanding of the occult philosophy. Freudian psychology in particular tends to be ahistorical. The same charge might be made against Jung. Brian Morris has argued that in contrast to Freud, 'Jung's theoretical outlook is . . . fundamentally ahistorical and asocial.'[67] This is not quite true. Jung's psychology may not be social in the sense of being interpersonal, but it is transpersonal. Jung showed little interest in the relations between atomised individuals, but he was pre-occupied by the notion of a psychic being shared by everyone. After all, one of the important ways in which Jung differed from Freud is in positing the existence of a *collective* unconscious; and he criticised Freud's attempts 'to reduce myth motifs to personal psychology'.[68] Jung regarded consciousness itself as being a historical phenomenon.[69] He 'ascribed a pivotal role to the evolutionary process' in his psychology,[70] and he recognised a degree of historical change in the psyche. He tells us, for example, that Christianity and Hinduism brought about 'a tremendous strengthening of consciousness',[71] and that the reduction in the fifteenth and sixteenth centuries of the four processes of classical alchemy to three represents a fundamental shift in psychic values.[72] In this sense, Jung's thought has an historical dimension that is entirely lacking in Freud. Nevertheless, Jung deals with a set of symbols that has a history of well over two thousand years, but treats it as if it has a single significance untouched by time. It is true that historical continuity can be demonstrated for this symbolism, but historical continuity is not the same thing as historical identity. The symbolism and its functions have quite clearly evolved over time. Psychological interpretations of alchemy, whether Freudian or Jungian, elide almost completely any sense of historical change and cultural variation within the given set of symbols, erecting a monolithic framework for understanding them. This may or may not be valid as a partial account of the phenomenon; it is certainly not adequate as a comprehensive interpretation.

There is also a danger when interpreting symbolic writings of projecting meanings into them which are simply not in the texts themselves, of giving 'a rationalistic reading in which the meaning of the symbolic text is described under the imagery of a contemporary understanding'.[73] The abundant sexual imagery of occult writings, and the incest symbolism of alchemy in particular, provide a rich hunting-ground for Freudian psychoanalysts. To anyone who shares the Freudian world-view, there is a plausibility about such assertions as 'the incestuous conjunction with the sister-mother and the slaying of the father are psychic acts resuscitated by the alchemist from the buried realms of unconscious fantasy'.[74] To those of us who do not happen to be Freudians, however, the unconscious fantasy involved here is as likely to be the psychoanalyst's as the alchemist's. The Freudian interpretation of alchemy depends entirely on the decoding of unconscious impulses allegedly within the psyche of someone who (usually) died a very long time ago. There is at the very least a problem of verification with this.

Jungian psychologists are at an advantage in this respect. Some writers who stand within the occult tradition are critical of Jung,[75] but the criticism seems to be the same one that Blake made about Swedenborg: he 'was wrong in endeavouring to explain to the rational faculty what the reason cannot comprehend'.[76] This is precisely the source of Jung's importance in the continuing history of the occult philosophy. Jungian psychology has the same structure as earlier occultism. To speak of the individuation and integration of the personality as the alchemists' objective may be to distort their project by imposing a modern idiom on it, but (unlike Freudian accounts) it does bear some relation to their consciously stated goals. As John Gruchy observed, 'the cultural crisis of the West as Jung saw it is a religious crisis'.[77] His psychology was an attempt to resolve this crisis by formulating the basis of what might be regarded as a secular spirituality. To achieve this, he drew on the centuries-old tradition of Western Gnosticism. Just as Swedenborg reformed the occult philosophy and made it palatable to eighteenth- and nineteenth-century sensibilities, so Jung also reformed esoteric thought, giving it a renewed lease of life in the twentieth century.[78]

8 Society, religion and history in occult thought

Alchemy is commonly regarded as a search for personal enrichment, but the alchemists themselves warned that anyone who desires occult knowledge 'for the purpose of procuring wealth and pleasure' should not 'think that he will ever attain to it'. On the contrary,

> In this furnace of the Cross, a man, like earthly gold, attains to the true black Raven's Head, *i.e.*, loses all beauty and honour in the eyes of the world; and that not only during forty days and nights, but often during his whole life, which is thus often more full of sorrow and suffering than of comfort and joy.[1]

Far from seeking personal wealth, one alchemist went so far as to hope 'that in a few years gold (not as given by God, but as abused by man) will be so common that those who are so mad after it shall contemptuously spurn aside this bulwark of Antichrist'.[2] The true alchemist seeks sanctity rather than wealth: 'he on whom the Most High has conferred the knowledge of this Mystery esteems mere money and earthly riches as lightly as the dirt of the streets. His heart and all his desires are bent upon seeing and enjoying the heavenly reality of which all these things are but a figure.'[3] Thomas Charnock advises the would-be adept that 'if you thinke to obtaine your Intent, / Fear God and keepe his Comandement'.[4] Alchemy was not intended for personal benefit, and we are told repeatedly that the Art should be used for 'the glory of [God and] His most Holy Name, and for the good of thy suffering fellow man'.[5] If you 'desire to struggle with this process', John Dastin advised, you 'ought not to approach it unless you have a mind that is pure and dedicated to God, and humbly beseech him for help'.[6] Purity was an essential prerequisite of success for the alchemist:

> Iyfe thow wilt thys warke begyn,
> Than schrevy the clene of alle thy Seyne:
> Contryte in hert wyth alle thy thowght,
> And ever thenke on hym that the der bowght.[7]

We are told that the alchemist should be 'Sober, Honest, and Meeke'.[8] The medieval alchemists sometimes recommended a fairly conventional piety: 'take thee to thy Beades and praye', Pierce the Black Monk admonished, and proceed with 'Prayers, Penaunces, and Piety'.[9] George Ripley advised the aspiring alchemist to

> Live clene in soule, to God doe none offence;
> Exalt thee not but rather keepe thee Lowe,
> Ells wyll thy God in thee no Wysdome sowe.[10]

The ungodly excluded themselves from mastery of the Art: 'God gives not this gift to the wicked, who despise His word, but to the godly who strive to live honestly and quietly in this wicked and impure world, and to lend a helping hand to the needy brethren'.[11]

The alchemical outlook sometimes implied a degree of withdrawal from mundane activities. One alchemist advises a quietist asceticism: 'let your minds and thoughts be turned away from all things earthly, and, as it were, created anew and consecrated to God alone'.[12] The alchemist, according to Henry Pinell, should 'live a serious and private life, free from all other employment and businesse in the world'.[13] The alchemical art, however, required more than a personal cleanliness of spirit and an ascetic quietism. It also demanded the practice of social virtues:

> And he that will come thereby,
> Must be meeke, and full of mercy:
> Both in spyrit and in Countenaunce,
> Full of Cheriti and good Governaunce . . .
> And all the ryches that he ys sped,
> To do God worschyppe with Almes deede.[14]

William Bloomfield admonished those who aspired to obtain the Stone that they should 'to the Poore be not unkind . . . be gentle to all men . . . Fatherles and Widows have alwaies in thy minde.'[15] A late seventeenth-century alchemist informs us that, although 'Divine Truths are adumbrated' in the spagyric art, 'it gives not the possession thereof, which is alone Entailed upon that Divine excellency that never fails; Charity'.[16]

The illuminists emphasised above all the virtue of charity, by which they meant an active love for our fellow creatures rather than a casual, patronising and conscious-salving pretence at caring. Charity, according to Thomas Tryon, 'is the first and last true step in Religion'. It is the supreme attribute of the divinity, since God 'gives freely to all his Off-spring, without Respect of Person; and receives nothing'.[17] God is a 'Will to all Goodness', and William Law observed that 'all Contrivances of Holiness, all Forms of religious Piety, signify nothing' unless informed by this will. Law pointed out that 'there is not one command in all the Gospel for *Public Worship*;

and perhaps it is a Duty that is least insisted upon in Scripture of any other . . .
Whereas that *Religion* or *Devotion* which is to govern the *ordinary Actions* of
our life is to be found in almost every verse of Scripture.'[18] On one occasion
Law's indiscriminate alms-giving induced his neighbours to petition the local
Justice to take action against him for encouraging paupers to flock to the
parish.[19] Law had his own answer to those of his contemporaries who
wished to confine alms-giving to the 'deserving' poor: 'where has the Scripture made *merit* the rule of charity?'[20] The ideal of benevolence to all
remained a central tenet of occult thought into the nineteenth century. It
was the aim of the Theosophical Society, for example, 'To form the nucleus
of a Universal Brotherhood of Humanity, without distinction of race, colour,
or creed.'[21]

William Blake summarised his ethical outlook at the end of one of his
poems, 'William Bond':

> Seek love in the Pity of others' Woe,
> In the gentle relief of another's care,
> In the darkness of night & the winter's snow,
> In the naked & outcast, Seek love there.[22]

This ethical emphasis in occult thought should not be construed as constituting a religion of works; the occultists are not concerned with acquiring merit,
either in the eyes of God or those of man. In this respect, Blake's position
is typical in being one of a radical antinomianism which recognises that
Christianity is not at heart an ethical religion:

> Mutual Forgiveness of each Vice,
> Such are the Gates of Paradise.
> Against the Accuser's chief desire,
> Jehovah's fingers wrote the Law:
> Then wept! then rose in Zeal & Awe,
> And in the midst of Sinai's heat
> Hid it beneath his Mercy Seat.
> O Christians, Christians, tell me Why
> You rear it on your Altars high.[23]

The message of Christianity is that 'Good & Evil are no more!'[24] because
'The Spirit of Jesus is continual forgiveness of Sin.'[25] E. P. Thompson was
right to locate Blake's antinomianism in the radical sectarian milieu of
eighteenth-century London, although his particular emphasis on the
Muggletonians is unwarranted. Where Thompson erred was in seeing this
context as somehow antithetical to what he called the 'polite tradition' of
early modern occultism, represented by Jane Lead and the Philadelphians.[26]
Blake's position is simply an emphatic version of the theodicy and soteriology of occultism as a whole, polite or otherwise. It was a fundamental

tenet of the occult philosophers that God was not a vindictive Father who wanted to punish his children for their failings. God damned no-one; at most, people damned themselves by turning their backs on God, whose infinite love was freely available to everyone. From the end of the seventeenth century, occultists like Lady Conway and Jane Lead were extending this position into a belief in universal salvation. God not only wanted to save everyone, eventually he would succeed in doing so.[27] The idea that the Messiah would restore everything to its original purity, including Samael and the other demons, was in fact a long-standing Cabalist idea.[28]

Some occult writers exhibited a lack of tolerance towards people who disagreed with them religiously. Giordano Bruno may not have been an orthodox Catholic, but he was nevertheless violently anti-Protestant, largely because of the Reformers' disparagement of good works.[29] Other occultists were equally anti-Catholic, objecting to what they regarded as a religion of empty ceremonies and priestly despotism. James Freake told Robert Childe that in Rome 'you have seen much ceremony, and little religion; and in the wilderness of New England, you have seen among some, much religion and little ceremony'.[30] The author of the Rosicrucian manifestoes had little time for 'Romish seducers'.[31] Quirinus Kuhlmann called for interdenominational toleration, but only among Protestants; he had no hesitation in identifying the Pope as Antichrist.[32]

Many occultists were deeply attached to the established churches of their homelands. Thomas Vaughan, for example, declared that he was 'neither Papist, nor Sectary, but a true resolute Protestant in the best sense of the Church of England'.[33] Such attachments did not necessarily preclude an ecumenical spirit, which was much more characteristic of the occult milieu than the occasional expressions of intolerance. Tolerance was in fact a general feature of what Lewis White Beck has called the 'Protestant Counter Reformation', exemplified by such figures as Sebastian Franck, Valentin Weigel and Jacob Boehme.[34] In an age when Europe was being torn apart by wars of religion, an age in which pretenders to Christian faith contrived to serve the God who is Love by torturing and killing each other, the Hermeticists sought to promote a universal tolerance and the reunification of a divided Christendom.[35] The Familists, it has been suggested, were attempting to follow a 'third way', avoiding the murderous dogmatism of both the Reformation and Counter-Reformation.[36] This attitude was to remain a characteristic of the occult milieu. Writers like Thomas Tryon recognised that the 'fierce Contentions, and brutal Outrages, which Men exercise against one another' were simply signs of human degeneracy: everyone speaks with confidence, the blind judging colours and the deaf judging sounds.[37] William Law was concerned with dissuading people from converting to Rome,[38] but he could nevertheless 'allmost wish that we had no spiritual Books but those that have been wrote by Catholicks'.[39] Lavater thought that 'everyone ought to have his own individual faith, like his own face'; although he criticised the

Church of Rome for its intolerance, he encouraged waverers to become Catholic rather than lose their faith altogether.[40] This occultist tolerance permeated Pietist circles, ultimately to be transformed into the liberal Protestantism of writers like Friedrich Schleiermacher. Schleiermacher regarded different forms of Christianity as being complementary rather than contradictory; even non-Christian religions had their value, and Christ himself was only one among a number of mediators between God and man.[41] An ecumenical spirit also informed the ideas of other Romantics. Coleridge declared that 'Never will God reject a soul that sincerely loves him, be his speculative opinions what they will.'[42] Victor Hugo admitted 'the possibilities of all the beauties of human virtues in a faith different from our own'.[43]

Occultist ecumenicalism was based on a distinction between ritualism and the inner spirituality that the mystics regarded as the essence of true religion. Agrippa tended to consider all ritual, Christian or otherwise, as exemplifying 'the same basic activity'.[44] An angel informed John Dee that the wise looked to neither Catholics nor Protestants, but 'up to the God of heaven and earth and to his Son, Jesus Christ, who has given the Spirit of his abundant graces to those who live a natural life in purity and a life of grace in their works'.[45] God acts in many ways, according to Thomas Bromley, from which it followed 'that none are to be confined to one exact path'.[46] John Pordage 'could not express the title of Saints to any one Sect or Society of men, but apply it to all that are called, chosen, and faithful, who shew their interest in Christs death and resurrection'.[47] Richard Roach argued that

> Mysticks in all Parts & of all Denominations . . . have Overlook[e]d and shot beyond ye Particularities of their own Church or Party as in an Outward Visible Form, and kept to ye Interior or Spiritual Way: in wch there may be Observ[e]d as great a Harmony & Unity even among those of Externally Different Denominations, as there is among those in the Outward Way & Forms a Disunity & Disharmony.[48]

The Philadelphian Society, of which Roach was a member, was expressly ecumenical in outlook, and did not seek to persuade 'others to *Dissent* from that Communion, which they are previously oblig'd to adhere to'.[49] Louis de Saint-Martin, nominally a Catholic, believed that Christianity 'has no sects'; Catholicism was no more than a first step on the spiritual path, and it was ultimately necessary to go beyond external forms to an inner spirituality.[50] Many illuminists (following Joachim of Fiore) expected a new stage in revelation or a higher form of religion to appear. For Franz von Baader, for example, 'Judaism is to Christianity what the latter is to a third, superior term in which each of the two must be transfigured.'[51]

The 'unbounded eclecticism' of later movements like the Theosophical Society or the Golden Dawn[52] was characteristic of the occult philosophy throughout its history. The alchemists had long been in the habit of pillaging mythology for their symbolism, a tendency satirised by Jonson in

The Alchemist.[53] The great medieval French alchemist Nicolas Flamel interpreted the legend of Theseus as an allegorical description of part of the
alchemical process. In the early seventeenth century Michael Maier identified
Oedipus as a representation of the Philosopher's Stone, asserting that the
sages had invented the myth 'by way of allegory to lay bare the secrets of
their learning'. About the same time, Burgavius was interpreting pagan
mythology as Hermetic allegory, an approach which was continued in the
eighteenth century by illuminists like Pernéty in his *Dictionnaire mytho-
hérmetique* (1758).[54] Such ideas were to lead occultists to the view that the
Christian religion did not enjoy a monopoly of spiritual truth. Antoine
Court de Gébelin believed that pagan mythologies expressed 'precisely the
same history as that given by Moses'.[55] Alchemists frequently included
'wise Gentiles' among the sages, notably Hermes Trismegistus, Pythagoras
and Plato, as well as Islamic writers like Avicenna, Rasis and Geber.[56]
The Behmenist Dionysius Andreas Freher thought that 'a faithfull collection of the divine doctrine taught by some holy souls among the heathen,
would make a sort of naturall Bible'. Freher mentions Diogenes, Epicurus,
Chrysippus, Antisthenes, Socrates, Zeno, Pythagoras and Epicurus. Of these,
Diogenes led 'a life so holy that it is hard to find one more conformable to
that of Jesus Christ'.[57]

Initially there was a strong tendency to Christianise such pagan sages.
Leone Ebreo thought that Plato had acquired his doctrines from Moses,
and Blaise de Vignère spoke of Pythagoras as 'having quaffed full draughts
from the living sources of Mosaicall tradition'.[58] Robert Fludd believed
that several pagans had acknowledged the Trinity, and that Plato and
Hermes Trismegistus had studied the Mosaic writings.[59] Henry Pinell went
even further. Observing that 'all moderne Philosophers grounded their
discourses' on the Hermetic *Emerald Tablet*, Pinell felt no danger of being
seduced by paganism, since Thrice-Great Hermes 'is said to be Moses'.[60]
Among the occultists none of the pagan seers enjoyed greater esteem than
Hermes Trismegistus, whom Gabriel Harvey regarded as 'ye very perfectiste
philosopher nexte unto God himselfe'.[61] The idea that Hermes was a pagan
prophet of Christianity can be traced at least as far back as Lactantius;
Augustine accepted Hermes' foreknowledge of Christ, but regarded it as
being of demonic rather than divine provenance.[62] Hermeticists naturally
favoured Lactantius's view. John French, in his preface to John Everard's
translation of Hermes' *Divine Pymander*, wrote that 'If God ever appeared
in any man, he appeared in him', and there was 'more true knowledge of
God and Nature' in the Hermetic texts than in any book except the Bible.
Everard himself was accused of 'sayeing that the Trismegiste was a more
Cleere author for the doctrine of the blessed Trinitye then Moses', a
charge which he did not deny.[63]

Many of the pagan sages praised by the occult philosophers were figures
from Graeco-Roman antiquity. This is not surprising, given the continuing
prestige of classical culture in post-Renaissance Europe, and writers like

Virgil had long been accorded an honorary place among the prophets of Christianity. The occult philosophers also cast their nets wider in their search for pagan Christians, perhaps encouraged by the belief that wisdom was of Eastern origin.[64] According to the Chevalier Ramsay, there were certain basic religious principles, and 'all nations had from the beginning some idea of those principles more or less confus'd'. Ramsay's *The Travels of Cyrus* sought to demonstrate that pagan religions were really garbled versions of Christian revelation. Ramsay seems to have co-ordinated comparative religious insight along an East–West axis: 'the Theology of the Orientals is more pure than that of the Egyptians, that of the Egyptians less corrupted than that of the Greeks, and that of the Greeks more exalted than that of the Romans'.[65] In praising oriental religion Ramsay was thinking primarily of Zoroastrianism. Other eighteenth-century occultists noted the similarities between their own religious system and the religions of India. P. E. Jablonski, for example, compared the Hermetic texts to the Hindu Vedas.[66] Among the Romantics, Ballanche asserted the identity 'of the ideas which rest at the bottom of Indian doctrines with those which are enclosed in the writings of our modern theosophers'.[67] According to Novalis, with Christ India would bloom in the North.[68] In the nineteenth century, Francis Barham believed that Buddhism was 'the Reformed Religion of the ancient, corrupted and effete "patriarchal Christianity", Druidism, or Brahmism of the East, descended to them in a direct line from Shem, the son of Noah'. Buddhism differed from Christianity only in its ignorance of the particular soteriological role of Christ.[69]

The view that all religions were approximations to Christianity was accompanied by the belief that righteous heathens could find salvation without submitting to the Gospel. Agrippa asserted that God had 'permitted no creature in the world to be without religion', and that 'Every religion hath something of good.' Although Christianity was the only true religion, God 'doth not altogether reject' others.[70] According to Boehme, it was perfectly possible for 'Jews, Turks, or Heathen' to be saved: 'Or dost thou think that God is the God of *Christians* only? Do not the *Heathen* also live in God, *whosoever doth* right or *righteousness God* loveth and *accepteth him*.'[71] Dutoit-Membrini believed that even heathens could have some knowledge of God, since they possessed 'a great supplement to revelation, be it in nature, be it in themselves'.[72] William Blake thought that 'the Innocent civilized Heathen & the Uncivilized Savage, who, having not the law, do by Nature the Things contain'd in the Law' will be found 'in Eternity'.[73]

Many of the occultists' forays into comparative religion are clearly examples of what John Mee has called 'conservative syncretism', intended to confirm the special claims of Christianity. Even conservative syncretism, however, could have a radical effect. As Desirée Hirst observed, Christian Cabalism began with a desire to convert the Jews and ended in the partial Judaising of Christianity.[74] If the attempt to give a Christianised reading to paganism maintained the primacy of Christian revelation, the doctrine of the righteous heathen undermined its claim to exclusive soteriological value. By the late eighteenth century, there was a new willingness to see all religions as equally valid expressions of a single, universal substratum of spiritual truth. This is a position adumbrated in the writings of Lord Herbert of Cherbury, and it is usually associated with deism and the notion of 'natural religion'.[75] It was also characteristic of the occult milieu. Indeed, it may be worth considering the possible links between deism and occultism. Although we generally associate the one with a cool rationalism and the other with mythopoeic extravagance, the two movements often shared common ground – both figuratively and, in the Masonic lodges, literally. We might apply Pope's criticism of deism to the mystical humanism of Romantic esotericism; both tended to make 'God Man's Image, Man the final cause'. In fact, despite the deeply religious sensibility of the Romantics, in some ways they brought about a more radical breach with transcendental religion than the deists, and there is some truth to Altizer's remark that William Blake was 'the first Christian atheist'.[76] The sceptical attitude of eighteenth-century deism towards the supernatural had been foreshadowed in the attacks on belief in witchcraft made by John Webster and other writers with developed occult interests, and it has been observed that the deist Thomas Woolston presented his arguments against miracles with 'a patina of mystical and cabbalistic jargon'.[77] There are certainly occult sources for the thought of John Toland, who is generally regarded as one of the founding fathers of English deism. Toland was an admirer of Giordano Bruno, and like many occultists he believed that there was a single esoteric doctrine underlying the diverse exoteric teachings of the different religions.[78] Given his avowed pantheism (a word he introduced into English to describe his own religion), we might in fact regard Toland as representing the secularisation of occultism rather than as simply fostering a sceptical deism.

A virtually dechristianised occultism can be found as early as the sixteenth century in Giordano Bruno's writings. Bruno thought that the secret of true religion could be found among the ancient Egyptians, and he condemned Jewish monotheism for its repudiation of the immanence of God in nature.[79] Such frank paganism was rare in early modern occultism, but by the late eighteenth century there was a clear trend away from Christianity among the illuminists. The French Revolutionary sect of Théophilanthropes, established by J. B. Chemin-Dupontés in 1796, was an attempt to construct a syncretic religion based on the common principles of all religious faiths. Its dual aim, 'that of encouraging men to worship God and love their fellows', was simply a version of a standard formula repeated endlessly in alchemical tracts. As Christopher McIntosh observes, the Théophilanthropes prefigured later occult movements.[80] By the nineteenth century, Fabre d'Olivet could assemble a motley variety of sages who allegedly expounded the same fundamental truths. In his writings we can find Christ brushing shoulders with Orpheus, Pythagoras, Plato, Zoroaster, Krishna, Moses, the Buddha and Odin.[81] The spiritualist Emma Hardinge-Britten published *Six Lectures on*

Theology and Nature in 1860, arguing that all religions derive from one original source. Later in the nineteenth century, Papus believed that 'Every priest of an ancient creed . . . knew perfectly well that only one religion existed, and that the cultus merely served to translate this religion to the different nations according to their different temperaments.'[82] Edouard Schuré's *Grands Initiés* was devoted to the theme that the founders of all the great religions had taught the same basic doctrine.[83]

By the nineteenth century, the syncretic trend in Western occultism was undergoing a fundamental shift. Whereas earlier occultists had regarded non-Christian religions as embodying faint echoes of Christianity, writers like N. A. Notovitch were now arguing that Christ had learnt his doctrines from Tibetan Buddhists.[84] This orientalising of Western occultism was the work above all of Helena Blavatsky and the Theosophical Society. The aim of the Theosophical Society was 'to reconcile all religions, sects, and nations under a common system of ethics, based on eternal verities'.[85] It has been argued that the result was 'the occultism of the Renaissance with a kind of Indian veneer'.[86] The veneer, however, was impenetrably thick, and with Blavatskian Theosophy we reach the point where independent Western occultism begins to collapse, to be replaced in Western culture by the Gnosticisms of the East.[87]

Not all Western occultists were sympathetic to this orientalisation of their tradition. The Order of the Golden Dawn may have originated in a Christian Hermeticist schism from the Theosophical Society.[88] Even members of the Golden Dawn, however, were not immune to Eastern influences. In his later life W. B. Yeats's attachment to Western esotericism may have waned under the influence of Shri Purohit Swami.[89] The Western occult tradition itself has come to be reinterpreted in the light of Eastern religious conceptions. W. P. Swainson, for example, explained Boehme's Three Principles in terms of Siva the Destroyer, Brahma the Creator and Vishnu the Preserver.[90] More recently, Peter Malekin has compared Boehme's distinction between reason and understanding to the Buddhist concepts of *vikalpa* and *prajña*, and Boehme's Abyss becomes equivalent to 'the ego-less *alayua-vijñana*'. Malekin also calls on the *Tao Te Ching*, the *Bhagavad Gita* and the *Tibetan Book of the Bardö Plane* as aids to our understanding of Boehme.[91] This is not in fact a genuinely comparative approach to religion, in which differences are as important as similarities and absolute identities are rarely sought. This way of thinking belongs to the myth of a perennial philosophy or *prisca theologia*, the anthropologically naïve notion that mystical systems have 'neither birthday nor native land'.[92] Such a notion has an obvious appeal to those who believe in a particular system; universality is implicitly a claim to veracity, or at least to an innate psychological validity. In terms of history or sociology, however, this approach is inherently detrimental, eliding as it does all trace of the specific cultural matrix of particular religious practices or beliefs. The notion of a *prisca theologia* is a phenomenon to be explained, not a principle of explanation.

The Christian occultists' ecumenical project was a failure. As Richard Baxter observed, John Pordage's group 'professed to wait for such a Coming down of the Holy Ghost upon them, as should send them out as his Missionaries to unite, and reconcile, and heal the Churches, and do Wonders in the World: But its [sic] fifteen years ago, and yet they are latent and their work undone.'[93] It is true that the occult philosophers pioneered the idea of religious pluralism, and in this they seem more akin to our own culture than do the Calvins or Loyolas of the early modern world. The reality of religious pluralism in our society, however, perhaps owes more to the rise of secularism, entailing among believers and unbelievers alike a growing indifference to other people's religion. Nevertheless, the occult philosophy did play an important role in preparing the ground for the reception of Eastern spiritualities in the West.

The occult philosophy has sometimes been associated with religious, political and social radicalism, and the examples of Paracelsus and Campanella have suggested a connection between 'animism, magic and political subversion'.[94] Certainly Giordano Bruno had no time for absolutism, whether in Church or State.[95] Paracelsus was even more radical in his outlook, advocating not only popular sovereignty, but also common ownership of property and the abolition of the death penalty. He showed some sympathy for the Anabaptists and, despite his advocacy of pacifism, supported the German Peasants' Revolt of 1525, in which he may have participated as a field-surgeon.[96] Some of the apparent radicalism in the occult milieu was really no more than an emphatic asceticism, espousing 'the grace of poverty'. Such asceticism, however, easily slips into the idiom of social radicalism:

> Therefore let the doctrine of the blessed life be taught not to those who love riches, for they will find no pleasure in it, but only to those who delight in poverty and who wish to dwell in the community of the poor and in justice, so that no one may be above another in the satisfaction of his needs, but that each may suffer with the other, help him and weep with him.[97]

A similar egalitarian idiom can be found in several occult writings. The Rosicrucian *Confessio Fraternitatis*, attributed to Valentin Andreae, tells us that God 'exalteth the lowly, and pulleth down the proud with disdain'.[98] In *The Chemical Wedding of Christian Rosenkreutz* we read that

> The joyful time is drawing on,
> When every one shall equal be,
> None wealthy, none in penury.[99]

The social ideal suggested by this passage is one of universalising the position enjoyed by those who occupy the middle ground of the social structure.

Occultist egalitarianism reached a high point among the radical spiritualists of Interregnum England.[100] The Ranter Abiezer Coppe poured scorn on the Eucharist, declaring that 'The True Communion among men, is to have all things common, and to call nothing one has, ones [sic] own.'[101] Roger Crab, a Behmenist, declared that '*To love God above all and to love thy neighbour as thy self* is impossible for any man to do, whilest he encroacheth to himself more Land, or finer Houses, or better clothing or dyet than his neighbours.'[102] The most celebrated example of social radicalism among occult-minded spiritualists is Gerrard Winstanley, who led a small group of followers to dig the commons in 1649. The Diggers' objective was to restore the earth to its prelapsarian state as 'a Common Treasury' for everyone.[103]

Occultist radicalism did not end with the Commonwealth in England. In his *Mémoires pour servir à l'histoire du Jacobinisme* (1797–8), the Abbé Barruel proposed the theory that the French Revolution had been caused by a conscious conspiracy of Freemasons and illuminists. Barruel's hypothesis was clearly overdrawn, and it has received little sympathy from later historians. Paradoxically, one of the nineteenth-century groups to take this notion seriously, the Naundorffists, were themselves deeply indebted to the occult tradition. Supporting Charles Naundorff's claim to be Louis XVII, they regarded the Revolution as an act of revenge by the Templars on the family that had destroyed their order.[104] Such fantasies are obviously excessive, but there is a demonstrable connection between Masonry, occultism and social agitation before the Revolution. Antoine Court de Gébelin was not only a leading occultist and prominent Mason; he was also a supporter of the American Revolution and a collaborator of Benjamin Franklin.[105] As Christopher McIntosh observed, the Masons 'occupied a unique position in the social structure; for in freemasonry the ideals of democracy and autocracy met'.[106] In this the Masons were legitimate heirs of the occult tradition, with its peculiar mixture of universalism and élitism. Several occultists were vigorous supporters of the Revolution. Suzette Labrousse thought that the Revolutionary Constitution was 'more the work of God than man'.[107] There was also a strong radical strain in the French mesmerist movement, which may have functioned as a vehicle for covert political opposition in pre-Revolutionary France. The government was sufficiently worried by mesmerism to appoint a Royal Commission to investigate it in 1784, and the membership of the movement's Societies of Universal Harmony went some way to justifying the government's anxieties. They included such future Revolutionary leaders as Lafayette, Brissot and Carra.[108]

Between the English Civil War and the French Revolution, the apparent radicalism of the occultists tended to be introverted in nature. As G. D. H. Cole observed of the sectarian communist experiments in America, their aim was to lead the elect 'out of the wicked world, not to save the world as a whole'.[109] Typical in this respect was the German-American group known as *Das Weib in der Wüste*, established by the Behmenist Johannes

Kelpius at the end of the seventeenth century. The group attempted to establish an ideal society, practising Christian communism.[110] The name they adopted (a reference to the 'woman in the wilderness' of Revelation 12:6) aptly symbolises the ambiguity of their political and social outlook. If it implied a millenarian hope for the imminent transformation and sanctification of society, it also suggested a quietistic acceptance of the saints' current exile in a social desert. The Shakers, another sectarian group showing clear Behmenist influences, also established communist communities in America after their emigration in the 1770s.[111] Such groups aimed more at reestablishing prelapsarian social relationships among themselves than at turning the world upside down. At the same time, however, they were to provide models for nineteenth-century thought on the ideal society.[112]

Much of the history of utopian socialism in fact coincides with that of nineteenth-century esotericism. In England, the followers of James Pierrepont Greaves, 'the sacred socialist', established a communitarian experiment called 'Concordium' at Ham in 1843.[113] A similar experiment was undertaken at the same time by Amos Bronson Alcott's followers in America.[114] A number of other American utopian experiments were involved in the spiritualist movement: the Mountain Cove community in Virginia, the Kiantone Movement in New York and the Harmonial Society in Arkansas.[115] It has been argued that Charles Fourier's *Theory of the Four Movements* 'is a reminder that "socialism" began as an attempt to discover a successor, not to capitalism, but to the Christian Church';[116] in Fourier's case, that successor was patently occultist. Much the same might be said of the Saint-Simonians. Although Saint-Simon himself was not an illuminist, after his death the movement veered swiftly from the 'predominantly rationalistic, even mechanistic' spirit of his writings towards an overt occultism under the leadership of Barthélemy-Prosper Enfantin.[117] Partly under Saint-Simonian influence, Victor Hugo moved leftwards politically at the same time as becoming occultist in his religious outlook. He summarised the movement underlying *Les Misérables* as 'Starting point: matter; goal: soul. Hydra at the beginning, angel at the end.' Hugo makes it clear that this is not simply a matter of personal regeneration, but also of social progress, which he identified with divine Providence. For Hugo, democratic insurgents become 'priests', and 'The French Revolution is an act of God.'[118]

The involvement of radicals with occultism sometimes seems to have led to a withdrawal from social agitation. In the 1840s Alphonse-Louis Constant was prominent in socialist and feminist circles in France, suffering imprisonment three times for his activities. He subsequently assumed the name Eliphas Lévi and became the most influential nineteenth-century French occultist. The period of Lévi's purely magical works coincided with an increasing conservatism in his outlook, but it would be wrong to conclude that he adopted occultism only in retreat from radicalism. Even his earlier socialist writings were occultist in orientation, and he saw his radical agitation as a preparation for the imminent reign of the Paraclete.[119] In England,

Annie Besant's conversion to Blavatskian Theosophy was accompanied by a partial withdrawal from socialist activity. The initial attraction of Theosophy for Besant, however, may have been that it provided a spirituality which entailed a radical social gospel. Helena Blavatsky herself had argued that Christ and the Buddha 'were ardent philanthropists and political *altruists – preaching most unmistakably Socialism* of the noblest and highest type'.[120] If Besant's conversion to Theosophy led her to be less active in the socialist movement, this perhaps involved more a redirection than a diminution of her radical energies. After moving to India, Besant became increasingly active in Indian nationalist politics.[121]

While there was a genuine radicalism among the illuminists, it was often a radicalism of compassion rather than revolution, and it did not necessarily imply a complete egalitarianism. The *Zohar* compared rich and poor to male and female, who had originally been united as the image of God in the form of Adam Kadmon:

> For as the male and female act in co-operation, showing compassion to each other, and mutually exchanging benefits and kindnesses, so must man here below act rich and poor in co-operation, bestowing gifts upon each other and showing kindness to each other.

The lesson to be drawn from this was not that economic differentials should be reduced, but that the rich should fulfil their responsibilities to the poor. When a rich man 'shows pity to the poor', the *Zohar* tells us, he 'will retain forever unchanged the original form of the first man, and by that impress of the likeness of Adam he will exercise dominion over all creatures of the world'.[122] This is an attitude that can easily degenerate into the one satirised by Blake, in which someone 'cherishes pity itself rather than those for whom he feels it':[123]

> Pity would be no more,
> If we did not make somebody poor:
> And mercy no more could be,
> If all were as happy as we.[124]

Even when occult writers seem to be making unambiguous statements of social radicalism, it is important to interpret their words carefully. Johann Reuchlin thought that the Messiah 'will not only ignore the silly and mean absurdities of the time – public office, honour, government – as being empty and stupid, he will actually hold them in contempt'.[125] Reuchlin wrote these words in a book prefaced by a grossly obsequious dedication to Pope Leo X, and there is no evidence that he himself ever followed his Messiah in holding 'public office, honour, government' in contempt. Similarly Jacob Boehme complained that 'Those who are in Authority and power suck the very Marrow from the Bones of Men of low Degree and

Rank, and feed upon the sweat of their Browes.'[126] Many of Boehme's own friends and followers, however, were men 'in authority and power': people of the urban élite and petty nobility, including members of the Elector's court at Dresden.[127]

The association of occultism with radicalism has been challenged by some historians. Those who were interested in alchemy in England came from the whole political and religious spectrum, from Anglican Royalists to radical Puritans.[128] Although the Behmenists play a radical role in Christopher Hill's account of Interregnum England,[129] most English Behmenists believed in the Divine Right of Kings; apart from Roger Crab, the nearest any of them came to the world of radical politics was in being moderate Whigs.[130] Alchemy is replete with royal imagery, and there is nothing to suggest that any of the alchemists felt compelled to rephrase their writings 'in a republican idiom'.[131] Douglas Brook-Davis has traced the history of the 'Mercurian Monarch' in English literature, arguing that 'the Hermetic myth . . . lives as long as there was a historically effective belief in monarchical absolutism in Britain'.[132] It is perhaps no coincidence that Elias Ashmole's two main interests were alchemy and heraldry; both were concerned with a hierarchical world, the one cosmological and the other political. Ashmole was a Royalist during the Civil War, and his interest in Hermeticism, with its stable universe, may have offered him some comfort in a time of change and conflict.[133] Thomas Vaughan, a Royalist like his brother Henry, declared that 'A Witch is a Rebel in Physicks, and a Rebel a Witch in Politicks.'[134]

It is in fact as easy to construct an account of occultism in terms of reactionary or conservative politics as of democratic or socialist agitation. In eighteenth-century Germany, such orders as the *Gold-und-Rosenkreuz* were noted for their political conservatism.[135] Julie de Krüdener hailed Tsar Alexander I as 'the elect of the Lord', and it was partly under her influence that Alexander established the Holy Alliance. While in Paris the Tsar visited the mesmerist Nicolas Bergasse, who was rumoured to have drawn up a draft of the Alliance.[136] Franz von Baader was yet another illuminist involved in creating this 'piece of sublime mysticism and nonsense'.[137] Nineteenth-century nationalism often had an occult background.[138] Despite the evils nationalism has brought on the world in the twentieth century, this was arguably a progressive and liberal phenomenon in the nineteenth century; the same cannot be said for the shameful involvement of occultists like Guido von List and Jörg Lanz von Liebenfels in the anti-Semitic movements that spawned Nazism.[139] Perhaps twentieth-century German mystics restored some of their honour in the person of Claus von Stauffenberg, who led the bomb-plot against Hitler. Yet, if Stauffenberg's politics were certainly more humane than Hitler's, they were nevertheless élitist and reactionary.[140]

It can be seen that it is extremely difficult to assess the political outlook of the occult philosophers as a whole. If it is possible to interpret Hermetic cosmology, especially in its Neoplatonised form, as static and hierarchical, the alchemical cosmos could also be extremely dynamic.[141] If the hier-archical structure of the Neoplatonic-Hermetic world-view seems to imply a conservative legitimation of an inegalitarian society, it is also possible to argue that Hermeticism is 'by nature democratic', since the Hermetic cosmos is a whole in which every part is essential; indeed, every part *contains* the whole.[142] Many occultists, of course, would have no truck with politics in any form, regarding such matters as merely a distraction from the important business in life, spiritual regeneration. The problem is not simply that there was a great variety of illuminists, ranging from kings to paupers; the terms of the occult social discourse escape the categories of late nineteenth- and twentieth-century culture. Even politically absolutist Hermeticism was not conservative in the strict sense; its objective was not to maintain the status quo, but to institute a fundamental reform of human society.[143] Most occultists, moreover, whatever their political outlook, tended to have a fundamentally apocalyptic vision of the world and its history.

Millenarianism was a virtually universal characteristic of esotericism, although not all occultists were inclined to see themselves as actually living in the Last Days. In the seventeenth century Samuel Pordage suggested that the world would end in 2051, and the eighteenth-century French occul-tist A. P. J. de Vismes thought that the year 2000 would be a likely date for the onset of the millennium.[144] It was much more typical of the occult milieu, however, to regard the millennium as being imminent. Jacob Boehme made several prophecies intimating the imminence of the Last Days, and in 1697 one of the Philadelphians estimated that the millennium would occur about 1700.[145] Such expectations were premature, but, despite a long history of disappointment, occultists never wearied of examining the signs of the times and concluding that 'The judgements of God on a perverted and cor-rupt world have begun.'[146] In 1800 William Blake was telling John Flaxman that 'the time is arriv'd when Men shall again converse in Heaven & walk with Angels'; following the Peace of Amiens (1802) Blake wrote that 'The kingdoms of this World are now become the Kingdoms of God & his Christ, & we shall reign with him for ever & ever.'[147] Even in the twentieth century we find men like Aleister Crowley, who believed that he was inaugu-rating a new Aeon of 2,000 years in which 'Do what thou wilt shall be the whole of the law.'[148] Crowley's millenarianism refers back not only to Rabelais's Abbaye de Thélème, but also to the antinomian fantasies of medieval chiliasm.[149] In this it was thoroughly traditional. Already in the eighteenth century, however, we can hear a new note in some illuminist millenarianism. Antoine Court de Gébelin thought that he could 'see the dawn arrive', detecting its crepuscular light in people's growing weariness with 'the disorders and cruelties that were contrary to the rights of humanity and reason'.[150] In these words we hear the tone of the new, secularised millenarianism that was to dominate nineteenth-century democratic and socialist movements.

All millenarianism implies a comprehensive and providential scheme of history. In occultist thought, human history is part of a wider cosmic process, governed by the Fall and Redemption of man and the world. Ultimately the process is cyclical, representing a movement from spirit to matter and back to spirit again. The basic paradigm of occult historical thought can be found in the speculations of Empedocles in the ancient world. For Empedocles, the cosmos is a process of constitution, dissolution and reconstitution, governed by the opposing forces of Aphrodite (love) and Ares (strife).[151] The process here is not only cyclical, it is also dialectical, and this dialectical aspect of cosmic history is emphasised in occult thought under the impact of the doctrine of the coincidence of opposites.

Occult conceptions of history can be divided into two basic types. On the one hand we have thoroughly cyclical schemes in the manner of Empedocles, the cosmic process being envisaged as repeating itself eternally. This view of history can be found in the ideas of Restif de la Bretonne in the eighteenth century: the universe is an eternal flux, a constant process of emanation from and reabsorption into the divine.[152] A similar view of history was developed by Charles Fourier, partly under Restif's influence. Fourier believed that the cosmos and society evolved from 'ascending coherence' to 'coherence', and back down through 'descending incoherence' to 'incoherence'.[153] With Fourier, however, there is a clear emphasis on cosmic and social ascent. Once such an emphasis is carried to its extremes, the possibility is opened that the cosmos can escape from the eternal recurrence of its cycles. Whereas in the genuinely cyclical model history can have no end, in this progressive model there will be a final consummation of the cosmic process, as there is in traditional Christian eschatology.

Both the cyclical and progressive models can be found in occult thought, but the tendency of Christian occultism is to emphasise the progressive nature of cosmic history. An example of the genuinely cyclical model can be found in Helena Blavatsky's thought, which is perhaps more Hindu than Empedoclean in origin:

> As the sun arises every morning on our *objective* horizon out of its (to us) subjective and antipodal space, so does the Universe emerge periodically on the plane of objectivity, issuing from that of subjectivity – the antipodes of the former. . . . And as the sun disappears from our horizon, so does the Universe disappear at regular periods, when the 'Universal Night' sets in.[154]

In contrast to this we have Rudolf Steiner's Christian outline of cosmic history. Steiner saw the cosmos as evolving from the realm of pure spirit (Crystal Heaven) through seven epochs. This involves a progressive densification until the fourth and densest epoch, the present one of 'Earth'. With the incarnation of Christ, however, the universe has already begun its reascent to spirit through the final three epochs.[155]

Steiner's belief that there were exactly seven epochs was not arbitrary. It derives from the strongly numerological aspect of occult thought, in which 7 and 3 are numbers of particular importance. The Steinerian account can be related to Jacob Boehme's seven fountain-spirits, which constitute the structure of the godhead and the universe. As in Steiner's system, it is the fourth of these which is the pivotal point between the natural and spiritual worlds.[156] A preference for a sevenfold scheme can be found in other occult writers. The Philadelphians identified the seven churches in the Book of Revelation as seven ages in human history. The name they chose for themselves indicated the transition from the Sardian age (which had begun with Luther) to the Philadelphian age. The Philadelphians also adopted the common millenarian interpretation of the seven days of creation as symbolising seven historical epochs, each day representing a thousand years.[157] Similarly, in William Blake's writings, the seven 'Eyes of God' are seven ages in the historical process.[158] Eliphas Lévi also believed that history was constituted by seven ages, each lasting 354 years under the governance of its own Archangel. He calculated that the seventh age would begin in 1879, when an epoch of universal empire would flourish under the aegis of the Archangel Michael. With a nationalist flourish typical of other nineteenth-century occultists, he added that in this age 'all people will acknowledge and follow . . . the standard of France, ever victorious or miraculously raised from the dead'.[159]

A sevenfold scheme of history was not incompatible with a preference for a threefold one, since in occult thought seven easily reduces to three. Steiner's cosmic process, for example, consists of two triads linked by a third term. A more decided preference for three periods derived from the thought of Joachim of Fiore. Joachim divided world history into three 'dispensations', each associated with a different Person in the Trinity and a distinct stage in revelation. The first of these dispensations was that of the Father and the Law, embodied in the Old Testament. This was followed by that of the Son and the Gospel, finding expression in the New Testament. Finally, there would be a third dispensation, that of the Holy Ghost and the Everlasting Gospel, inscribed directly in the hearts of men and women.[160] The underlying structure of Joachimism is dialectical. The first dispensation establishes the thesis, in which law is imposed externally, and the second dispensation constitutes its antithesis, Christ coming to relieve us of the burden of the law by preaching the forgiveness of sin. Finally, the third dispensation represents a synthesis of the previous two, when the external imposition of the law and forgiveness are no longer necessary, since both are inscribed in the heart as authentic expressions of our innermost being. The synthesis can also be understood as a return to the thesis on a higher level; the goal of history thus becomes a sublimated form of its beginning. This is, of course, the basic structure of later speculative philosophies of history.

Mystics generally believed themselves to be living at the dawn of Joachim's third dispensation, and heterodox writers like Jane Lead found Joachimism useful in legitimating departures from the received Scriptures.[161] The influence of Joachimism was widespread in the sixteenth century, in the writings of men like Heinrich Vogel, Julius Sperber and Simon Studion.[162] The Joachimite conception of history permeated English radical thought in the seventeenth century, especially that of radicals in the spiritualist and occult milieu.[163] We can also find it in the nineteenth century. Joseph de Maistre, for example, thought that God had devised three stages of revelation. In the first of these, truth had been concentrated in the Israelites, and in the second it had become extended to the Gentiles; now the whole work was about to be accomplished in a third and final revelation.[164] In fact, echoes of Joachimism can be found not only in occult thought, but also in the apparently more secular historiography of writers like Jean Bodin in the sixteenth century and Auguste Comte in the nineteenth.

Bodin has been regarded as one of the founders of modern rational and critical history as distinct from the mystical historiography of earlier writers. Bodin's scheme, however, not only shows traces of Joachimism, it is also astrologically based. Human history is divided into three periods. In the first of these, from about 4000 BC to 2000 BC, the Southern peoples developed the religious sensibilities of humanity under the governance of the planet Saturn, assisted by Venus. In the next period, lasting until the birth of Christ, the planets Jupiter and Mercury presided over the development of the political arts by the peoples of the temperate zone. Finally the two thousand years of the Christian era witness the Northern peoples developing mechanical and martial skills under the governance of Mars and the moon.[165]

Bodin's use of astrology in his historical thought was far from being novel or unique. As Nicholas Campion suggests, astrology had long served 'as a comprehensive philosophy of history',[166] a function which has left a lasting legacy in secular historiography. Although practising historians are well aware of the limits of the time-honoured division of history into Ancient, Medieval and Modern, it is a structure of thought which appears to be too convenient to be abandoned. It is, of course, an historical scheme devised in the Renaissance by men contrasting the splendours of their own age and the ancient world with what they took to be the darkness of the intervening period. In the Renaissance itself, this theory of cultural rebirth and renewal was related to the astrological notion of great planetary conjunctions. This implied a cyclical view of history in which human societies were subject to revolutions in both the modern and traditional senses of the word, social revolutions that were determined by celestial ones. Any conjunction of the superior planets, especially that of Saturn and Jupiter, portended major political and religious change.[167]

It would be foolish to claim that Auguste Comte, the great apostle of nineteenth-century positivism, was in any sense an occultist. After all, he turned with contempt from the Saint-Simonians as they moved increasingly towards mysticism under Enfantin's leadership. Nevertheless it might be argued that Comte's historical thought, and that of the Saint-Simonians from which it derived, is a radically secularised version of the mystical historiography common among occultists. Comte posited a historical transition from a theological stage, through a metaphysical one, to a final positive epoch.[168] This is a threefold scheme of progressive revelation, with the omission of God as an external agent: the revelation now occurs on a purely anthropological level. We might wonder why Comte thought that there were three stages in human history. Modern historians tend to stress the problematic nature of periodisation, and particularly of simple schemes like Comte's. His perception of history as divided into three periods was anything but an objective, positivist inference from observed facts. We might suspect that Comte was predisposed to triadic thinking: that the notion of a tripartite history was so widespread and so deeply internalised in his culture that it inevitably imposed itself on his analysis of empirical data.

A secularisation of earlier mystical conceptions of history also seems to underlie Saint-Simonianism. Here again we find the familiar tripartite periodisation: antiquity, the Middle Ages and the modern world. Superimposed on this framework, however, is a dynamic and dialectical element. Each of the earlier historical periods exhibits 'two distinct and alternating states of society', the organic and the critical. The organic phase of the historical process is one in which all elements of a culture are subordinated to a single 'general theory' in which 'the goal of all social action is closely defined'. The prime example of an organic period was the Middle Ages, with the unifying primacy of Christianity. In the critical period, however, the principle of social co-ordination dissolves and society becomes 'a mere agglomeration of isolated individuals'. Such, for example, was the age ushered in by the Reformation, culminating in the Enlightenment. The Saint-Simonians thought they were living at the dawn of a final organic period, characterised by the rational organisation of industry.[169]

After Saint-Simon's death, his followers became frankly millenarian in outlook under the guidance of Barthélemy-Prosper Enfantin.[170] They began to stress the redemptive role that women were about to play in history. Olinde Rodrigues, for example, spoke of 'the woman of the future, throwing her life and her faith into the midst of the combatants in order to win them over to the love of God and humanity'.[171] Women's role in history went beyond this Sabine behaviour, and the Saint-Simonians expected the imminent arrival of a female messiah, the Mother, who was to complement the work of Enfantin, the Father. In recognition of this an empty chair was reserved for the Mother by the side of Enfantin's at Saint-Simonian meetings. In 1832 the movement became more proactive in the search for the female messiah, launching an Oriental mission to find her. The *Compagnons de la Femme*, as the members of this mission were called, failed in their appointed task, but their work was not entirely fruitless. It played a role in the introduction of Oriental themes in Western music through the work of Félicien David, and it also contributed to keeping alive a favourite Saint-

Simonian project, the building of a Suez Canal. Enfantin's messianic feminism was set in the context of a theology of the duality of divine gender. The Saint-Simonians were prone to dispense with grammatical convention by applying feminine adjectives to God ('Dieu bonne'), and the ship in which the *Compagnons* set sail for the East was consecrated in the name of 'God FATHER and MOTHER'.[172] This is simply an example of the theology of the occult philosophy, which had been spawning female messianism for over a century before Enfantin began his mission.[173]

Neither Comte nor Saint-Simon himself were in any sense occultists, and if they are at all indebted to esoteric thought it is only in the weak sense of applying a structure of ideas that originally may have had an occult provenance. There is a stronger case for direct influence among other philosophers of history, such as Giambattista Vico. Vico's understanding of history as cyclical in nature has affinities with views found in the occult tradition, and his ideas are generally permeated by Neoplatonic and Neo-Pythagorean modes of thought. It has been argued that Vico's most important contribution to the history of ideas, the concept of a 'culture', may owe something to a particular sociological construction of the doctrine of microcosmic correspondence.[174] The concept of cultural specificity in both time and space is essential to modern historical practice, but it is a concept which owes more to the Counter Enlightenment than the Enlightenment itself. Enlightenment historiography, with its rationalist homogenisation of human nature, was profoundly ahistorical. It is in those circles which rejected Enlightenment rationalism that we find the growth of historical relativism.[175]

If Vico founded cultural history and the speculative philosophy of history in its modern sense, it was the German Romantic philosophers who fully developed it. The seminal figure in this respect was Johann Gottfried Herder, who at one point seemed to deny the possibility of any philosophy of history whatsoever: 'the history of man is ultimately a theatre of transformations which only He [God], who animates these events and lives and feels himself in all of them, can review'.[176] He nevertheless developed his own *Ideas for the Philosophy of the History of Mankind* and, as the passage just cited indicates, they were ideas based on God's immanence in history. God is 'the primal force of all forces, the Soul of all souls',[177] and Herder tells us that 'The radiant image of God is present in everything that exists, closely wedded to its material form.' Everything is part of one great whole and, as in the traditional doctrine of correspondences, the whole is in fact implicit in each part: 'Everything fits together, and God discerns in the smallest of substances the entire course of things in the whole world.' For Herder, there was 'not a doubt but the creative life in all its shapes and forms and channels is but one spirit and one vital flame'.[178] Herder believed that man was 'the middling ring between two adjoining systems of Creation', the natural and spiritual worlds. This is clearly a reformulation of the idea of man's central place in the Great Chain of Being, at the top of a natural hierarchy and at the foot of a spiritual one. In this Herder resembles Pico della Mirandola in his *Oration on the Dignity of Man* and, like Pico, Herder had a profound sense of human freedom: 'man alone has made a goddess of *choice* in place of *necessity*'.[179] Herder sees this as not merely an individual choice, but part of a social and cosmic process. Man as a species is striving towards 'the attainment of humanity' (*Humanität*).[180] Herder conceives of humanity as constituting a single organic being, and his view of history can be compared to the occult conception of the cosmic process as culminating in the re-formation of the primordial cosmic man: Adam Kadmon of the Cabala. Like the occultists, Herder's understanding of history is cosmic, organic and teleological. The cosmos evolves through a progressive series of changes in which ever higher organisms are produced by their predecessors. The universe first produces the solar system, which becomes the unique locus of cosmic development. On earth there is a progression from merely mineral existence, through plant and animal life, to human beings. People owe their unique status among animals to the fact of their habitually erect posture, which permits 'the invisible organic power pervading everything' to penetrate them more thoroughly. Man himself is striving towards *Humanität*, which constitutes 'the realization of the purpose of the world and the control over it'. Man's *Humanität* 'expresses the essence of himself as a human being, and . . . thus reflects the image of the Creator of our earth'.[181]

Much of Herder's philosophy of history can be interpreted as a recasting of occult mystical ideas in a more philosophical form. Jacob Boehme's ideas permeated the Pietist circles in which Herder moved. In Boehme's theosophy, man stands between the lower ternary of fountain-spirits which constitute the natural world and the higher ternary which forms the spiritual world. His task is to move forward from the one to the other, restoring himself to his proper status as the image of God, Herder's *Humanität*. Whatever the source of Herder's ideas, it was above all to Boehme that later German philosophers of history were most indebted. In the occult philosophy, the cosmogonic process is one in which the divine being becomes fully conscious of itself in the creation. We have already seen something of this view expressed by Herder. Friedrich Schelling, in his *System of Transcendental Idealism* (1800) provides another version of it by interpreting history as a process in which the Absolute was evolving into full existence. The occult philosophy was dialectical in structure, emphasising the interplay and ultimate coincidence of opposites. Boehme, for example, described the whole cosmogonic process as one driven by a dialectical dynamic within his seven fountain-spirits. J. G. Fichte, in his *Characteristics of the Present Age*, transcribed this structure of thought into the realm of human history, which proceeded through the dialectical process of thesis, antithesis and synthesis.

G. W. F. Hegel's philosophy of history, the high point of German speculation on the topic, is largely a synthesis of Schelling's and Fichte's ideas, and it derives ultimately from the occult philosophy. The fundamental elements of the Hegelian system are all to be found in esoteric mysticism, and Hegel himself referred to Boehme as 'the first truly German philosopher'.[182] By this, of course, Hegel did not mean that Boehme was the first German to philosophise, but the first philosopher to attain insight into the basic nature of reality. Hegel's religious outlook was one of dynamic panentheism – what Peter Singer calls his 'strange vision' of God 'as an essence that needs to manifest itself in the world, and, having made itself manifest, to perfect the world in order to perfect itself'.[183] This was no more than a restatement of German Pietist theosophy. Both Boehme and Hegel understand reality as a cosmic process in which the godhead (Boehme) or Spirit (Hegel) become manifest in the creation (Boehme) or realised in history (Hegel). In his early writings Hegel refers to Spirit before its realisation in the cosmic process as 'nothing',[184] a favourite term of Boehme's for the godhead before its manifestation in the creation.[185] Both writers, of course, use the term 'nothing' in a special sense, referring to an undifferentiated plenitude of being rather than non-being as such. Boehme identified the fundamental malaise of the human condition as a severence of inner and outer; Hegel saw it as the divorce between subject and object.[186] For both men the cosmic process is essentially dialectical: as Boehme puts it, 'without contrariety there is no manifestation'.[187] For both, the goal of the process is a harmonisation of the contraries that constitute reality, and for both, man plays the central role in this process. Boehme tells us that man stands between the spiritual and natural worlds, which are in reality two aspects of God; and Hegel thought that man was the 'middle term' between Spirit and Nature, which are really two aspects of the Absolute.[188] Man's role in the cosmic process is to reunite these apparent contraries. He does so through an act of self-negation which is simultaneously an act of self-affirmation. Man, according to Boehme, must destroy his self-will and conform his will to God's. According to Hegel, man must exercise his free individuality in accordance with reason, or freely subsume his individuality in an organic community.[189]

The structure of the Behmenist and Hegelian systems is virtually identical; so too is much of the content. There are, however, differences. An obvious one relates to terminology. When he is not using bizarre neologisms or symbols drawn from alchemy, Boehme employs a fairly traditional religious language; Hegel, on the other hand, expresses himself in abstract philosophical terms. This is not a trivial difference. As Alexandre Koyré observed, Boehme speaks 'a poetic language';[190] it is both symbolic and emotive. Hegel complained that Boehme was a 'complete barbarian' in his manner of expressing ideas. Apart from reminding us of pots and kettles, this remark indicates a basic difference between the two men. Hegel assumes that 'it is only in the concept, the thought, in which philosophy has its truth, in which the Absolute can become expressed, and [in which it] also *is* how it is in itself'.[191] Hegel devalues symbolic discourse and, for all his irrationalities, his outlook is nevertheless rational and utterly prosaic. If the godhead can be approached only through symbols, its ineffable mystery remains intact. If a concept is the most authentic expression of the Absolute, the Absolute is completely expressible.

This suggests a related difference between Hegel and Boehme. The theosopher had a deep sense of God's immanence, but he never abandoned a belief in the ultimate transcendence of the divine being. The philosopher, on the other hand, constructs the transcendence of the Absolute as a purely historical phenomenon, since history is precisely the progressive immanentalising of Spirit. For the Romantic philosophers as a whole, 'There is no *being*, only *becoming*',[192] and all becoming is ultimately God's coming-to-be in the world. The result of this conception is a radical immanentalism. 'If God doesn't exist in the world', Herder tells us, 'then he exists nowhere'; 'I know no extramundane God.'[193] What David Walsh calls the 'mysticism of inner-worldly fulfilment'[194] really exists only *in potentia* in the traditional occult philosophy; it is the Romantics who bring this potential to fruition. Romantic immanentalism, moreover, is really a mystical humanism since, in Lorenz Oken's words, 'Man is God fully manifested.'[195] Similarly, Friedrich Schlegel wrote that 'The Being of God is as evident as that of Nature, for both are parts of humanity.'[196] Or, to quote a later poet, the Anthroposophist Christian Morgenstern,

> So bin ich Gott, mit allem was ich bin
> und mein und Gottes ist der gleiche Sinn.
> Die Welt ist nicht ein Hier, Gott nicht ein Dort,
> er ist du selbst, wird mit dir fort und fort.
> Und nirgends weiss er irgendwie von sich,
> denn als in Wesen so wie du und mich.[197]

(Thus I am God, with all that I am, and mine and God's are the same mind. The world is not a Here, God not a There, he is you yourself, evolves with you on and on. And he nowhere knows anything of himself other than in beings like you and me.) The emphatic panentheism of occult philosophy is transformed into what has been called 'panenanthropism'.[198] God has been incorporated into the world, and the world subsumed in human consciousness. Man, microcosm and microtheos, has swallowed up both God and the world.

9   The occult and Western culture

Occultism is a religion of ecstasy, and like all ecstatic religions it offers its adherents the possibility of undergoing 'those transports of mystical experience in which man's whole being seems to fuse in a glorious communion with the divinity'.[1] We might therefore attempt to understand the sociology of the occult in terms of Ioan Lewis's analysis of ecstatic religions. Lewis regards these as 'religions of the oppressed' which function to enable marginalised groups, and especially women, 'to advance their interests and improve their lot by escaping, even if only temporarily, from the confining bonds of their alloted stations in society'.[2] The occult philosophy could indeed offer the appearance of an immediate power to the powerless. Nor was this power always illusory. At the very least, any religion, and magical religion in particular, can build confidence in its adherents. This is why magic flourishes in uncertain circumstances: even its illusions offer an avenue of escape from the debilitating doubts of sober realism.

There are, however, difficulties in applying Lewis's theory of ecstatic religion to the Western occult tradition. Mary Douglas has argued that ecstatic religions are not simply a response to 'strain, deprivation or tension', and Lewis's compensation theory has a problem explaining 'the throng of well-to-do women who so often predominate in these movements'.[3] The Behmenists are a good example of this. They certainly accorded women a high place, and the Philadelphian Society may well have provided an empowering environment for them; in this sense, the sociological profile conforms to Lewis's theory. But the Behmenists were not for the most part 'dispossessed' or 'oppressed' members of society, but respectable and prosperous people.[4] So also were the Familists, an earlier movement permeated by occult mentalities.[5] The same might be said of the Romantics, who modernised and partly secularised the occult tradition.[6] At the end of the nineteenth century the Order of the Golden Dawn consisted mostly of middle-class intellectuals.[7] If we want to find occultists in our own society, we would be advised to look among the middle classes. The occult is not a phenomenon peculiar to the ignorant poor; its adherents today are most likely to be young, well-educated professionals.[8] The occult philosophy, in fact, has been characteristic of the culture of the 'middling sort' since the

Renaissance. It expresses one of the ways in which members of this sector of society perceive themselves and their position in the society as a whole. It is certainly not the only expression of middle-class self-perceptions, nor even the dominant one. Since the eighteenth century occultism has become decidedly marginalised; but its marginality is perhaps the secret of its social function rather than the badge of its social irrelevance.

To speak of the marginalisation of occultism in contemporary Western culture is not to suggest that it is insignificant. Even if we disregard various secularised offshoots of esoteric thought, it is evident that occultism remains an important strand in our cultural life. Occult mentalities permeate New Age spirituality, for example.[9] Admittedly, those who frequent New Age circles are more likely to hear talk of karma and kundalini than of Boehme's Three Principles or his seven fountain-spirits. What passes for native American and Celtic spiritualities is also popular in such circles. When these cultural forms are examined closely, however, it can be seen that they embody a similar structure of ideas to traditional esotericism. The symbolic dress of occult thought has been changed, but the underlying body of ideas remains the same. The browser in the 'Mind and Spirit' section of any bookshop will find volumes on Eastern mysticisms, Amerindian spirituality, Celtic religion and wicca nestling alongside works on Cabala, Hermeticism, alchemy and the whole panoply of traditional Western occultism. These various traditions are in fact generally treated as glosses on each other by their New Age adherents.

If the marketability of books can be used as a gauge, a visit to a bookshop may also suggest something about the relative importance of 'alternative' spiritualities and Christian orthodoxy itself in modern Western culture. In most mainstream bookshops, the 'Mind and Spirit' section is at least equal in size to that devoted to orthodox Christian devotional and theological works. Yet most people would agree that orthodox Christianity is somehow central to our culture, while alternative spiritualities are marginal. To reiterate: if we speak of these alternative spiritualities as marginal, it is to say nothing about their relative importance. They are marginal in the sense that they exist on what is constructed as the margins of Western culture. Which is to say, they are perhaps better described as marginalised than marginal as such.

This marginalisation can be seen in several ways. I have argued that the occult philosophy has played a vital role in the history of modern culture; even if much of this argument is dismissed as exaggerated, we must surely accept the role played by esotericism in German Romantic philosophy, or its importance as a source of Jungian psychology, or its place in the worldview of major poets like Yeats and Morgenstern; to deny this would be to deny a debt that was acknowledged. Yet, while it is patently true that occultism has been significant in these ways, most histories of the Western intellectual tradition avoid the topic as if with embarrassment. After all, it would seem to contradict the West's favourite self-projection as rational or empirical. Similarly, it has been observed that in our own times 'The occult is alive and well and living next door.'[10] It is by no means difficult to find; and yet we frequently hear expressions of surprise at the discovery that it still exists in our enlightened age. Recently, for example, there have been amused reports of the growing popularity of Cabala among American celebrities. It was not that the phenomenon was not there to be seen before, only that those who identify with mainstream culture usually decline to notice it. The supercilious tone of such reports points to another aspect of the marginalisation of the occult. To the impartial sceptic, occultism is not inherently more incredible or superstitious than Catholicism, Protestantism or Islam. Nor does it share the shameful history of persecution and bloodshed of these religions. Yet there is a licence in our culture to mock the religious sensibilities of the occult philosopher in a way that would be deemed a gross breach of good manners if applied to the devout Catholic or Muslim. This double standard is surely based on a social rationale rather than a rational discrimination of ethical principle.

This is not to argue that those who adopt an occult world-view should be regarded as unwitting victims in the process of marginalisation, forced against their will into the cultural periphery. The marginalisation of the occult philosophy serves a social function for its adherents no less than its opponents. Occultism no longer in any sense expresses the central tendencies of the wider culture, as it had arguably done in the sixteenth century. On the contrary, to adopt the occult philosophy has come to involve a conscious choice to opt out of mainstream culture. Occultism has survived, not despite its marginalisation, but because of it. Like its Romantic offspring, it has become a cultural protest against modern Western society.

We can perhaps see this more clearly by reflecting on the orientalising of Western esotericism. There can be no doubt that a growing number of young people have found mainstream Christianity and Judaism to be 'devoid of a meaningful spiritual dimension', and have consequently 'embarked on a mystical quest which has led them to Eastern religions or the new religious movements'.[11] This cannot be, as the Cohn-Sherboks imply, simply a function of ignorance of the Judaeo-Christian mystical tradition. When this process began, after all, the Western mystical tradition was obviously more accessible to people than its Eastern counterparts. Ignorance may be as culturally patterned as knowledge, and as a historical process the orientalisation of Western spirituality has involved what appears to be a voluntary act of collective amnesia with regard to European traditions.

Eastern spiritualities remain an exotic phenomenon even in contemporary, multicultural European societies; they are readily available as a symbolic rejection of the dominant culture of the West. The vogue for Hindu and Buddhist spirituality among white, middle-class Europeans and Americans has been associated above all with youth culture and bohemianism. The growing interest in Eastern religions and the rise of New Age spirituality since the 1960s can be traced back to the popularity of such works as

Jack Kerouac's *Dhamma Bums*, uniting an ill-digested Buddhism with an unambiguous hostility to the American Dream. Similarly, the Rousseauist primitivism of supposedly American Indian spirituality clearly functions as a repudiation of the values of Western civilisation. The contemporary cult of the Goddess,[12] itself a vigorously syncretising movement which can be traced back to the occult tradition,[13] is a conscious feminist protest against an allegedly patriarchal society.

Even when, as in the cult of the Celtic, the sources of alternative spiritualities are Western, the reaction against the hegemonic culture of the West is unmistakable. The role of Celticism in the Western esoteric tradition is instructive. Stoddard Martin suggests that Celtic elements may have been introduced into occultism by the 'Celtic enthusiasts' of the Order of the Golden Dawn. S. L. Mathers, for example, adopted the name McGregor, took to wearing a kilt and constructed a fictitious Jacobite ancestry for himself.[14] A taste for Celtic spirituality in fact has had a much longer history in Western occultism. Since the time of Giovanni Nanni da Viterbo in the late fifteenth century the Druids have been seen as the guardians of an ancient wisdom.[15] Although William Blake believed Druidism had degenerated, he also thought that 'Adam was a Druid, and Noah'.[16] The Chevalier Ramsay introduced the 'Scottish rite' into Freemasonry in the belief that the Masonic tradition had been preserved in its pristine purity in his native land.[17] Ramsay may have been motivated by a patriotic impulse, and a naïve patriotism seems to have underlain early modern Druidism as a whole. It is surely no coincidence that the Druids enjoyed their highest esteem in France and Britain, the two countries which could claim a Druidic antiquity. Elias Ashmole, for example, was filled with patriotic pride at the thought of foreigners visiting Britain in search of the secret of the Philosophers' Stone, a secret which the British sages possessed thanks to their Druidic and Bardic ancestry.[18] As a naïve nationalism, early modern Druidism was an eccentric expression of the central tendencies of its wider culture. Modern 'Celtic' spirituality, on the other hand, is ecological rather than patriotic in orientation. Its appeal lies precisely in the fact that it originates in what is represented as the 'Celtic fringe', in a culture long since overwhelmed by the forces of modernity. Celticism is therefore an apt symbolic gesture of identification with the margins rather than the mainstream – an antithetical stance towards modern Western civilisation. Paradoxically, this rejection of Western civilisation is strongest among those who benefit most from it, the middle classes.

David Walsh has suggested that Behmenism represents a 'mysticism of inner-worldly fulfillment', seeking 'a self-generated salvation within time'.[19] Walsh's terminology derives from Max Weber's analysis of *The Protestant Ethic and the Spirit of Capitalism*. According to Weber's thesis, Protestantism involved a new commitment to the world, in contrast to the otherworldly orientation of medieval spirituality. Weber's argument has been much criticised, and there are serious difficulties in trying to establish a causal connection between Protestantism and capitalism. Both the Protestant Reformation and the Catholic Counter-Reformation can be interpreted as an attempt to Christianise the whole of society,[20] and in this sense both represent a shift from otherworldly to innerworldly concerns in religion. Nevertheless, there were elements in Protestant theology which were especially congenial to bourgeois attitudes. The insistence that humanity's relationship to God requires no mediation other than through Christ led to omni-sacerdotalism, the belief in the priesthood of all believers. As a consequence, sacraments were devalued and ordinary human activity itself became quasi-sacramentalised as a service to God.[21] The reformers stressed the traditional teaching that one's position in the world was a 'calling', part of a divinely sanctioned providential order, a notion which led to an emphasis on the duty to fulfil one's mundane responsibilities. In this way the reformers introduced an 'insistence on the sanctification of secular life'.[22]

Much of the debate about Weber's thesis has concentrated on the relationship between Calvinism and capitalism. According to Weber, however, it was not only Calvinists who played a role in developing the spirit of capitalism. With its emphasis on practical piety and its disregard of doctrinal orthodoxy, Pietism also encouraged a this-worldly orientation, extending 'ascetic conduct' into the 'non-Calvinist denominations'.[23] While Pietism is often associated with German Lutheran circles, it was in fact a pan-European and interdenominational movement,[24] found in much the same form wherever there were middle-class illuminists and occultists. The occult philosophy displayed to a marked degree a paradoxical innerworldly asceticism, commiting itself simultaneously to the immanent and the transcendent. It was in this way that it contributed to the secularisation of the Western world-view. The belief in a transcendent order of being is implicitly a disparagement of the mundane: 'why a Beyond if not as a means of befouling the Here-and-Now?'[25] The affirmation of the world requires an immanentalisation of value, and this immanentalisation was achieved not by simply repudiating the transcendent, but by locating transcendence at the very heart of the immanent. In this respect, Calvinism remained a largely otherworldly religion in which the Beyond was given an absolute priority over the Here-and-Now. Hence the Calvinist rejection of perfectionism. The illuminists, on the other hand, tended to believe in the possibility of sanctification in this life. The occult philosophy represented a profound attempt to sacramentalise the world, to permeate the profane with the sacred. The sacred and the profane, however, stand in necessary opposition to one another: each can only exist by not being what the other is.[26] Ultimately the immersion of God in the world does not divinise the mundane, but desacralises the divine. God becomes redundant, socially and politically, physically and metaphysically. As Amos Funkenstein observes of the seventeenth-century tendency to attribute dimensionality to God, 'Once God regained transparency or even a body, he was all the easier to kill.'[27]

So it is that the mysticism of innerworldly fulfilment, standing in awe and reverence before the divine, leads inexorably to the expulsion of the sacred from the profane; and it does so by virtue of the very attempt to effect their union. The whole process can be seen clearly in the occult discourse on nature. We begin with an insistence that the visible world signifies meanings beyond itself: it functions as a means of access to a world of transcendent values. Gradually the transcendent reference diminishes in importance, and value comes to be discovered in the world itself. But as soon as the world loses its transcendent support, its value and meaning become arbitrary. In itself it is meaningless, but this meaninglessness furthers rather than undermines the valorisation of the mundane. Since the world is free of value it is transformed into a neutral space into which values can be projected. The occult discourse on nature culminates in Romantic solipsism: the transcendence of value is replaced by its immanence, and this immanence is precisely that of the human subject – an order of signification derived from the interiority and autonomy of the self.

The immanentalisation of value in the human subject can be regarded as the metaphysical corollory of bourgeois social atomism. Middle-class society is premised on the supposed detachment of individuals from the social groupings to which they in fact belong, the rejection of overtly ascribed status for notionally achieved status, and an essentially meritocratic ethos. Self-help and the *carrière ouverte aux talents* are the twin watchwords of bourgeois society. The middle class, however, is unavoidably placed in a precarious position by the very principle which constitutes it as a class. The bourgeois produce nothing tangible. They merely organise other people's production, and the talents that open up their career in life are primarily intellectual. There is, by the nature of things, no natural monopoly in knowledge. To those whose power and status in society depend on their intellects, this situation is fraught with danger. In this the intellectual's position is paradigmatic of the middle-class condition as a whole. The social and political ascendency of the middle class is only possible once the stratification of society by estates, based on the ascription of status, has dissolved. The *carrière ouverte aux talents* is the essential precondition of bourgeois hegemony, but what is a *carrière ouverte* on an individual level becomes a *classe ouverte* on a collective level. The middle class is vulnerable to infiltration from below, and its members are themselves in constant danger of social derogation. An impoverished nobleman is still a nobleman; an impoverished bourgeois is just another proletarian. The solution to this problem is to attempt a reversion to a system of estates by the *de facto* incorporation of the class. We can see the urge to do this in the petty snobbery which seems to be most characteristic of the lower middle class, whose position on the borderline between classes requires them to assert their own superiority more insistently than those who inhabit the class hinterland.

Nothing is certain in the world of the early modern bourgeois, confronted as they are by increasingly incomprehensible market forces, forces which are no longer incarnated in the noise and dirt and haggling of the local square. Even if the bourgeois free themselves from the workshop and the ship, even if their destiny lies in the burgeoning professional stratum, they remain dependent (perhaps more so) on the whim of others in their need for patronage. Above them are the gentry and aristocratic élites, which are relatively impenetrable, at least in the short term. Below them is the rabble, ever ready to recruit from their numbers. It is easy to understand why the bourgeois of early modern Europe should develop an ideology of inner-worldly asceticism, not as a means to accumulation, but as a way of distancing themselves from a world which simultaneously enables and entraps them. In distancing themselves from the world they close themselves off and revel in the dream of another kind of world, a world of freedom and non-contingent selves.

The esoteric mystical movement is largely a phenomenon of the professional middle class. Those whose interests were in manufacturing or commerce tended to adopt a more prosaic and conventional religious outlook; and, in place of the implicit collectivism of the occult myth of the cosmic man, they favoured the ideology of possessive individualism,[28] developing a discourse in which the empirical self alone is recognised. The professional middle class is relatively more dependent on others than the manufacturing and commercial strata; or rather, its specific relations of dependence (patronage) are more immediate and visible than those of manufacturers and merchants (market forces). This may help to explain the appeal of esoteric mysticism to the professional strata. Feeling their dependence more acutely, the professional middle class experiences the self as an object buffeted by personal forces, and flees from this experience into the inner sanctum of a transcendental self.

Intellectuals share the general class-vulnerability of their compeers, but their position within their class has its own special fragility. Socially useless by commercial or industrial standards, ever prone to fall in ditches while wondering at the stars, intellectuals require and create their own legitimating cultural forms. One possibility open to them is to turn their backs contemptuously on the whole affair, and so modern intellectuals have a tendency to become bohemians. Another possibility is to follow the precedent of the medieval craftsmen, and raise their trade into a mystery. This is easily done by the creation of a jargon, a language whose function is precisely *not* to communicate, except to the initiated. It was this strategy, in a refined form, that was adopted by the occult philosophers. This is one of the reasons that they insist on secrecy, and why the alchemists devised their elaborate symbolic language.

To some extent, the occult philosophy in its pure form serves a merely compensatory function. Mystery is its own authority.[29] A palpable absurdity is a challengeable absurdity, and mystification is its best protection. Sceptics may dismiss it out of hand, but unless they themselves have been admitted to the mystery they have no authority for doing so. The seeker after occult truths, when finally admitted into the imperial court, may see that the emperor has no clothes, but by this time the initiate has undergone a process of acculturation which severs him from the common-sense world-view (which may itself be absurd by the standards of another culture) and induces a willingness to believe those who control the mystery. As the history of countless cults demonstrates, the mystagogue can thus achieve a position of status and power, which may be sufficient to compensate him for his marginalisation in the wider culture. Initiates in fact often make a virtue of their marginalisation, which becomes a sign of their own exalted status.

Occultist sectarian élitism is not always merely compensatory in function; it sometimes provided the basis for effective action in the wider world. One of the functions of symbolic language, according to Johann Reuchlin, is to create solidarity among the adepts; it was in this way that the Pythagoreans built for themselves 'a bond of indissoluble love and friendship'.[30] It was this function of esoteric symbolism that was institutionalised in the secret societies that burgeoned in the occult milieu from the seventeenth century onwards. The seminal event in this respect was the 'Rosicrucian furore' of the early seventeenth century. Although in origins the Brotherhood of the Rosy Cross seems to have been purely fictitious, Rosicrucianism was to become the basis of the Masonic movement.[31] Masonry gave 'a strong element of cohesion and central direction' to esotericism,[32] but secret societies did not only serve to perpetuate and propagate occult doctrine. They also functioned as powerful organisations for mutual aid and the promotion of various political and social programmes, and these functions may have become more important as the Masonic movement evolved from its occultist roots.

Occultism, as a magical movement, may have served other purposes in the genesis of modern bourgeois society. Malinowski argued that the basic function of magic was to build confidence in uncertain situations.[33] Similarly, Ernst Cassirer has observed that 'Faith in magic is one of the earliest and most striking expressions of man's awakening self-confidence. Here he no longer feels himself at the mercy of natural or supernatural forces. He begins to play his own part.'[34] The occult philosophy flourished in early modern Europe among an increasingly assertive sector of the population which nevertheless experienced life as precarious: the middling sort who, unlike the poor, were not absolved from social responsibility, and, unlike the nobles, were not compensated for their role in society by power and prestige. Theosophy and the occult sciences can be regarded as an abstraction of the conceptual framework of sorcery, a phenomenon which originates in 'resistance to society's pressure'.[35] It is a means of strengthening the individual against the given social consensus. Occultism continues this function of providing a magical armoury for those who are breaking free of social norms. This is why it became an important part of the world-view of some of those who were challenging the aristocratic order.

If the ideology of innerworldly asceticism was not developed in order to accumulate, accumulation was nevertheless one of its consequences. Gradually the bourgeoisie grew in power and wealth, and a world of relative uncertainties gave way to one of relative certainties. The notion of a transcendent self began to lose its appeal. The alternative discourse of a purely empirical self became the distinctive discourse of the middling sort of Europe. The empirical self remained an objectification of the living 'I' but this objectification is no longer experienced as an alienation of the self. In place of the mystic's characteristic diffidence towards the world as presently constituted, there is a self-confident involvement in the mundane order; and instead of the mystic's repugnance for the war of each against all which constitutes both the condition of life and the threat of death in the marketplace, there is now a celebration of the competitive self and its deeds. For the mystics, self-will (the psychological precondition of bourgeois life) is a source of conditionality and alienation. For the modern bourgeois, it is the basis of freedom and authenticity. Thus in the eighteenth century the traditional moral derogation of the self is cast aside, preserved only on the margins of middle-class society. At the centre of social discourse there is a new validation of the self as blindly beneficent, a source of unintended altruism. Self-interest is no longer seen as a cancer eating away at the fabric of society, but is promoted as the governing principle of all social intercourse. Mandeville's public benefits grow from private vices, Adam Smith's invisible hand silently regulates the new political economy, Ricardo's comparative advantage maximises the goods enjoyed by competing individuals or nations. Overt magic becomes totally marginalised when the bourgeoisie rises to power in the nineteenth century, and occultism is largely transformed into Romanticism.

The occult philosophy reflects and magnifies the contradictions in bourgeois culture as a whole. On the one hand it is vigorously universalising, and occasionally slips into a genuinely radical social egalitarianism; on the other hand it is equally vigorously élitist, tending towards a theocratic and meritocratic ideal. Its obsession with the self in its autonomy and interiority frequently leaves the impression of a mere solipsism; but it is also profoundly collective in its outlook, positing the reconstitution of the primordial cosmic man as the goal of the historical process. These contradictions are carried over into Romanticism. The Romantics were noted for their exaltation of the self, developing what has been called a 'cult of the Ego'.[36] On the other hand, many Romantics also devoted themselves to lamenting the passing of the supposedly organic Middle Ages, in which individuals were subsumed in their social relations.[37] The Hegelian philosophy of history is an attempt to overcome precisely this problem, by positing as the goal of history an organic community which will be the authentic expression of a fully developed individualism.[38]

More clearly than unadulterated occultism, Romanticism is a revolt against aristocratic culture. We can see this when we consider the historical development of German Romanticism as analysed by Norbert Elias. The eighteenth-century German aristocracy favoured a Francophile neo-classicism, with Johann Cristoph Gottsched as its 'high priest'.[39] Germany itself was economically backward, its development being hindered by the tur-moil following the Reformation and the Thirty Years' War. The German middle class was relatively small, poor and powerless, functioning basically as a court service-class, dependent on the aristocracy and excluded from the exercise of political power. The relatively high barriers between the middle class and the aristocracy placed the former in an anomalous position. They themselves wanted the ability to rise in the world, but at the same time they were afraid of the possible devaluation of their position by social mobility from below. Romanticism grew as a legitimation of the middle class *vis-à-vis* Francophile court society. Its emphasis on *das rein Geistige*, the purely spiritual, reflected the exclusion of the middle classes from politics and commerce; and its love-affair with popular German culture expressed the yearning to be free from the Francophile neoclassicism associated with aristocratic hegemony.[40]

Romanticism, however, was never simply a cultural protest of the bour-geoisie against the aristocratic order. Romantic medievalism appears to be an attempted reversion to feudal society, and Romanticism appealed to members of the nobility and gentry as well as to the middle classes. The Romantic movement was in fact more a protest against the emergent bourgeois order than against the remnants of a moribund feudalism. If it was primarily a middle-class phenomenon, it made its greatest appeal to those whose position was marginal in middle-class society: intellectuals, women and youths.[41] From nineteenth-century bohemians and *fin-de-siècle* Decadents to twentieth-century beatniks and hippies, middle-class society has produced movements of cultural protest against itself; it has always been sections of the middle classes themselves who have been most concerned to *épater les bourgeois*. These protest movements not only carry on the tradi-tion of the Romantic rebel, they are also the social locale of modern occult-ism. The marginalisation of occultism since the eighteenth century is thus the secret of its survival: it continues to exist as part of a culural protest against the conditions of bourgeois society. It is, however, a futile protest. Withdraw-ing from an effective political engagement with the world, it can never hope to change the conditions against which it rebels. Increasingly identified with youth, both occultism and contemporary forms of Romantic rebellion are tolerated as a life-cycle aberration. Both might even be said to be functional for middle-class society. They provide a cultural safety-valve, permitting the abreaction of negative responses to the dominant culture, and both, of course, are eminently marketable.

Notes

1 Introduction

1 Norman Cohn, *Europe's Inner Demons. The Demonization of Christians in Medieval Christendom*, rev. edn (London, 1993).

2 Christopher Marlowe, *Doctor Faustus*, ed. Roma Gill (London, 1989), i: 53.

3 Frances A. Yates, *The Occult Philosophy in the Elizabethan Age* (London, 1979), ch. 11.

4 Emmanuel Leroy Ladurie, 'Peasants', in Peter Burke (ed.), *The New Cambridge Modern History, XII, Companion Volume* (Cambridge, 1979), pp. 115–63, p. 159; J. F. C. Harrison, *The Second Coming. Popular Millenarianism, 1780–1850* (London, 1979), p. 39.

5 Marcel Mauss, *A General Theory of Magic*, trans. Robert Brain (London, 1972), pp. 64 ff.

6 There are, of course, also sociological differences: the witch was typically poor, uneducated and female; the occult philosopher tended to come from the middling orders of society, possessed a degree of learning, and was usually male.

7 Mauss, *A General Theory of Magic*, p. 28.

8 W. E. Monter, 'The Pedestal and the Stake: Courtly Love and Witchcraft', in Renate Bridenthal and Claudia Koonz (eds), *Becoming Visible. Women in European History* (Boston, MA, 1977), pp. 121–36; Clarke Garrett, 'Women and Witches: Patterns of Analysis', *Signs*, 3, 2 (1977), pp. 461–70; Alan Anderson and Raymond Gordon, 'Witchcraft and the Status of Women: The Case of England', *British Journal of Sociology*, 29, 2 (1978), pp. 171–84; Clive Holmes, 'Women, Witnesses and Witches', *Past and Present*, 140 (August 1993), pp. 45–78. The assumptions made about the predominance of women in witchcraft cases have been challenged in J. K. Swales and Hugh McLaughlin, 'Witchcraft and the Status of Women: A Comment', *British Journal of Sociology*, 30, 3 (1979), pp. 349–58.

9 Serge Hutin, *Les Disciples anglais de Jacob Boehme aux XVIIe et XVIIIe siècles* (Paris, 1960), p. 25; Antoine Faivre, *L'Esotérisme au XVIIIe siècle en France et en Allemagne* (Paris, 1973), p. 171. Kuhlmann's execution may have had more to do with his revolutionary millenarianism than his occultism as such.

10 B. J. Gibbons, *Gender in Mystical and Occult Thought. Behmenism and its Development in England* (Cambridge, 1996), p. 5.

11 Samuel Butler, *Characters and Passages from the Note-Books*, ed. A. R. Waller (Cambridge, 1908), pp. 97–108; Samuel Butler, *Hudibras*, ed. John Wilders (Oxford, 1967), i: 523–64; Jonathan Swift, *The Tale of a Tub*, ed. Herbert Davis, in *The Prose Works of Jonathan Swift*, 14 vols (Oxford, 1939–68), vol. 1, p. 79.

12 Paul Hazard, *European Thought in the Eighteenth Century. From Montesquieu to Lessing*, trans. J. Lewis May (Gloucester, MA, 1973); Peter Gay, *The Enlightenment. An Interpretation*, 2 vols (London, 1973), vol. 2, pp. 187–9.

13 Lewis White Beck, *Early German Philosophy. Kant and His Predecessors*, paperback edn (Bristol, 1996), p. 159. On the proximity of Enlightenment and esoteric culture, see Faivre, *L'Esotérisme au XVIIIe siècle en France et en Allemagne*, p. 26; Wouter Hanegraaff, *New Age Religion and Western Culture. Esotericism in the Mirror of Western Thought* (Leiden, 1996), pp. 411–15.

14 Keith Thomas, *Religion and the Decline of Magic. Studies in Popular Beliefs in Sixteenth- and Seventeenth-Century England*, paperback edn (Harmondsworth, 1973), ch. 18.

15 Desirée Hirst, *Hidden Riches. Traditional Symbolism from the Renaissance to Blake* (London, 1964), p. 162.

16 David Walsh, *The Mysticism of Innerworldly Fulfillment. A Study of Jacob Boehme* (Gainesville, FL, 1983), p. 5.

17 Elaine Pagels, *The Gnostic Gospels*, paperback edn (Harmondsworth, 1982), ch. 5.

18 Bentley Layton (ed.), *The Gnostic Scriptures* (London, 1987), Introduction, p. 8.

19 Brian P. Copenhaver (ed.), *Hermetica. The Greek Corpus Hermeticum and the Latin Asclepius* (Cambridge, 1995).

20 Frances A. Yates, *Giordano Bruno and the Hermetic Tradition* (London, 1964), p. 13.

21 Moshe Idel, Introduction to Johann Reuchlin, *On the Art of the Kabbalah. De arte cabalistica*, trans. Martin Goodman and Sarah Goodman (Lincoln, NE, 1993), pp. v–vi.

22 Joseph Leon Blau, *The Christian Interpretation of the Cabala in the Renaissance* (New York, 1944), p. 100.

23 E. J. Holmyard, *Alchemy* (Harmondsworth, 1957), pp. 102 ff.; F. Sherwood Taylor, *The Alchemists* (New York, 1992), chs. 7–8.

24 Titus Burckhardt, *Alchemy. Science of the Cosmos, Science of the Soul*, trans. William Stoddart (Shaftesbury, 1986), p. 20.

25 Chiara Crisciani and Claude Gagnon, *Alchimie et philosophie au moyen âge. Perspectives et problèmes* (Quebec, 1980), p. 36.

26 For early Christian Mysticism, see Andrew Louth, *The Origins of the Christian Mystical Tradition* (Oxford, 1981).

27 John Scotus Eriugena, *Periphyseon. On the Division of Nature*, trans. Myra L. Uhlfelder (Indianapolis, 1976). See also John J. O'Meara, *Eriugena* (Oxford, 1988); Dermot Moran, *The Philosophy of John Scotus Eriugena. A Study of Idealism in the Middle Ages* (Cambridge, 1989).

28 O'Meara, *Eriugena*, p. 217.

29 Beck, *Early German Philosophy*, chs. 2–3; Jeanne Ancelet-Hustache, *Master Eckhart and the Rhineland Mystics*, trans. Hilda Graef (London, 1957).

30 Steven E. Ozment, *Mysticism and Dissent. Religious Ideology and Social Protest in the Sixteenth Century* (New Haven, 1973).

31 For an introduction to classical Greek philosophy, see F. M. Cornford, *Before and After Socrates*, paperback edn (Cambridge, 1976); A. H. Armstrong, *An Introduction to Ancient Philosophy*, paperback edn (London, 1965).

32 Plotinus, *The Enneads*, trans. Stephen MacKenna, paperback edn (Harmondsworth, 1991); Lloyd P. Gerson, *Plotinus* (London, 1994).

33 M. R. Wright (ed.), *Empedocles. The Extant Fragments* (New Haven, 1981), pp. 30–4.

34 Charles A. Kahn (ed.), *The Art and Thought of Heraclitus. An Edition of the Fragments with Translation and Commentary* (Cambridge, 1979).

35 W. J. Verdenius, *Parmenides. Some Comments on his Poem* (Amsterdam, 1964).

36 J. A. Philip, *Pythagoras and Early Pythagoreanism* (Toronto, 1966).

37 Reuchlin, *On the Art of the Kabbalah*, p. 39.

38 J. E. McGuire, 'Neoplatonism and Active Principles: Newton and the Corpus Hermeticum', in R. S. Westman and J. E. McGuire (eds), *Hermeticism and the Scientific Revolution* (Los Angeles, CA, 1977), pp. 95–142, p. 106.

39 Paul-Henri Michel, *The Cosmology of Giordano Bruno*, trans. R. E. W. Maddison (London, 1973), p. 42.

40 Zdenek V. David, 'The Influence of Jacob Boehme on Russian Religious Thought', *Slavic Review*, 21, 1 (March 1962), pp. 43–64.

41 U. Szulakowska, 'The Tree of Aristotle: Images of the Philosopher's Stone and their Transference in Alchemy from the Fifteenth to the Twentieth Century', *Ambix*, 33, 2/3 (1986), pp. 55–77, p. 63.

42 H. G. Schenk, *The Mind of the European Romantics*, paperback edn (Oxford, 1979), p. xxii.

43 Layton, *The Gnostic Scriptures*, pp. 8–9; Giovanni Filoramo, *A History of Gnosticism*, trans. Anthony Alcock (Oxford, 1990), pp. 38–9; Hans Jonas, *The Gnostic Religion. The Message of the Alien God and the Beginnings of Christianity*, 2nd edn (London, 1992), p. 32.

44 A. J. Festugière, *La révélation d'Hermès Trismégiste*, 4 vols (Paris, 1944–54), vol. 1, p. 84.

45 Jonas, *The Gnostic Religion*, pp. 241 ff.

46 M. H. Abrams, *Natural Supernaturalism. Tradition and Revolution in Romantic Literature* (New York, 1971), pp. 183–4.

47 Giordano Bruno, *The Expulsion of the Triumphant Beast*, trans. Arthur D. Imerti, paperback edn (Lincoln, NE, 1992), pp. 235, 240.

48 Cited in Beck, *Early German Philosophy*, p. 149.

49 Jacob Boehme, *Signatura Rerum. The Signature of All Things*, trans. John Ellistone (London, 1648), 8: 2, 3: 40.

50 Jacob Boehme, *Mysterium Magnum. Or, An Exposition of the First Book of Moses Called Genesis*, trans. John Ellistone and John Sparrow (London, 1655), 1: 8.

51 Richard Coppin, *Divine Teachings*, 3 Parts (London, 1649), part iii, p. 14.

52 George Cheyne, *Philosophical Principles of Religion Natural and Revealed* (London, 1715), p. 75.

53 George Cheyne, *An Essay on Regimen. Together With Five Discourses, Medical, Moral, and Philosophical* (London, 1740), p. 313.

54 Cited in Auguste Viatte, *Les Sources occultes du romantisme*, 2nd edn, 2 vols (Paris, 1965), vol. 1, p. 275.

55 *The Emerald Tablet* is reprinted in several works on alchemy; the translation used here can be found in Burckhardt, *Alchemy*, pp. 196–7. This is particularly useful in comparing the Latin and Arabic versions of the document. In the latter, this sentence from clause 1 reads: 'The highest comes from the lowest and the lowest from the highest.'

56 Boehme, *Signatura Rerum*, 1: 6.

57 Paracelsus, *Selected Writings*, ed. Jolande Jacobi (London, 1951), p. 95.

58 Boehme, *Signatura Rerum*, 9: 1.

59 Samuel Taylor Coleridge, *Shakespeare Criticism*, ed. T. M. Raysor, 2 vols (London, 1960), vol. 1, p. 198.

60 Charles Fourier, *The Theory of the Four Movements*, ed. Gareth Stedman Jones and Ian Patterson (Cambridge, 1996), pp. 38, 16.

61 Cited in Neal C. Gillespie, *Charles Darwin and the Problem of Creation* (Chicago, 1979), p. 14.

62 Cited in François Wendel, *Calvin*, trans. Philip Mairet, paperback edn (London, 1965), p. 161.
63 On this misunderstanding with specific reference to the Diggers and Ranters, see B. J. Gibbons, 'Debate. Fear, Myth and Furore: Reappraising the Ranters', *Past and Present*, 140 (August 1993), pp. 178–94, pp. 182–4.
64 Peter Sterry, *The Clouds In Which Christ Comes* (London, 1648), p. 3; Peter Sterry, *The Teachings of Christ in the Soul* (London, 1648), p. 4.
65 For Toland's pantheism and indebtedness to occult thought, see Robert E. Sullivan, *John Toland and the Deist Controversy. A Study in Adaptation* (Cambridge, MA, 1982), especially ch. 6.
66 Jonas, *The Gnostic Religion*, pp. 181 ff.
67 *Ibid.*, pp. 51–4.
68 Gershom Scholem, *Major Trends in Jewish Mysticism*, paperback edn (New York, 1961), pp. 207 ff.
69 Gershom Scholem, *Kabbalah* (New York, 1974), pp. 106–7.
70 Joseph Dan, *Gershom Scholem and the Jewish Mystical Tradition* (New York, 1987), p. 214.
71 Jacob Boehme, *The Aurora. That Is, The Day-spring*, trans. John Sparrow (London, 1656), 10: 3.
72 See, for example, the Anglo-German Philadelphian credo, cited in Nils Thune, *The Behmenists and the Philadelphians. A Contribution to the Study of English Mysticism in the Seventeenth and Eighteenth Centuries* (Uppsala, 1948), p. 119.
73 Gibbons, *Gender in Mystical and Occult Thought*, pp. 90–1.
74 Jacob Boehme, *Quaestiones Theosophicae*, in *De Electione Gratiae and Quaestiones Theosophicae*, trans. John Rolleston Earle (London, 1930), 3: 2.
75 Joseph Dan (ed.), *The Early Kabbalah* (Mahwah, NJ, 1986), Introduction, pp. 46, 51.
76 [Moses de Leon], *The Zohar*, trans. Harry Sperling and Maurice Simon, 5 vols (London, 1931–4), vol. 1, p. 72.
77 S. L. McGregor, Introduction to his translation of Knorr von Rosenroth (ed.), *The Kabbalah Unveiled*, paperback edn (London, 1991), p. 16.
78 See Gibbons, *Gender in Mystical and Occult Thought*.
79 Beck, *Early German Philosophy*, pp. 62–3.
80 Imerti, Introduction to Bruno, *The Expulsion of the Triumphant Beast*, pp. 35–6.
81 Bruno, *The Expulsion of the Triumphant Beast*, p. 91.
82 William F. Huffmann, *Robert Fludd and the End of the Renaissance* (London, 1988), p. 106.
83 Viatte, *Les Sources occultes du romantisme*, vol. 2, pp. 28–30.
84 William Blake, 'The Marriage of Heaven and Hell', in William Blake, *Complete Writings*, ed. Sir Geoffrey Keynes, paperback edn (Oxford, 1966), p. 149.
85 Fourier, *The Theory of the Four Movements*, p. 117.
86 F. W. J. Schelling, *On the World Soul*, cited in Robert Stern's Introduction to Schelling, *Ideas for a Philosophy of Nature* (Cambridge, 1988), pp. ix–x.
87 See David Pym, *The Religious Thought of Samuel Taylor Coleridge* (Gerrards Cross, 1978), pp. 25, 96 note.
88 Eliphas Lévi, *The History of Magic*, trans. A. E. Waite, paperback edn (London, 1986), p. 358; Christopher McIntosh, *Eliphas Lévi and the French Occult Revival* (London, 1972), p. 150.
89 Papus, *The Tarot of the Bohemians* (1896), trans. A. P. Morton, paperback edn (London, 1994), p. 21.

90 Norbert Elias, *The Civilizing Process. The History of Manners and State Forma-tion and Civilization*, trans. Edmund Jephcott, paperback edn (Oxford, 1994), p. 204.
91 D. P. Walker, *Spiritual and Demonic Magic from Ficino to Campanella*, paper-back edn (Notre Dame, 1975), p. 76.
92 Frances Yates, 'The Hermetic Tradition in Renaissance Science', in Charles S. Singleton (ed.), *Art, Science and History in the Renaissance* (Baltimore, 1967), pp. 255–74.
93 Daniel O'Keefe, *Stolen Lightning. The Social Theory of Magic* (Oxford, 1982), p. 528.
94 Stoddard Martin, *Orthodox Heresy. The Rise of 'Magic' as Religion and its Relation to Literature* (London, 1989), pp. 195 ff.
95 Ernst Benz, *The Mystical Sources of German Romantic Philosophy*, trans. Blair R. Reynolds and Eunice M. Paul (Allison Park, PA, 1983).
96 Walsh, *The Mysticism of Innerworldly Fulfillment*, p. 1.
97 G. W. F. Hegel, *Vorlesungen über die Geschichte der Philosophie*, ed. Eva Moldenhauer and Karl Markus, in Hegel's *Werke*, 21 vols (Frankfurt-am-Main, 1971–81), vol. 20, p. 94. See also E. S. Haldane, 'Jacob Boehme in his Relation to Hegel', *Philosophical Review*, 6 (1897), pp. 146–61; Ingrid Schüssler, 'Böhme und Hegel', *Jahrbuch der schlesischen Friedrich-Wilhelms-Universität*, 10 (1965), pp. 45–58.
98 Beck, *Early German Philosophy*, p. 153.
99 F. W. J. von Schelling, *On the History of Modern Philosophy*, trans. Andrew Bowie (Cambridge, 1994), p. 183.
100 Robert F. Brown, *The Later Philosophy of Schelling. The Influence of Boehme on the Works of 1809–1815* (Lewisberg, 1977); Wilhelm Schulze, 'Der Einfluss Boehmes und Oetingers auf Schelling', *Blätter für württembergische Kirchen-geschichte*, 56 (1956), pp. 171–80.
101 Claud Sutton, *The German Tradition in Philosophy* (London, 1974), pp. 78–9.
102 Arthur Schopenhauer, *The World as Will and Idea*, trans. R. B. Haldane and J. Kemp, 3 vols (London, 1948), vol. 1, p. 248.
103 Beck, *Early German Philosophy*, p. 156; Paul Tillich, 'Existential Philosophy', *Journal of the History of Ideas*, 12, 5 (1942), pp. 44–70, p. 58.
104 William Kluback and Jean T. Wilde, Introduction to Martin Heidegger, *What is Philosophy?* (London, 1956), p. 7.
105 Richard Holmes, *Coleridge* (Oxford, 1982), pp. 57–9.
106 Giovanni Pico della Mirandola, 'Oration on the Dignity of Man', in E. Cas-sirer, P. O. Kristellar and J. H. Randall, Jr. (eds), *The Renaissance Philosophy of Man* (Chicago, 1948), pp. 224–5.
107 Jean-Paul Sartre, *Existentialism and Humanism*, trans. Philip Mairet, paperback edn (London, 1973), p. 26.
108 Charles Taylor, *Sources of the Self. The Making of the Modern Identity*, paper-back edn (Cambridge, 1992), p. 200.
109 Jonas, *The Gnostic Religion*, ch. 13.
110 Peter Malekin, Introduction to his edition of Jacob Boehme, *The Key and Other Writings* (Durham, 1988), p. 10.
111 O'Keefe, *Stolen Lightning*, pp. 39 ff.
112 John Webster, *Academarum Examen, Or The Examination of Academies* (London, 1653), pp. 28 ff.
113 On occult linguistics see Peter Schaublin, *Zur Sprache Jacob Boehmes* (Winterthur, 1963); Steven A. Konopacki, *Descent into Words. Jacob Boehme's Transcendental Linguistics* (Ann Arbor, 1979); Brian Vickars, 'Analogy versus Identity: The Rejection of Occult Symbolism, 1580–1680', in Brian Vickars

(ed.), *Occult and Scientific Mentalities in the Renaissance* (Cambridge, 1984), pp. 95–163; Hugh Ormsby-Lennon, 'Renaissance Linguistics: Twilight of a Renaissance Tradition', in Ingrid Merkel and Allen G. Debus (eds), *Intellectual History and the Occult in Early Modern Europe* (Washington, 1988), pp. 311–41.

114 Isaiah Berlin, *Vico and Herder. Two Studies in the History of Ideas* (London, 1976), p. 167.

115 F. M. Barnard (ed.), *Herder on Social and Political Culture* (Cambridge, 1969), p. 176.

116 Ioan P. Couliano, *Eros and Magic in the Renaissance*, trans. Margaret Cook (Chicago, 1987).

117 Roy Porter, Introduction to George Cheyne, *The English Malady* (London, 1991), p. vii.

118 For Cheyne, see G. S. Rousseau, 'Immortal Dr Cheyne', in Richard H. Popkin (ed.), *Millenarianism and Messianism in English Literature and Thought* (Leiden, 1988), pp. 81–126; David E. Shuttleton, '"My Own Crazy Carcass": The Life and Works of Dr George Cheyne (1672–1743)', unpublished Ph.D. thesis (University of Edinburgh, 1992); B. J. Gibbons, 'Mysticism and Mechanism: The Religious Context of George Cheyne's Representation of the Body and its Ills', *British Journal for Eighteenth-Century Studies*, 21, 1 (1998), pp. 1–23.

119 Anne-Marie Jaton, *Johann Caspar-Lavater. Philosoph – Gottesmann – Schöpfer der Phisiognomik* (Zurich, 1993), pp. 121 ff.

120 Wolf-Dieter Muller-Jahnke, 'Die Signaturenlehre des Paracelsus', in Heinz Dopsch, Kurt Goldammer and Peter F. Kramml (eds), *Paracelsus (1493–1541). Keines andern Knecht . . .* (Salzburg, 1993), pp. 167–9.

121 Viatte, *Les Sources occultes du romantisme*, vol. 1, pp. 223 ff.; Robert Darnton, *Mesmerism and the End of the Enlightenment in France* (Cambridge, MA, 1968), pp. 67 ff.

122 Hanegraaff, *New Age Religion and Western Culture*, ch. 2.

123 Martin, *Orthodox Heresy*, p. 21.

124 O'Keefe, *Stolen Lightning*, passim.

125 McIntosh, *Eliphas Lévi and the French Occult Revival*, p. 152.

126 James Hall, *A History of Ideas and Images in Italian Art* (London, 1983), pp. 261–6; Edgar Wind, *Pagan Mysteries in the Renaissance*, paperback edn (Harmondsworth, 1967); Mirella Levi d'Ancona, *Botticelli's Primavera. A Botanical Interpretation including Astrology, Alchemy and the Medici* (Florence, 1983).

127 See, for example, Gerald E. Bentley, Jr., 'William Blake and the Occult Philosophers', B.Litt. thesis (Oxford, 1954); Hirst, *Hidden Riches*; Bryan Aubrey, 'The Influence of Jacob Boehme on the Work of William Blake', Ph.D. thesis (Durham, 1981); Gibbons, *Gender in Mystical and Occult Thought*, pp. 191–8.

128 Edward Lucie-Smith, *Symbolist Art* (London, 1972), ch. 9; Fred Gettings, *The Hidden Art. A Study of Occult Symbolism in Art* (London, 1978), pp. 130 ff.; Rose-Carol Washton Long, *Kandinsky. The Development of an Abstract Style* (Oxford, 1980), ch. 2; Nadia Choucha, *Surrealism and the Occult* (Oxford, 1991).

129 Walker, *Spiritual and Demonic Magic*, passim.

130 Gilchrist, *Alchemy*, pp. 72, 75; Faivre, *L'Esotérisme au XVIIIe siècle en France et en Allemagne*, p. 43; Jacques Chailley, *La Flûte enchantée. Opéra maçonnique* (Paris, 1968).

131 Gilchrist, *Alchemy*, pp. 108–12; Lyndy Abraham, *Marvell and Alchemy* (Aldershot, 1990).

132 The programme of a 1983 Theatre Set-Up production, cited in Gilchrist, *Alchemy*, p. 109.

133 Charles Nicholl, *The Chemical Theatre* (London, 1980).
134 John S. Mebane, *Renaissance Magic and the Return of the Golden Age. The Occult Tradition in Marlowe, Jonson and Shakespeare* (Lincoln, NE, 1989).
135 Douglas Brooke-Davies, *The Mercurian Monarch. Magical Politics from Spenser to Pope* (Manchester, 1983).
136 Elizabeth Holmes, *Henry Vaughan and the Hermetic Philosophy*, 2nd edn (New York, 1967); E. C. Pettet, *Of Paradise and Light. A Study of Vaughan's Silex Scintillans* (Cambridge, 1960), ch. 4.
137 Arthur O. Lovejoy, 'On the Discrimination of Romanticisms', *Publications of the Modern Languages Society of America*, 39 (1924), pp. 229–53, p. 236; Lilian R. Furst, *Romanticism in Perspective. A Comparative Study of Aspects of the Romantic Movements in England, France and Germany* (London, 1979), pp. 15, 18.
138 Viatte, *Les Sources occultes du romantisme*, vol. 1, p. 6. On occult trends in English Romanticism, see Paul Davies, *Romanticism and Esoteric Tradition. Studies in Imagination* (Hudson, NY, 1998).
139 Maurice Bowra, *The Romantic Imagination*, paperback edn (Oxford, 1961), pp. 145, 281–3.
140 See below, pp. 92–9.
141 Kathleen Raine, *Blake and Tradition*, 2 vols (Princeton, NJ, 1962), is a useful introduction to the occult context of Blake's work despite its misleadingly Neoplatonic interpretation. Coleridge's philosophical inheritance is discussed in John H. Muirhead, *Coleridge as Philosopher* (London, 1930); the esoteric background to his work is dealt with in Alice D. Snyder, 'Coleridge on Giordano Bruno', *Modern Language Notes*, 42 (1927), pp. 427–36; Alice D. Snyder, 'Coleridge on Böhme', *Publications of the Modern Language Association of America*, 45 (1930), pp. 616–18; John Beer, 'Coleridge and Boehme's *Aurora*', *Notes and Queries*, 208 (1963), pp. 183–7; Richard Haven, 'Coleridge and Jacob Boehme: A Further Comment', *Notes and Queries*, 211 (1966), pp. 176–8; Thomas McFarland, *Coleridge and the Pantheist Tradition* (Oxford, 1969).
142 Ernest Lee Tuveson, *Avatars of Thrice-Great Hermes. An Approach to Romanticism* (Lewisberg, 1982), ch. 6.
143 Lothar Hönnighausen, *The Symbolist Tradition in English Literature. A Study of Pre-Raphaelitism and fin de siècle* (Cambridge, 1988), ch. 6; George Mills Harper (ed.), *Yeats and the Occult* (Toronto, 1975); James Olney, *The Rhizome and the Flower. The Perennial Philosophy – Yeats and Jung* (Berkeley, CA, 1980); Patrick J. Keane, *Yeats's Interactions with Tradition* (Columbia, 1987).
144 Heinrich Heine, *Die romantische Schule*, ed. Helga Weidmann (Stuttgart, 1979), p. 86; see also Marshall Brown, *The Shape of German Romanticism* (Ithaca, NY, 1979), pp. 133 ff.
145 Rolf Zimmerman, *Das Weltbild des jungen Goethe. Studien zur Hermetischen Tradition des deutschen 18. Jahrhunderts* (Munich, 1969).
146 Maurice Besset, *Novalis et la pensée mystique* (Paris, 1947); Jacques Roos, *Les aspects littéraires du mysticisme philosophique et l'influence de Boehme et de Swedenborg au début du romantisme. William Blake, Novalis, Balanche* (Strasbourg, 1953).
147 Martin, *Orthodox Heresy*, ch. 6.
148 Erich P. Hofacker, *Christian Morgenstern* (Boston, MA, 1978), especially ch. 7.
149 Viatte, *Les Sources occultes du romantisme*; Auguste Viatte, *Victor Hugo et les illuminés de son temps* (Geneva, 1973).
150 Karl-Erik Sjöden, *Swedenborg en France* (Stockholm, 1985), p. 157.

151 Charles Baudelaire, *Les Fleurs du mal*, ed. Adrien Cart and S. Hamel (Paris, 1972), p. 19.

152 Alain Mercier, *Les Sources ésotériques et occultes de la poésie Symboliste (1870–1914)*, 2 vols (Paris, 1969–74); John Senior, *The Way Down and Out. The Occult in Symbolist Literature* (New York, 1959); Enid Starkie, *Arthur Rimbaud*, reprint of 3rd edn (London, 1973), Part 2, ch. 3.

153 Arthur Rimbaud, *Poésies. Une Saison en enfer. Illuminations*, ed. Louis Forestier (Paris, 1965), pp. 202–4.

154 J. K. Huysmans, *Là-Bas (Down There)*, ed. Robert Irwin (Sawtry, 1986); McIntosh, *Eliphas Lévi and the French Occult Revival*, ch. 6; Francis King and Isabel Sutherland, *The Rebirth of Magic* (London, 1982), ch. 5.

155 On magic and fantasy fiction, see Lin Carter, *Imaginary Worlds. The Art of Fantasy* (New York, 1973).

156 King and Sutherland, *The Rebirth of Magic*, pp. 152–3, 194 ff.

157 William James, *The Varieties of Religious Experience*, paperback edn (London, 1960), p. 404; cf. F. C. Happold, *Mysticism. A Study and an Anthology*, revised edn (Harmondsworth, 1970), p. 17.

158 Anders Nygren, *Agape and Eros*, trans. Philip S. Watson (London, 1982), p. 35.

159 Gilchrist, *Alchemy*, p. 53.

160 Hirst, *Hidden Riches*, p. 293.

161 Marcello Truzzi, 'Definitions and Dimensions of the Occult: Towards a Sociological Perspective', reprinted in Edward A. Tiryakian (ed.), *On the Margin of the Visible. Sociology, the Esoteric and the Occult* (New York, 1974), pp. 243–55, p. 244. Wouter Hanegraaff has noted the same tendency, distinguishing between 'esotericism' and 'occultism' on this basis; he uses esotericism to refer to a traditional world-view based on the doctrine of correspondences, and occultism to denote the nineteenth- and twentieth-century reformulation of this world-view in terms of causality: *New Age Religion and Western Culture*, especially ch. 15. For a good example of 'scientific' occultism, see Colin Wilson, *The Occult* (London, 1979).

162 O'Keefe, *Stolen Lightning*, p. 561. On the orientalising of Western occultism, see my discussion, pp. 119–21.

163 Viatte, *Victor Hugo et les illuminés de son temps*, p. 20.

164 Cited in Martin, *Orthodox Heresy*, p. 76.

165 Hirst, *Hidden Riches*, p. 293.

166 Tuveson, *The Avatars of Thrice-Great Hermes*, pp. 50–5.

167 Gettings, *The Hidden Art*, p. 11.

168 Denis Saurat, *Literature and Occult Tradition* (London, 1930), p. 7.

169 J. H. Brennan, *The Occult Reich* (New York, 1974); Nicholas Goodrick-Clarke, *The Occult Roots of Nazism. Aryan Cults and their Influence on Nazi Ideology* (London, 1985).

170 Christopher McIntosh, *The Rosicrucians. The History and Mythology of an Occult Order*, 2nd edn (Wellingborough, 1987), p. 141; Martin, *Orthodox Heresy*, ch. 9.

171 Jeffrey B. Russell, *A History of Witchcraft. Sorcerors, Heretics and Pagans*, paperback edn (London, 1981), chs. 8 and 9.

172 Theodore Adorno, 'Theses Against Occultism', *Telos*, 19 (Spring 1974), pp. 7–12, p. 9.

2   Nature in occult thought

1 On early modern attitudes to nature, see Keith Thomas, *Man and the Natural World. Changing Attitudes in England, 1500–1800* (London, 1983).

2 William Shakespeare, *The Tempest*, ed. Stephen Orgel (Oxford, 1994), I: i: 16–17.

3 John Milton, *Paradise Lost*, ed. Christopher Ricks (Harmondsworth, 1968), ix: 782–4.

4 James Garden, *Comparative Theology, Or the True and Solid Grounds of Pure and Peaceable Theology*, 2nd edn (Bristol, 1756), pp. 31–2.

5 Martin Luther, *Works*, ed. Jaroslav Pelikan and Helmut T. Lehmann, 55 vols (St Louis and Philadelphia, 1957–86), vol. 1, p. 208.

6 See Harry H. Levin, *The Myth of the Golden Age in the Renaissance* (London, 1970).

7 Milton, *Paradise Lost*, x: 651 ff.

8 Thomas Tryon, *Letters Upon Several Occasions* (London, 1700), pp. 79, 127.

9 Jacob Boehme, *Concerning the Three Principles of the Divine Essence*, trans. John Sparrow (London, 1648), Preface, 13.

10 William Law, *The Works of the Reverend William Law*, 9 vols (Brockenhurst and Canterbury, 1892–3), vol. 8, p. 9.

11 Francis Lee, *Dissertations Theological, Mathematical, and Physical*, 2 vols (London, 1752), vol. 1, p. 198.

12 Samuel Pordage, *Mundorum Explicatio. Or the Explanation of an Hieroglyphical Figure* (London, 1661), p. 71.

13 See below, pp. 76–81.

14 Pordage, *Mundorum Explicatio*, p. 57.

15 G. H. Sabine (ed.), *The Works of Gerrard Winstanley* (Ithaca, NY, 1941), p. 169.

16 Anonymous, 'Experience and Philosophy', in Elias Ashmole (ed.), *Theatrum Chemicum Britannicum* (London, 1652), pp. 336–41, p. 339.

17 Paracelsus, *Selected Writings*, ed. Jolande Jacobi (London, 1951), p. 87.

18 Philalethes, 'Three Treatises', in Derek Bryce (ed.), *Concerning the Secrets of Alchemy and Other Tracts from the Hermetic Museum* (Lampeter, 1989), pp. 174–218.

19 Thomas Vaughan, *Aula Lucis, Or, The House of Light* (London, 1651), p. 6.

20 Thomas Vaughan, *Magia Adamica: Or the Antiquitie of Magic and the Descent Thereof from Adam downwards proved* (London, 1650), sigs. C3^r–C3^v.

21 Thomas Vaughan, *Anthroposophia Theomagica: Or a Discourse of the Nature of Man and his State after Death* (London, 1650), p. 11.

22 Jacob Boehme, *Signatura Rerum. The Signature of All Things*, trans. John Ellistone (London, 1648), 3: 38.

23 Basil Valentine, 'The Great Stone of the Ancient Sages', in Derek Bryce (ed.), *The Book of Lambspring and The Golden Tripod* (Lampeter, 1987), pp. 43–85, 45.

24 Paracelsus, *Three Books Written to the Athenians* (London, 1657), p. 2.

25 Paracelsus, *Archidoxes*, trans. J. H. (London, 1661), pp. 154–5.

26 Vaughan, *Anthroposophia Theomagica*, pp. 24–5.

27 Thomas Vaughan, *Anima Magica Abscondita* (London, 1650), p. 28.

28 Elias Ashmole (ed.), *The Way to Bliss* (London, 1658), pp. 29–31.

29 [Moses de Leon], *The Zohar*, trans. Harry Sperling and Maurice Simon, 5 vols (London, 1931–4), vol. 1, p. 113.

30 Auguste Viatte, *Les Sources occultes du romantisme*, 2nd edn, 2 vols (Paris, 1965), vol. 1, pp. 102, 257.

31 Charles Fourier, *The Theory of the Four Movements*, ed. Gareth Stedman Jones and Ian Patterson (Cambridge, 1996), pp. 44–7.

32 Vaughan, *Anthroposophia Theomagica*, sig. B4^r.

33 Anonymous, 'The Glory of the World', in Derek Bryce (ed.), *The Glory of the World and Other Alchemical Tracts from the Hermetic Museum* (Lampeter, 1987), pp. 7–85, p. 24.

34 Gerrard Malynes, 'Philosophy about the Essence or Existence of Metals', in *Chymical, Medicinal, and Chyrurgical Addresses to Samuel Hartlib, Esq.* (London, 1655), sigs. *1ᵛ–*2ʳ.

35 On medieval and early modern understandings of reproductive biology, see Audrey Eccles, *Obstetrics and Gynaecology in Tudor and Stuart England* (London, 1982); Danielle Jacquart and Claude Thomasset, *Sexuality and Medicine in the Middle Ages*, trans. Matthew Adamson (Cambridge, 1988); Thomas Laqueur, *Making Sex. Body and Gender from the Greeks to Freud* (Cambridge, MA, 1990).

36 For early modern domestic ideology, see Levin L. Schücking, *The Puritan Family. A Study from Literary Sources*, trans. Brian Battershaw (London, 1969); Steven E. Ozment, *When Fathers Ruled. Family Life in Reformation Europe* (Cambridge, MA, 1983); Margo Todd, *Christian Humanism and the Puritan Social Order* (Cambridge, 1987), ch. 4.

37 Alexandre Koyré, *Mystiques, spirituels alchimistes. Schwenckfeld, Sébastian Franck, Weigel, Paracelse* (Paris, 1955), pp. 64–5.

38 Cited in Viatte, *Les Sources occultes du romantisme*, vol. 1, pp. 123, 205, 242.

39 Law, *The Works*, vol. 8, p. 14.

40 Francis Mercury van Helmont, *Cabalistical Dialogue in Answer to a Learned Doctor in Philosophy and Theology that the World was Made of Nothing* (London, 1682), p. 4.

41 Ann, Lady Conway, *The Principles of the Most Ancient and Modern Philosophy Concerning God, Christ, and the Creatures* (London, 1692), p. 93.

42 George Cheyne, *Philosophical Principles of Religion Natural and Reveal'd* (London, 1715), p. 119.

43 S. L. McGregor Mathers, 'Preface to the New Edition' of his translation of Christian Knorr von Rosenroth (ed.), *The Kabbalah Unveiled*, paperback edn (London, 1991), p. viii.

44 Viatte, *Les Sources occultes du romantisme*, vol. 1, pp. 59, 276.

45 Martin Luther, *Works*, vol. 1, p. 204.

46 Milton, *Paradise Lost*, x: 651 ff.

47 Boehme, *Concerning the Three Principles of the Divine Essence*, 7: 4.

48 Mungo Murray, letter to Colin Campbell (1701), cited in David E. Shuttleton, '"My Own Crazy Carcass": The Life and Works of Dr George Cheyne (1672–1743)', unpublished Ph.D. thesis (University of Edinburgh, 1992), p. 287.

49 Tryon, *Letters Upon Several Occasions*, p. 154.

50 Thomas Tryon, *Some Memoirs of the Life of Mr. Tho. Tryon, Late of London, Merchant* (London, 1705), p. 24.

51 Sabine (ed.), *The Works of Gerrard Winstanley*, pp. 155–6.

52 [de Leon], *The Zohar*, vol. 1, pp. 9–13.

53 Elizabeth Holmes, *Henry Vaughan and the Hermetic Tradition*, 2nd edn (New York, 1967), pp. 44 ff.

54 Henry Cornelius Agrippa, *Three Books of Occult Philosophy*, trans. I. F., ed. Donald Tyson (St Paul, MN, 1993), p. 213.

55 John Webster, *Academarum Examen. Or the Examination of Academies* (London, 1653), pp. 28 ff.

56 Mary Cary, *A New and More Exact Mappe or Description of New Jerusalems Glory* (London, 1651), p. 293.

57 Thomas, *Man and the Natural World*, pp. 138–9.

58 Jean Calvin, *Commentary on the Book of the Prophet Isaiah*, trans. William Pringle, 4 vols (Edinburgh, 1850), vol. 1, p. 384.
59 Colleen McDannell and Bernhard Lang, *Heaven. A History* (New Haven, 1988), pp. 146 ff.
60 Luther, *Works*, vol. 16, pp. 122–3; Calvin, *Commentary on the Book of the Prophet Isaiah*, vol. 1, p. 384.
61 Luther, *Works*, vol. 16, p. 263.
62 Cited in Holmes, *Henry Vaughan and the Hermetic Tradition*, p. 61.
63 Henry Vaughan, 'The Book', in *The Complete Poems*, ed. Alan Rudrum, rev. edn (Harmondsworth, 1983), p. 310.
64 Leonard Barkan, *Nature's Work of Art. The Human Body as the Image of the World* (New Haven, 1975), pp. 3, 48.
65 Mary Douglas, *Purity and Danger. An Analysis of Concepts of Pollution and Taboo*, paperback edn (Harmondsworth, 1970), p. 139.
66 Marcel Mauss, *A General Theory of Magic*, trans. Robert Brain (London, 1972), pp. 64–5.
67 Tryon, *Letters Upon Several Occasions*, p. 40.
68 *Ibid.*, p. 21.
69 Valentin Weigel, *Astrologie Theologized; Wherein is set forth what Astrologie and the Light of Nature is* (London, 1649), p. 28.
70 Paracelsus, *Selected Writings*, p. 226.
71 Urszula Szulakowska, 'The Tree of Aristotle: Images of the Philosophers' Stone and their Transference in Alchemy from the Fifteenth to the Twentieth Century', *Ambix*, 33, 2/3 (November 1986), pp. 53–77, pp. 54, 63. Not that pure astrology is as deterministic as Szulakowska suggests. The whole point of medical and mundane astrology is to allow people to control events rather than be controlled by them: Nicholas Campion, 'Astrological Historiography in the Renaissance: The Work of Jean Bodin and Louis Le Roy', in Annabella Kitson (ed.), *History and Astrology. Clio and Urania Confer* (London, 1989), pp. 89–136, pp. 92–3.
72 Koyré, *Mystiques, alchimistes spirituels*, pp. 54–5.
73 John G. Burke, 'Hermetism as a Renaissance World View', in Robert S. Kinsman (ed.), *The Darker Vision of the Renaissance. Beyond the Fields of Reason* (Berkeley, CA, 1984), pp. 95–117, p. 101.
74 Agrippa, *Three Books of Occult Philosophy*, pp. 589–90.
75 Cited in Viatte, *Les Sources occultes du romantisme*, vol. 1, p. 277.
76 Paracelsus, *Selected Writings*, pp. 166–7.
77 Robert Bruce Barnes, *Prophecy and Gnosis. Apocalypticism in the Wake of the Lutheran Reformation* (Stanford, CA, 1988), p. 52.
78 Chiara Crisciani and Claude Gagnon, *Alchimie et philosophie au moyen âge. Perspectives et problèmes* (Montreal, 1980), p. 50.
79 Stanislas Klossowski de Rola, *Alchemy. The Secret Art* (London, 1973), p. 16.
80 Michael Sendivogius, 'The New Chemical Light', in Bryce (ed.), *Concerning the Secrets of Alchemy*, p. 147.
81 Anonymous, 'The Glory of the World', pp. 9, 30.
82 Ernest Lee Tuveson, *The Avatars of Thrice Great Hermes. An Approach to Romanticism* (Lewisberg, 1982), pp. xiii, 4 ff.
83 Alexander Gode-Von Aesch, *Natural Science in German Romanticism* (New York, 1966), p. 211.
84 John S. Mebane, *Renaissance Magic and the Return of the Golden Age* (Lincoln, NE, 1989), p. 23.
85 Novalis, *Hymns to the Night and Other Selected Writings*, trans. Charles E. Passage (Indianapolis, 1960), p. 72.

86 Sabine (ed.), *The Works of Gerrard Winstanley*, pp. 116–17.
87 Richard Coppin, *Divine Teachings*, 3 Parts (London, 1649), Part 3, p. 14.
88 Peter Sterry, *The Clouds in Which Christ Comes* (London, 1648), p. 6.
89 Law, *The Works*, vol. 8, p. 6.
90 Marcus Woodward (ed.), *Gerard's Herbal. The History of Plants*, paperback edn (London, 1994), p. 1.
91 Nicholas Culpeper, *Complete Herbal*, paperback edn (Ware, 1995), p. vii.
92 Cited in Jeanne Ancelet-Hustache, *Master Eckhart and the Rhineland Mystics*, trans. Hilda Graef (London, 1957), p. 163.
93 Boehme, *Concerning the Three Principles of the Divine Essence*, 5: 18.
94 John Everard, *Some Gospel-Treasures Opened* (London, 1653), p. 383.
95 Tryon, *Letters Upon Several Occasions*, p. 8.
96 Vaughan, *Anthroposophia Theomagica*, pp. 21, 56.
97 Henry Vaughan, 'Corruption', in *The Complete Poems*, p. 197.
98 Vaughan, 'Religion', in *The Complete Poems*, p. 155.
99 M. M. Mahood, 'Vaughan: The Symphony of Nature', in Alan Rudrum (ed.), *Essential Articles for the Study of Henry Vaughan* (Hamden, CT, 1987), pp. 5–45, p. 9.
100 Vaughan, 'And do they so?', in *The Complete Poems*, pp. 188–9.
101 Vaughan, 'Rules and Lessons', in *The Complete Poems*, p. 193.
102 Vaughan, 'The Tempest', in *The Complete Poems*, p. 220.
103 Holmes, *Henry Vaughan and the Hermetic Tradition*, p. 47.
104 Vaughan, 'The Tempest', in *The Complete Poems*, p. 220.
105 Vaughan, 'I walked the other day', in *The Complete Poems*, p. 242.
106 Vaughan, 'Rules and Lessons', in *The Complete Poems*, p. 195.
107 Vaughan 'The Retreat', in *The Complete Poems*, p. 173.
108 Alan Rudrum, 'Vaughan's "The Night": Some Hermetic Notes', in Rudrum (ed.), *Essential Articles for the Study of Henry Vaughan*, pp. 141–53, p. 141.
109 Mahood, 'Vaughan: The Symphony of Nature', p. 40. On the Romantics' understanding of importance of a child-like vision in restoring 'the pristine experience of paradise', see M. H. Abrams, *Natural Supernaturalism. Tradition and Revolution in Romantic Literature* (New York, 1971), pp. 379 ff.
110 L. C. Martin, 'Henry Vaughan and the Theme of Infancy', in Rudrum (ed.), *Essential Articles for the Study of Henry Vaughan*, pp. 46–58, p. 56.
111 S. S. Sandbank, 'Henry Vaughan's Apology for Darkness', in Rudrum (ed.), *Essential Articles for the Study of Henry Vaughan*, pp. 128–40, p. 131.
112 Georgia B. Christopher, 'In Arcadia Calvin . . . : A Study of Nature in Henry Vaughan', in Rudrum (ed.), *Essential Articles for the Study of Henry Vaughan*, pp. 170–188, pp. 170, 181; cf. Christopher Hill, 'Henry Vaughan', in Christopher Hill, *Writing and Revolution in 17th Century England* (Brighton, 1985), pp. 206–25, pp. 219, 221.
113 Alan Rudrum, 'Henry Vaughan, the Liberation of the Creatures, and Seventeenth-Century English Calvinism', *The Seventeenth-Century*, 4, 1 (Spring 1989), pp. 35–54, p. 50.
114 L. C. Martin, 'Henry Vaughan and "Hermes Trismegistus",' in Rudrum (ed.), *Essential Readings for the Study of Henry Vaughan*, pp. 59–67, pp. 64–5.
115 Sir Thomas Browne, *The Major Works*, ed. C. A. Patrides (Harmondsworth, 1977), p. 74.
116 E. C. Pettet, *Of Paradise and Light. A Study of Vaughan's Silex Scintillans* (Cambridge, 1960), ch. 4; Holmes, *Henry Vaughan and the Hermetic Tradition*, p. 16.
117 Mahood, 'Vaughan: The Symphony of Nature', pp. 13, 44.

118 Cited in H. G. Schenk, *The Mind of the European Romantics*, paperback edn (Oxford, 1979) p. 167.
119 N. E. Restif de la Bretonne, *La Découverte australe par un Homme-volant* (Paris), p. 40.
120 Cited in Basil Willey, *The Eighteenth-Century Background*, paperback edn (London, 1986), p. 63.
121 Alexander Pope, 'An Essay on Man', i: 267–8, in *The Poetical Works of Alexander Pope*, ed. Sir Adolphus William Ward (London, 1961), p. 199.
122 William Godwin, *Memoirs of the Author of A Vindication of the Rights of Woman* (London, 1978), pp. 33–4.
123 Paul Tillich, *The Shaking of the Foundations*, paperback edn (Harmondsworth, 1962), pp. 89–90, 92.
124 William Blake, annotations to Wordsworth's poems, in *Complete Writings*, ed. Sir Geoffrey Keynes, rev. edn (Oxford, 1972), p. 783.
125 George Mills Harper, *The Neoplatonism of William Blake* (Chapel Hill, NC, 1961), p. 5.
126 Stuart Curran, 'Blake and the Gnostic Hyle: A Double Negative', in Nelson Hilton (ed.), *Essential Articles for the Study of William Blake* (Hamden, CT, 1986), pp. 15–32, p. 28.
127 Kathleen Raine, *William Blake* (London, 1970), p. 113.
128 William Blake, 'The Marriage of Heaven and Hell', in *Complete Writings*, p. 152.
129 Blake, 'A Vision of the Last Judgement', in *Complete Writings*, p. 617.
130 Blake, 'The Marriage of Heaven and Hell', p. 150.
131 J. G. Davies, *The Theology of William Blake* (Oxford, 1948), p. 100.
132 Blake, 'The Marriage of Heaven and Hell', p. 154.
133 Blake, 'Auguries of Innocence', in *Complete Writings*, p. 431.
134 Blake, 'The Marriage of Heaven and Hell', p. 153.
135 Abrams, *Natural Supernaturalism*, p. 379.
136 William Blake, letter to Thomas Butts, in *Complete Writings*, p. 817.
137 William Blake, letter to Dr Trusler, in *Complete Writings*, p. 793. On the occult concept of the imagination, see below, pp. 92–9.
138 Zachary Leader, *Reading Blake's Songs* (Boston, MA, 1981), pp. 28 ff.
139 William Blake, letter to Thomas Butts, in *Complete Writings*, p. 806.
140 Blake, 'A Vision of the Last Judgement', p. 617.
141 Henry Crabb Robinson, *Diary, Reminiscences, and Correspondence*, ed. Thomas Sadler, 3 vols (London, 1869), vol. 2, p. 306.
142 Blake, 'A Vision of the Last Judgement', pp. 605, 614.
143 Samuel Taylor Coleridge, *Collected Letters of Samuel Taylor Coleridge*, ed. Earl Leslie Griggs, 6 vols (Oxford, 1971), vol. 4, p. 883.
144 Coleridge, *Collected Letters of Samuel Taylor Coleridge*, vol. 6, pp. 897–8.
145 Robert F. Brown, *The Later Philosophy of Schelling. The Influence of Boehme on the Works of 1809–1815* (Lewisberg, 1977); on German Idealism generally, see Ernst Benz, *The Mystical Sources of German Romantic Philosophy*, trans. Blair R. Reynolds and Eunice M. Paul (Allison Park, PA, 1983).
146 B. J. Gibbons, *Gender in Mystical and Occult Thought. Behmenism and its Development in England* (Cambridge, 1996), pp. 89–92.
147 F. W. J. Schelling, *On the History of Modern Philosophy*, ed. Andrew Bowie (Cambridge, 1994), p. 180.
148 Samuel Taylor Coleridge, 'Religious Musings', in *The Works of Samuel Taylor Coleridge*, ed. Martin Corner (London, 1994), pp. 106–25, pp. 113–14.
149 Coleridge, 'Religious Musings', pp. 109, 111.
150 Samuel Taylor Coleridge, 'Frost at Midnight', in *The Works*, pp. 240–2, p. 242.

151 Samuel Taylor Coleridge, *Biographia Literaria*, ed. G. Watson (London, 1965), p. 289.
152 David Jaspers, *Coleridge as Poet and Religious Thinker* (London, 1985), pp. 66–7; Richard Holmes, *Coleridge* (Oxford, 1982), p. 55.
153 Samuel Taylor Coleridge, *The Friend*, in *The Collected Works of Samuel Taylor Coleridge*, vol. 4, ed. Barbara E. Rooke, 2 Parts (London 1961), Part 1, p. 520.
154 Coleridge, 'Religious Musings', pp. 124, 115, 110.
155 William Wordsworth, *The Prelude*, in Stephen Gill (ed.), *William Wordsworth* (Oxford, 1986), pp. 464, 542.
156 Blake, annotations to Wordsworth's poems, in *Complete Writings*, p. 783.
157 Cited in John H. Muirhead, *Coleridge as Philosopher* (London, 1930), p. 44, note.
158 Earl A. Wasserman, 'Nature Moralized: The Divine Analogy in the Eighteenth Century', *ELH*, 20, 1 (March 1953), pp. 39–76, pp. 68–9.
159 Amos Bronson Alcott, extracts from 'Journals', in George Hochfield (ed.), *Selected Writings of the American Transcendentalists* (New York, 1966), pp. 92–104, pp. 94, 97–8.
160 Amos Bronson Alcott, 'The Doctrine and Discipline of Human Culture', in Hochfield (ed.), *Selected Writings of the American Transcendentalists*, p. 141.
161 Amos Bronson Alcott, 'Orphic Sayings', in Hochfield (ed.), *Selected Writings of the American Transcendentalists*, pp. 308–19, p. 314.
162 Mark Holloway, *Heavens on Earth. Utopian Communities in America, 1680–1880* (London, 1951), pp. 19, 130–2.
163 Joseph von Eichendorff, 'Wünschelrute', in *Gedichte*, ed. Konrad Nussbächer (Stuttgart, 1957), p. 58.
164 Eichendorff, 'Abschied', in *Gedichte*, p. 65.
165 Eichendorff, 'Morgengebet', in *Gedichte*, p. 119.
166 Honoré de Balzac, *Séraphita, Louis Lambert and The Exiles*, trans. Clara Bell (Sawtry, 1995), pp. 18, 147, 138.
167 Victor Hugo, 'Ce que dit la bouche d'ombre', in *Les Contemplations*, ed. Pierre Albouy (Paris, 1973), pp. 386–7.
168 Victor Hugo, *Les Misérables*, 2 vols (London, 1994), vol. 1, p. 349.
169 Hugo, 'Explication', in *Les Contemplations*, p. 148.
170 Hugo, 'Ce que dit la bouche d'ombre', pp. 388–9.
171 Hugo, *Les Misérables*, vol. 1, p. 114.
172 Hugo, 'Ce que dit la bouche d'ombre', p. 394.
173 Cited in Auguste Viatte, *Victor Hugo et les illuminés de son temps*, 2nd edn (Geneva, 1973), p. 235.
174 Hugo, 'Ce que dit la bouche d'ombre', p. 389.
175 Maurice Bowra, *The Romantic Imagination*, paperback edn (Oxford, 1961), p. 12.
176 Albert Gérard, cited in Schenk, *The Mind of the European Romantics*, p. 165; cf. Aiden Day, *Romanticism* (London, 1996), p. 4.

3 Science, magic and the occult

1 Christopher Marlowe, *Dr Faustus*, ed. Roma Gill, 2nd edn (London, 1989), i: 77.
2 William Shakespeare, *The Tempest*, ed. Stephen Orgel (Oxford, 1987), V: i: 41–8.
3 Marlowe, *Dr Faustus*, i: 59.
4 Pierre Poiret, 'La Vie Continuée', in *La Vie de dam*[lle] *Antoinette Bourignon par elle-même* (Amsterdam, 1683), pp. 185–7.

5 Robert Turner, Preface to Henry Cornelius Agrippa, *His Fourth Book of Occult Philosophy* (London, 1655).
6 Anonymous, *The Book of Secrets of Albertus Magnus of the Virtues of Herbs, Stones, and Certain Beasts*, ed. Michael R. Best and Frank H. Brightman (Oxford, 1973), p. 3.
7 Henry Cornelius Agrippa, *Three Books of Occult Philosophy*, trans. I. F., ed. Donald Tyson (St Paul, MN, 1993), p. li.
8 Mircea Eliade, *Yoga. Immortality and Freedom*, trans. Willard R. Trask, paperback edn (London, 1989), p. xvi.
9 Hans Jonas, *The Gnostic Religion. The Message of the Alien God and the Beginnings of Christianity*, 2nd edn (London, 1992), pp. xv, 11 ff.
10 Eliade, *Yoga*, pp. 88–9.
11 Gershom Scholem, *Major Trends in Jewish Mysticism*, rev. edn (New York, 1961), p. 99.
12 Honoré de Balzac, *The Wild Ass's Skin*, trans. Herbert J. Hunt (Harmondsworth, 1977), p. 52.
13 Cited in Stoddard Martin, *Orthodox Heresy. The Rise of 'Magic' as Religion and its Relation to Literature* (London, 1989), p. 64.
14 Robert Turner, *Elizabethan Magic. The Art and the Magus* (Shaftesbury, 1989), p. 81.
15 John S. Mebane, *Renaissance Magic and the Return of the Golden Age. The Occult Tradition and Marlowe, Jonson and Shakespeare* (Lincoln, NE, 1989), p. 50.
16 Paracelsus, *Selected Writings*, ed. Jolande Jacobi, paperback edn (Princeton, NJ, 1979), p. 213.
17 William R. Shea, 'Trends in the Interpretation of Seventeenth-Century Science', in M. L. Righini Bonelli and William R. Shea (eds), *Reason, Experiment and Mysticism in the Scientific Revolution* (London, 1975), pp. 1–17, p. 12.
18 William F. Huffmann, *Robert Fludd and the End of the Renaissance* (London, 1988), p. 168.
19 Robert K. Merton, 'Puritanism, Pietism and Science', in C. A. Russell (ed.), *Science and Religious Belief. A Collection of Recent Historical Studies* (London, 1973), pp. 20–54.
20 Frances A. Yates, 'The Hermetic Tradition in Renaissance Science', in Charles S. Singleton (ed.), *Art, Science and History in the Renaissance* (Baltimore, 1967), pp. 255–74.
21 Charles Webster, *From Paracelsus to Newton. Magic and the Making of Modern Science* (Cambridge, 1982).
22 Allen G. Debus, *Man and Nature in the Renaissance* (Cambridge, 1978).
23 Charles B. Schmitt, 'Reappraisals in Renaissance Science', *History of Science*, 16 (1978), pp. 200–14, p. 206.
24 Thomas Spratt, *The History of the Royal Society*, ed. J. I. Cape and H. W. Jones (London, 1959), p. 341.
25 Mordechai Feingold, 'The Occult Tradition in the English Universities of the Renaissance', in Brian Vickers (ed.), *Occult and Scientific Mentalities in the Renaissance* (Cambridge, 1984), pp. 73–94.
26 Graham Rees, 'Francis Bacon's Biological Ideas: A New Manuscript Source', in Vickers (ed.), *Occult and Scientific Mentalities in the Renaissance*, pp. 297–314.
27 Stuart Clark, 'The Scientific Status of Demonology', in Vickers (ed.), *Occult and Scientific Mentalities in the Renaissance*, pp. 351–74.
28 Charles Webster, *The Great Instauration. Science, Medicine and Reform, 1626–1660* (London, 1975), pp. 1 ff.

29 Frances A. Yates, *The Rosicrucian Enlightenment*, paperback edn (St Albans, 1975), chs. 11 and 13.
30 Cited in Merton, 'Puritanism, Pietism and Science', p. 23.
31 L. M. Principe, 'Robert Boyle's Alchemical Secrecy: Codes, Ciphers and Concealments', *Ambix*, 39, 2 (July 1992), pp. 63–74.
32 Lotte Mulligan, '"Reason", "Right Reason", and Revelation in Mid-Seventeenth-Century England', in Vickers (ed.), *Occult and Scientific Mentalities in the Renaissance*, pp. 375–401, p. 376.
33 Brian Vickers, Introduction to Vickers (ed.), *Occult and Scientific Mentalities in the Renaissance*, pp. 1–55, pp. 5–6.
34 Antoine Faivre, *L'Esotérisme au XVIIIe siècle en France et en Allemagne* (Paris, 1973), p. 44.
35 E. P. Thompson, *Witness Against the Beast. William Blake and the Moral Law* (Cambridge, 1993), p. 39.
36 G. Bowles, 'Physical, Human, and Divine Attraction in the Life and Thought of George Cheyne', *Annals of Science*, 31, 6 (November 1974), pp. 473–88; B. J. Gibbons, 'Mysticism and Mechanism: The Religious Context of George Cheyne's Representation of the Body and its Ills', *British Journal for Eighteenth-Century Studies*, 21, 1 (1998), pp. 1–23.
37 William Law, *The Works of the Reverend William Law*, 9 vols (Brockenhurst and Canterbury, 1892–3), vol. 6, p. 201; vol. 8, p. 19.
38 Francis Lee, *Dissertations Theological, Mathematical, and Physical*, 2 vols (London, 1752), vol. 1, p. 194.
39 Robert Darnton, *Mesmerism and the End of the Enlightenment in France* (Cambridge, MA, 1968), pp. 10 ff.
40 Ernst Benz, *The Theology of Electricity*, trans. Wolfgang Taraba (Allison Park, PA, 1989); Erik Davis, *TechGnosis. Myth, Magic and Mysticism in the Age of Information* (London, 1999), ch. 3.
41 Lewis White Beck, *Early German Philosophy. Kant and his Predecessors*, paperback edn (Bristol, 1996), p. 364.
42 Karl Marx and Friedrich Engels, *Selected Works* (London, 1970), p. 378.
43 Robert E. Sullivan, *John Toland and the Deist Controversy. A Study in Adaptations* (Cambridge, MA, 1982), ch. 6.
44 Hans Eichner, 'The Rise of Modern Science and the Genesis of Romanticism', *PMLA*, 97 (1982), pp. 8–30, p. 9.
45 Brian P. Copenhaver, 'Natural Magic, Hermetism, and Occultism in Early Modern Science', in David C. Lindberg and Robert S. Westman (eds), *Reappraisals of the Scientific Revolution* (Cambridge, 1990), pp. 261–301, p. 287.
46 John Hedley Brooke, *Science and Religion. Some Historical Perspectives* (Cambridge, 1991), p. 63.
47 Thomas Vaughan, *Magia Adamica: Or the Antiquitie of Magic and the Descent thereof from Adam downwards Proved* (London, 1650), sig. B3^v.
48 Cited in Henry M. Pachter, *Magic into Science. The Story of Paracelsus* (New York, 1951), p. 7.
49 Paracelsus, *Essential Readings*, ed. Nicholas Goodrick-Clarke (Wellingborough, 1990), p. 70.
50 Henry Nollius [Heinrich Nolle], *Hermetical Physick*, trans. Henry Vaughan, in L. C. Martin (ed.), *The Works of Henry Vaughan*, 2nd edn (Oxford, 1957), pp. 550, 580.
51 Nicholas H. Clulee, 'At the Crossroads of Magic and Science', in Vickers (ed.) *Occult and Scientific Mentalities in the Renaissance*, pp. 57–71.
52 Cited in Pachter, *Magic into Science*, p. 40.

53 Paracelsus, *Selected Writings*, p. 131.
54 Nicholas H. Clulee, *John Dee's Natural Philosophy. Between Science and Religion* (London, 1988), pp. 171 ff.
55 Thomas Tryon, *Letters Upon Several Occasions* (London, 1700), p. 2.
56 Peter J. French, *John Dee. The World of an Elizabethan Magus* (London, 1972), p. 103.
57 Clulee, *John Dee's Natural Philosophy*, p. 150.
58 Georg Joachim Rheticus, *Narratio Prima*, in Edward Rosen (ed.), *Three Copernican Treatises* (New York, 1959), pp. 109–96, p. 147. Fernand Hallyn, *The Poetic Structure of the Cosmos. Copernicus and Kepler*, trans. Donald M. Leslie (New York, 1990), p. 62.
59 Nicholas Copernicus, *On the Revolutions*, trans. E. Rosen (Baltimore, 1978), p. 22.
60 Robert S. Westman, 'Magical Reform and Astronomical Reform: The Yates Thesis Reconsidered', in R. S. Westman and J. E. McGuire, *Hermeticism and the Scientific Revolution* (Los Angeles, CA, 1977), pp. 5–91, p. 16.
61 French, *John Dee*, p. 103; Brian Easlea, *Witch Hunting, Magic and the New Philosophy. An Introduction to the Debates of the Scientific Revolution* (Brighton, 1980), pp. 59 ff.; Ioan P. Couliano, *Eros and Magic in the Renaissance*, trans. Margaret Cook (Chicago, 1987), p. 205.
62 N. I. Matar, '"Alone in Our Eden": A Puritan Utopia in Restoration England', *The Seventeenth Century*, 3, 1 (Spring 1988), pp. 47–61, p. 195.
63 Cited in Hallyn, *The Poetic Structure of the World*, p. 130.
64 William Harvey, *The Circulation of the Blood and Other Writings*, trans. Kenneth Franklin, rev. edn (London, 1990), p. 3.
65 Huffmann, *Robert Fludd and the End of the Renaissance*, pp. 65 ff.
66 Richard Overton, *Mans Mortalitie*, ed. Harold Fish (Liverpool, 1968), pp. 49–52.
67 Cited in J. M. Armistead, 'The Occultism of Dryden's "American" Plays in Context', *The Seventeenth Century*, 1, 2 (July 1986), pp. 127–52, p. 145.
68 Arthur Quinn, 'On Reading Newton Apocalyptically', in Richard H. Popkin (ed.), *Millenarianism and Messianism in English Literature and Thought, 1650–1800* (Leiden, 1988), pp. 176–92, pp. 183–5.
69 Margaret Llasera, 'Concepts of Light in the Poetry of Henry Vaughan', *The Seventeenth Century*, 3, 1 (Spring 1988), pp. 47–61, p. 48.
70 Thomas Vaughan, *Aula Lucis, Or, The House of Light* (London, 1651), p. 6.
71 Thomas Vaughan, *Anthroposophia Theomagica: Or A Discourse on the Nature of Man and his State after Death* (London, 1650), p. 7.
72 Agrippa, *Three Books of Occult Philosophy*, p. 365.
73 Tryon, *Letters Upon several Occasions*, p. 23.
74 George Cheyne, 'Conjectures on Natural Analogy', in *An Essay on Regimen. Together with Five Discourses, Medical, Moral, and Philosophical* (London, 1740), p. 234.
75 Cited in Auguste Viatte, *Les Sources occultes du romantisme*, 2nd edn, 2 vols (Paris, 1928), vol. 2, p. 54.
76 Samuel T. Coleridge, *Biographia Literaria*, ed. George Watson, rev. edn (London, 1975), p. 286.
77 Anonymous, 'The Glory of the World', in Derek Bryce (ed.), *The Glory of the World and Other Alchemical Tracts* (Lampeter, 1987), p. 55.
78 Law, *The Works*, vol. 5, p. 171.
79 *Ibid.*, vol. 8, p. 113.
80 Jacob Boehme, *Signatura Rerum. The Signature of All Things*, trans. John Ellistone (London, 1651), 4: 8.

81 Judith V. Field, 'Kepler's Rejection of Numerology', in Vickars (ed.), *Occult and Scientific Mentalities in the Renaissance*, pp. 273–96.

82 I. Bernard Cohen, *The Birth of a New Physics* (Harmondsworth, 1992), pp. 133–4.

83 Hallyn, *The Poetic Structure of the World*, p. 167.

84 Cohen, *The Birth of a New Physics*, p. 145.

85 Hallyn, *The Poetic Structure of the World*, p. 163.

86 Alexandre Koyré, *From the Closed World to the Infinite Universe*, paperback edn (Baltimore, 1968), p. 31; Cohen, *The Birth of a New Physics*, p. 44.

87 Hallyn, *The Poetic Structure of the World*, pp. 212–14.

88 Nick Kollerstrom, 'Kepler's Belief in Astrology', in Annabella Kitson (ed.), *History and Astrology. Clio and Urania Confer* (London, 1989), pp. 152–70, p. 155.

89 Edward Rosen, 'Kepler's Attitude Toward Astrology and Mysticism', in Vickers (ed.), *Occult and Scientific Mentalities in the Renaissance*, pp. 253–72.

90 Kollerstrom, 'Kepler's Belief in Astrology', p. 163.

91 Hallyn, *The Poetic Structure of the World*, p. 239.

92 Cited in Alexander Gode-Von Aesch, *Natural Science in German Romanticism* (New York, 1966), p. 252.

93 Henri Talon (ed.), *Selections from the Journals and Papers of John Byrom* (London, 1950), pp. 221–2.

94 Serge Hutin, *Les Disciples anglais de Jacob Boehme* (Paris, 1960), pp. 147–50.

95 Richard Westfall, *The Life of Isaac Newton*, paperback edn (Cambridge, 1994), pp. 111–19.

96 Betty Jo Dobbs, *The Foundations of Newton's Alchemy. Hunting the Green Lyon* (Cambridge, 1975); David Castillejo, *The Expanding Force in Newton's Cosmos* (Madrid, 1981).

97 Cited in Richard Westfall, 'Newton and Alchemy', in Vickers (ed.), *Occult and Scientific Mentalities in the Renaissance*, pp. 315–35, p. 322.

98 Richard S. Westfall, 'The Role of Alchemy in Newton's Career', in Bonelli and Shea (eds), *Reason, Experiment and Mysticism in the Scientific Revolution*, pp. 189–232, pp. 216 ff.

99 Quinn, 'On Reading Newton Apocalyptically', pp. 183–5.

100 See, for example, F. Sherwood Taylor, *The Alchemists. Founders of Modern Chemistry* (London, 1951); H. J. Holmyard, *Alchemy* (Harmondsworth, 1957); Robert P. Multhauf, *The Origins of Chemistry* (London, 1966).

101 See Hannaway, *The Chemists and the Word*.

102 Brooke, *Science and Religion*, p. 68.

103 Holmyard, *Alchemy*, ch. 4; Serge Hutin, *A History of Alchemy*, trans. Tamara Alferoff (New York, 1962), pp. 108–9.

104 Cited in Alan Menhennet, *The Romantic Movement* (London, 1981), p. 21.

105 Lee, *Dissertations*, vol. 1, p. 194.

106 Hutin, *Les Disciples anglais de Jacob Boehme*, p. 264.

107 Cited in Gode-Von Aesch, *Natural Science in German Romanticism*, p. 58.

108 Viatte, *Les Sources occultes du romantisme*, vol. 1, p. 256.

109 Bentley Glass, Owsei Tamkin and William L. Straus, Jr. (eds), *Forerunners of Darwin, 1745–1859* (Baltimore, 1959).

110 Cited in Janet Oppenheim, *The Other World. Spiritual and Psychical Research in England, 1850–1914* (Cambridge, 1985), p. 381.

111 Frank Miller Turner, *Between Science and Religion. The Reaction to Scientific Naturalism in Late Victorian England* (New Haven, 1974), p. 80.

112 J. F. C. Harrison, *Robert Owen and the Owenites in Britain and America. The Quest for the New Moral World* (London, 1969), p. 127; J. F. C. Harrison,

The Second Coming. Popular Millenarianism, 1780–1850 (London, 1979), p. 159; Dennis Hardy, *Alternative Communities in Nineteenth-Century England* (London, 1979).

113 Cited in Turner, *Between Science and Religion*, p. 94.
114 Cited in Turner, *Between Science and Religion*, p. 100.
115 Gershom Scholem, *On the Kabbalah and its Symbolism* (New York, 1965), pp. 16–17.
116 Cited in Turner, *Between Science and Religion*, pp. 195–8.
117 See, for example, Stephen Larsen, Introduction to Emanuel Sedenborg, *The Universal Human and The Soul–body Interaction* (New York, 1984); Michael Stanley, Introduction to Emanuel Swedenborg, *Essential Readings* (Wellingborough, 1988).
118 Oppenheim, *The Other World*, ch. 8.
119 Martin, *Orthodox Heresy*, pp. 195 ff.
120 Wolfgang Pauli, 'The Influence of Archetypal Ideas on the Scientific Theories of Kepler', in C. G. Jung and W. Pauli, *The Interpretation of Nature and the Psyche* (New York, 1955), pp. 147–240, pp. 153, 208.
121 Daniel O'Keefe, *Stolen Lightning. The Social Theory of Magic* (Oxford, 1982), p. 559.
122 Christopher McIntosh, *Eliphas Lévi and the French Occult Revival* (London, 1972), p. 158.
123 Cherry Gilchrist, *The Elements of Alchemy* (Shaftesbury, 1991), pp. 123–5.
124 Fritjof Capra, *The Tao of Physics* (London, 1983); James Lovelock, *Gaia. A New Look at Life on Earth* (Oxford, 1979). On 'New Age science', see Wouter J. Hanegraaff, *New Age Religion and Western Culture. Esotericism in the Mirror of Secular Thought* (Leiden, 1996), ch. 3.
125 O'Keefe, *Stolen Lighning*, p. 104.
126 Sir Thomas Browne, *The Major Works*, ed. C. A. Patrides (Harmondsworth, 1977), p. 99.
127 Brian Morris, *Anthropological Studies in Religion. An Introductory Text* (Cambridge, 1987), pp. 149–50.
128 O'Keefe, *Stolen Lightning*, pp. 96 ff.
129 Robert S. Westman, 'Nature, Art and Psyche: Jung, Pauli, and the Kepler–Fludd Polemic', in Vickers (ed.), *Occult and Scientific Mentalities in the Renaissance*, pp. 177–229, p. 214.
130 Thomas S. Kuhn, *The Structure of Scientific Revolutions*, 2nd edn (Chicago, 1970).
131 Mauss, *A General Theory of Magic*, p. 33.
132 Owen Hannaway, *The Chemists and the Word. The Didactic Origins of Chemistry* (Baltimore, 1975), p. 15.
133 Balzac, *The Wild Ass's Skin*, p. 124.
134 Seyyed Hossein Nasr, *Man and Nature. The Spiritual Crisis in Modern Man*, paperback edn (London, 1990), p. 21.
135 Novalis, 'Christendom or Europe?', in *Hymns to the Night and Other Selected Writings*, trans. Charles E. Passage (Indianapolis, 1960), p. 53.
136 Mary Shelley, *Frankenstein*, ed. Maurice Hindle (Harmondsworth, 1992), pp. 38–9; on the occult background to *Frankenstein*, see Radu Florescu, *In Search of Frankenstein. Exploring the Myths Behind Mary Shelley's Monster* (London, 1999).
137 Henri Frankfort, H. A. Frankfort, John A. Wilson and Thorkild Jacobsen, *Before Philosophy. The Intellectual Adventure of Ancient Man*, paperback edn (Harmondsworth, 1967), p. 15.

138 Vickers, Introduction to Vickers (ed.), *Occult and Scientific Mentalities in the Renaissance*, p. 9.
139 H. G. Schenk, *The Mind of the European Romantics*, paperback edn (Oxford, 1979), pp. 22 ff.
140 Samuel Taylor Coleridge, *The Collected Letters of Samuel Taylor Coleridge*, ed. Earl Leslie Griggs, 6 vols (Oxford, 1971), vol. 4, p. 575.
141 W. B. Yeats, *Explorations* (London, 1962), p. 325.
142 W. B. Yeats, 'Fragments', in W.B. Yeats, *The Poems*, ed. Daniel Allbright (London, 1994), p. 260.
143 Patrick J. Keane, *Yeats's Interactions with Tradition* (Columbia, 1987), pp. 39 ff.

4   The body in occult thought

1 Erich Fromm, *The Art of Loving* (London, 1957), p. 53; Erich Fromm, *Psycho-analysis and Zen Buddhism*, paperback edn (London, 1974), pp. 128–9.
2 Marcel Mauss, 'A Category of the Human Mind: The Notion of Person, the Notion of Self', trans. W. D. Wills, in Michael Carrithers, Steven Collins and Steven Lukes (eds), *The Category of the Person. Anthropology, Philosophy, History* (Cambridge, 1985), pp. 1–25, p. 3.
3 Annie Mignard, 'Propos élémentaires sur la prostitution', *Les Temps modernes*, 354 (1976), pp. 1526–47, p. 1544.
4 Helmut J. Schneider, 'Deconstruction of the Hermeneutical Body: Kleist and the Discourse of Classical Aesthetics', in Veronica Kelly and Dorothea von Mücke (eds), *Body and Text in the Eighteenth Century* (Stanford, CA, 1994), pp. 209–26, p. 212.
5 Aleister Crowley, *Magick in Theory and Practice* (New York, 1976), p. 143.
6 Gershom Scholem, *Kabbalah* (New York, 1974), p. 153.
7 Samuel Pordage, *Mundorum Explicatio. Or, The Explanation of an Hieroglyphical Figure* (London, 1661), p. 40.
8 Jacob Boehme, 'Six Mystical Points', in *Six Theosophical Points and Other Writings*, trans. John Rolleston Earle (London, 1919), 1: 4.
9 William Law, *The Works of the Reverend William Law*, 9 vols (Brockenhurst and Canterbury, 1892–3), vol. 8, p. 16.
10 George Cheyne, 'Philosophical Conjectures About the Nature and Qualities of the Original Animal Body', in *An Essay on Regimen. Together with Five Discourses, Medical, Moral, and Philosophical* (London, 1740), p. 7.
11 Antoine Faivre, *L'Esotérisme au XVIIIe siècle en France et en Allemagne* (Paris, 1973), p. 107.
12 Thomas H. Luxon, *Literal Figures. Puritan Allegory and the Reformation Crisis in Representation* (Chicago, 1995), p. 124.
13 Cited in Amos Funkenstein, 'The Body of God in 17th Century Theology and Science', in Richard H. Popkin (ed.), *Millenarianism and Messianism in English Literature and Thought, 1650–1800* (Leiden, 1988), pp. 149–75, p. 156.
14 Augustine, *Confessions*, trans. R. S. Pine-Coffin (Harmondsworth, 1961), p. 63.
15 Christopher Hill, Barry Reay and William Lamont, *The World of the Muggletonians* (London, 1983), p. 30.
16 Funkenstein, 'The Body of God in 17th Century Theology and Science'.
17 Jacob Boehme, *Signatura Rerum. The Signature of All Things*, trans. John Ellistone (London, 1651), 3: 4.
18 Thomas Tryon, *Letters Upon Several Occasions* (London, 1700), p. 65.
19 Cheyne, 'Philosophical Conjectures About the Nature and Qualities of the original animal Body', p. 7.

20 George Cheyne, 'Philosophical Conjectures on Natural Analogy', in *An Essay on Regimen*, p. 313.
21 Isaac Newton, *Opticks. Or A Treatise of the Reflections, Refractions, Inflections 7 Colours of Light*, ed. Sir Edmund Whittaker (London, 1931), p. 370.
22 Anonymous, 'The Sophic Hydrolith', in Derek Bryce (ed.), *The Glory of the World and Other Alchemical Tracts* (Lampeter, 1987), p. 108.
23 Humphrey Ellis, *Pseudochristus* (London, 1650), p. 39.
24 Anonymous, 'The Glory of the World', in Bryce (ed.), *The Glory of the World and Other Alchemical Tracts*, p. 10.
25 I. A. Dorner, *History of the Development of the Doctrine of the Person of Christ*, vol. 2, p. 319.
26 William Blake, 'The Everlasting Gospel', in Geoffrey Keynes (ed.), *Complete Writings*, rev. edn (Oxford, 1966), p. 756.
27 Alexandre Koyré, *Mystiques, alchimistes spirituels. Schwenckfeld, Sébastian Franck, Weigel, Paracelse* (Paris, 1955), pp. 16 ff.
28 Cited in Auguste Viatte, *Les Sources occultes du romantisme*, 2nd edn, 2 vols (Paris, 1965), vol. 1, p. 47.
29 Cited in Luxon, *Literal Figures*, p. 73.
30 Charles Fourier, *The Theory of the Four Movements*, ed. Gareth Stedman Jones and Ian Patterson (Cambridge, 1996), p. 99.
31 Samuel Taylor Coleridge, *Biographia Literaria*, ed. George Watson, paperback edn (London, 1975), p. 74.
32 F. M. Barnard (ed.), *Herder on Social and Political Culture* (Cambridge, 1969), pp. 272–3.
33 Joseph Priestley, *Disquisitions Relating to Matter and Spirit* (London, 1777).
34 Anonymous, 'The Glory of the World', p. 17.
35 Boehme, *Signatura Rerum*, 1: 13.
36 *Ibid.*, 9: 1.
37 Law, *The Works*, vol. 8, p. 16.
38 *Ibid.*, vol. 5, p. 138.
39 Michael Sendivogius, 'The New Chemical Light', in Derek Bryce (ed.), *Concerning the Secrets of Alchemy and Other Tracts from the Hermetic Museum* (Lampeter, 1989), p. 123.
40 Antoine-Joseph Pernéty, *La Conoissonce de l'homme moral par celle de l'homme physique*, 2 vols (Berlin, 1776), vol. 1, pp. 93–4.
41 William Blake, 'The Marriage of Heaven and Hell', in *Complete Writings*, p. 149.
42 Joseph Dan (ed.), *The Early Kabbalah* (New York, 1986), p. 59.
43 Gershom Scholem, *On the Kabbalah and its Symbolism*, trans. Ralph Mannheim (New York, 1965), p. 128.
44 Jacob Boehme, *Concerning the Three Principles of the Divine Essence*, trans. John Sparrow (London, 1648), 25: 33.
45 Fourier, *The Theory of the Four Movements*, pp. 285–6.
46 Barbara Maria Stafford, *Body Criticism. Imaging the Unseen in Enlightenment Art and Medicine* (Cambridge, MA, 1993), p. 86.
47 Wolf-Dieter Muller-Jahnke, 'Die Signaturenlehre des Paracelsus', in Heinz Dopsch, Kurt Goldammer and Peter F. Kramml (eds), *Paracelsus (1493–1541). 'Kein anderes Knecht . . . '* (Salzburg, 1993), pp. 167–9.
48 Stafford, *Body Criticism*, p. 234.
49 Jim Tester, *A History of Western Astrology*, paperback edn (Woodbridge, 1999); Emile Grillot de Givry, *Illustrated Anthology of Sorcery, Magic and Alchemy* (London, 1991), pp. 240–79; Kurt Seligmann, *The History of Magic*.

A Catalogue of Sorcery, Witchcraft, and the Occult, paperback edn (New York, 1997), pp. 374–409.

50 Rosalie Osmond, *Mutual Accusation. Seventeenth-Century Body and Soul Dialogues in their Literary and Theological Contexts* (Toronto, 1990), p. 11.
51 Lodovico Maria Sinistrari, *Demonality*, trans. Montague Summers (London, 1927), pp. 42–3.
52 *Ibid.*, p. 28.
53 G. R. S. Mead, *The Subtle Body in Western Tradition*, paperback edn (London, 1967), pp. 37–8.
54 *Ibid.*, p. 38.
55 *Ibid.*, pp. 3, 36.
56 Paracelsus, *Essential Readings*, ed. Nicholas Goodrick-Clarke (Wellingborough, 1990), p. 64.
57 Paracelsus, *Selected Writings*, ed. Jolande Jacobi (London, 1951), p. 90.
58 Paracelsus, *Essential Readings*, p. 117.
59 *Ibid.*, p. 113.
60 Owen Hannaway, *The Chemists and the Word. The Didactic Origins of Chemistry* (Baltimore, 1975), p. 28.
61 Paracelsus, *Selected Writings*, p. 292.
62 Paracelsus, *Essential Readings*, pp. 119–20.
63 Paracelsus, *Selected Writings*, p. 113.
64 *Ibid.*, p. 292.
65 Jacob Boehme, *Mysterium Magnum. Or An Explanation of the First Book of Moses Called Genesis*, trans. John Ellistone and John Sparrow (London, 1654), Author's Preface, p. 9.
66 Jacob Boehme, *The Fifth Book of the Author* [*On the Incarnation of Jesus Christ*], trans. John Sparrow (London, 1659), 1: 2: 50.
67 Jacob Boehme, *Two Theosophical Epistles* (London, 1654), 1: 17.
68 Boehme, *Concerning the Three Principles of the Divine Essence*, 4: 19.
69 Pordage, *Mundorum Explicatio*, p. 31.
70 Cited in George Garden, *An Apology for M. Antonia Bourignon* (London, 1699), p. 46.
71 B. J. Gibbons, 'Mysticism and Mechanism: The Religious Context of George Cheyne's Representation of the Body and its Ills', *British Journal for Eighteenth-Century Studies*, 21, 1 (1998), pp. 1–23.
72 Cheyne, 'Philosophical Conjectures About the Nature and Qualities of the Original Animal Body', p. 6.
73 *Ibid.*, p. 4.
74 Anita Guerrini, 'Isaac Newton, George Cheyne, and the "Principa Medicinae"', in Roger French and Andrew Wear (eds), *The Medical Revolution of the Seventeenth Century* (Cambridge, 1989), pp. 222–45, p. 233.
75 George Cheyne, *The English Malady* (London, 1733), p. 38.
76 George Cheyne, *Philosophical Principles of Natural Religion* (London, 1705), pp. 72 ff.
77 Cheyne, *The English Malady*, p. 38.
78 Cheyne, *Philosophical Principles of Natural Religion*, p. 95.
79 See above, pp. 45–6.
80 Thomas Norton, 'The Ordinal of Alchemy', in Derek Bryce (ed.), *The Book of Lambspring and The Golden Trypod* (Lampeter, 1987), p. 138.
81 Henry Cornelius Agrippa, *Three Books of Occult Philosophy*, trans. I. F., ed. Donald Tyson (St Paul, MN), pp. 44, 585.
82 John Dastin, 'The Alchemical Art', trans. Wilfred Theissen, *Ambix*, 38, 2 (July 1991), pp. 73–8, p. 75.

83 Basil Valentine, 'The Twelve Keys', in Bryce (ed.), *The Book of Lambspring and The Golden Trypod*, p. 46.

84 Cheyne, *The English Malady*, p. 87.

85 Cited in Garden, *An Apology for M. Antonia Bourignon*, p. 46.

86 Jacob Boehme, 'Concerning the Election of Grace', in *De Electione Gratiae and Quastiones Theosophicae*, trans. John Rolleston Earle (London, 1930), 5: 116.

87 Boehme, *The Fifth Book of the Author*, 1: 2: 53.

88 Cited in Viatte, *Les Sources occultes du romantisme*, vol. 1, pp. 125–6.

89 Sendivogius, 'The New Chemical Light', p. 157.

90 Thomas Vaughan, *Anthroposophia Theomagica: Or A Discourse of the Nature of Man and his State after Death* (London, 1650), p. 36.

91 Cited in Garden, *An Apology for M. Antonia Bourignon*, pp. 46–7.

92 Andrew Michael Ramsay, *The Travels of Cyrus*, trans. Nathaniel Hooke, 4th edn, 2 vols (London, 1727), vol. 2, p. 10.

93 Fourier, *The Theory of the Four Movements*, p. 70.

94 Cited in Brian Easlea, *Witch-Hunting, Magic and the New Philosophy. An Introduction to the Debates of the Scientific Revolution, 1450–1750* (Brighton, 1980), p. 76.

95 Mircea Eliade, *Dreams and Mysteries. The Encounter Between Contemporary Faiths and Archaic Realities*, trans. Philip Mairet (London, 1960), pp. 174–5; see also Herbert Silberer, *The Problems of Mysticism and its Symbolism*, trans. Smith Ely Jeliffe (New York, 1917), pp. 71 ff.; Joseph Campbell, *The Masks of God*, 4 vols (London, 1960–5), vol. 1, pp. 103 ff.

96 B. J. Gibbons, *Gender in Mystical and Occult Thought. Behmenism and its Development in England* (Cambridge, 1996).

97 Andrew Michael Ramsay, *The Philosophical Principles of Natural and Revealed Religion*, 2 vols (Glasgow, 1749), vol. 2, p. 223.

98 On imagination in occult thought, see below, pp. 92–9.

99 Boehme, *The Fifth Book of the Author*, 1: 3: 69.

100 Edward Taylor, *Jacob Behmen's Theosophick Philosophy Unfolded* (London, 1691), p. 24.

101 Cited in Viatte, *Les Sources occultes du romantisme*, vol. 1, p. 60.

102 Antoinette Bourignon, *La Vie de Dam^{lle} Antoinette Bourignon, écrite par elle-même* (Amsterdam, 1683), pp. 315–16.

103 Gibbons, *Gender in Mystical and Occult Thought*, pp. 178, 182; George Cheyne, 'Philosophical Conjectures on Spiritual Nature', in Cheyne, *An Essay on Regimen*, p. 153.

104 Boehme, *Concerning the Three Principles of the Divine Essence*, 4: 7.

105 Jacob Boehme, '177 Theosophical Questions', in *De Electione Gratiae and Quastiones Theosophicae*, 12: 17.

106 Taylor, *Jacob Behmen's Theosophick Philosophy Unfolded*, p. 28.

107 Sendivogius, 'The New Chemical Light', p. 157.

108 Thomas Bromley, *The Way to the Sabbath of Rest* (London, 1655), p. 15.

109 George Cheyne, *The Natural Method of Curing the Diseases of the Body*, 5th edn (London, 1753), p. 79.

110 Ramsay, *The Travels of Cyrus*, vol. 2, p. 13.

111 Boehme, 'Concerning the Election of Grace', 6: 135.

112 Cited in Garden, *An Apology for M. Antonia Bourignon*, p. 49.

113 Taylor, *Jacob Behmen's Theosophick Philosophy Unfolded*, pp. 28–9.

114 Francis Lee, *Dissertations Theological, Mathematical, and Physical*, 2 vols (London, 1752), vol. 1, pp. 198–9.

115 Boehme, *The Fifth Book of the Author*, 1: 6: 39.

116 Taylor, *Jacob Behmen's Theosophick Philosophy Unfolded*, p. 23.

117 Cheyne, *An Essay on Regimen*, pp. xxxiii–xxxiv

118 Cheyne, *The English Malady*, pp. 112 ff.

119 George Cheyne, *An Essay on Gout. With An Account of the Nature and Qualities of the Bath Water*, 3rd edn (London, 1721), pp. 2–4, 11.

120 G. S. Rousseau, 'Mysticism and Millenarianism: Immortal Dr Cheyne', in Popkin (ed.), *Millenarianism and Messianism in English Thought and Literature*, pp. 81–126, p. 87.

121 Robert Schofield, *Mechanism and Materialism. British Natural Philosophy in an Age of Reason* (Princeton, 1970), p. 62.

122 Cited in Shuttleton, 'My Own Crazy Carcass', p. 287.

123 Cheyne, *The English Malady*, p. 94.

124 See below, pp. 78–80.

125 Brian P. Copenhaver, *Hermetica. The Greek Corpus Hermeticum and the Latin Asclepius in a New English Translation*, paperback edn (Cambridge, 1995), p. 16.

126 Dorner, *History of the Development of the Doctrine of the Person of Christ*, Division 2, vol. 2, p. 318.

127 Boehme, *Concerning the Three Principles of the Divine Essence*, 7: 7.

128 Cited in Robert Turner, *Elizabethan Magic. The Art and the Magus* (Shaftesbury, 1989), p. 101.

129 Roger Crab, *The English Hermite and Dagon's Downfall*, ed. Andrew Hopton (London, 1991), p. 26.

130 Henry Vaughan, 'Repentence', in *The Complete Poems*, p. 206.

131 Vaughan, 'Cock-Crowing', in *The Complete Poems*, p. 206.

132 Vaughan, 'The Incarnation, and Passion', in *The Complete Poems*, p. 168.

133 Vaughan, 'Distraction', in *The Complete Poems*, p. 208.

134 Vaughan, 'The Burial of an Infant', in *The Complete Poems*, p. 208.

135 Vaughan, *Anthroposophia Theomagica*, pp. 46–7.

136 William Blake, 'To Tirzah', in *Complete Writings*, p. 220.

137 William Blake, annotations to Berkeley's *Siris*, in *Complete Writings*, p. 775.

138 Honoré de Balzac, *Séraphîta*, p. 113.

139 Victor Hugo, *Les Misérables*, 2 vols (Ware, 1994), vol. 1, p. 11.

140 H. P. Blavatsky, *The Key to Theosophy* (Pasadena, CA, 1987), p. 29.

141 Novalis, 'Fragmente', in *Hymns to the Night and Other Selected Writings*, trans. Charles E. Passage (Indianapolis, 1960), p. 71

142 Leone Ebreo, *The Philosophy of Love* (*Dialoghi d'Amore*), trans. F. Friedberg-Seeley and Jean H. Barnes (London, 1937), pp. 345 ff.

143 Anonymous, 'The Sophic Hydrolith', p. 98.

144 Law, *The Works*, vol. 8, p. 113.

145 *Ibid.*, vol. 5, p. 140.

146 Gibbons, *Gender in Mystical and Occult Thought*, pp. 69–72, 138–41.

147 Ralph P. Locke, *Music, Musicians and the Saint-Simonians* (Chicago, 1986), pp. 89–90; Francis King and Isabel Sutherland, *The Rebirth of Magic* (London, 1982), ch. 12; Colin Wilson, *The Occult* (London, 1972), p. 178.

148 On Crowley, see John Symonds, *The Great Beast. The Life and Magick of Aleister Crowley*, rev. edn (London, 1973); Gerald Suster, *The Legacy of the Beast. The Life, Work and Influence of Aleister Crowley* (London, 1988), especially ch. 6.

5   The body in health and death

1 Cited in Robert E. Cousins, 'Robert Turner of Holshott (1620–1665?)', in Robert Turner (ed.), *Elizabethan Magic. The Art and the Magus* (Shaftesbury,

1989), pp. 128–50, p. 143. The editor of the book and subject of this article are, of course, different individuals.

2 Nicholas Culpeper, *Complete Herbal* (Ware, 1995), p. vi.

3 Alan Chapman, 'Astrological Medicine', in Charles Webster (ed.), *Health, Medicine and Mortality in the Sixteenth Century* (Cambridge, 1979), pp. 275–300.

4 Robert Darnton, *Mesmerism and the End of the Enlightenment in France* (Cambridge, MA, 1968), p. 177.

5 *Ibid.*, p. 4.

6 Chapman, 'Astrological Medicine', p. 278; Antoine Faivre, *L'Esotérisme au XVIIIe siècle en France et en Allemagne* (Paris, 1973), p. 140.

7 Darnton, *Mesmerism and the End of the Enlightenment in France*, p. 58. On fascination, see Henry Cornelius Agrippa, *Three Books of Occult Philosophy*, trans I. F., ed. Donald Tyson (St Paul, MN, 1993), p. 148; Emile Grillot de Givry, *Illustrated Anthology of Sorcery, Magic and Alchemy* (London, 1991), pp. 325–6.

8 H. G. Schenk, *The Mind of the European Romantics*, paperback edn (Oxford, 1966), p. 180.

9 Charles Webster, 'Paracelsus Confronts the Saints: Miracles, Healing and the Secularization of Magic', *Social History of Medicine*, 8, 3 (December 1995), pp. 403–21, p. 421.

10 *Ibid.*, p. 419.

11 Paracelsus, *Selected Writings*, ed. Jolande Jacobi (London, 1951), p. 123.

12 Allen G. Debus, *The English Paracelsians* (London, 1965), p. 30.

13 Henry M. Pachter, *Magic into Science. The Story of Paracelsus* (New York, 1951), pp. 5–6.

14 Howard H. Brinton, *The Mystic Will. Based on a Study of the Philosophy of Jacob Boehme* (New York, 1930), p. 73.

15 Samuel Hahnemann, *Organon of the Rational Art of Healing*, trans. C. E. Wheeler (London, 1913).

16 Paracelsus, *Selected Writings*, p. 140.

17 Anonymous, 'Fama Fraternitatis', trans. Thomas Vaughan, in Frances A. Yates, *The Rosicrucian Enlightenment*, paperback edn (St Albans, 1975), pp. 282–96, p. 288.

18 E. J. Holmyard, *Alchemy* (Harmondsworth, 1957), p. 32; H. J. Shepherd, 'Alchemy: Origin or Origins?', *Ambix*, 17, 2 (July 1970), pp. 69–84, pp. 78–9.

19 Michael Maier, 'Concerning the Secrets of Alchemy', in Derek Bryce (ed.), *Concerning the Secrets of Alchemy and Other Tracts from the Hermetic Museum* (Lampeter, 1989), p. 37.

20 Anonymous, 'The Glory of the World', in Derek Bryce (ed.), *The Glory of the World and other Alchemical Tracts* (Lampeter, 1987), pp. 79–80.

21 Anonymous, 'The Sophic Hydrolith', in Bryce (ed.), *The Glory of the World and other Alchemical Tracts*, p. 88.

22 Helvetius, 'The Golden Calf', in Bryce (ed.), *Concerning the Secrets of Alchemy and other Tracts from the Hermetic Museum*, p. 10.

23 Anonymous, *A Short Enquiry Concerning the Hermetic Art* (Edmonds, WA, 1983), p. 3.

24 Henri Talon (ed.), *Selections from the Journals and Papers of John Byrom* (London, 1950), p. 149.

25 Cited in Pachter, *Magic into Science*, p. 214.

26 Webster, 'Paracelsus Confronts the Saints', pp. 415–16.

27 Maier, 'Concerning the Secrets of Alchemy', p. 39.

28 Paracelsus, *Essential Readings*, ed. Nicholas Goodrick-Clarke (Wellingborough, 1990), p. 54.
29 Agrippa, *Three Books of Occult Philosophy*, p. 441.
30 Turner, *Elizabethan Magic*, p. 101.
31 Heinrich Nolle, *Hermetical Physick: Or, The Right Way to Preserve and to Restore Health*, trans. Henry Vaughan, in L. C. Martin (ed.), *The Works of Henry Vaughan*, 2nd edn (Oxford, 1957), pp. 547–92, p. 587.
32 Kathleen Raine, *The Human Face of God. William Blake and the Book of Job* (London, 1982), pp. 212–13.
33 William Law, *The Works of the Reverend William Law*, 9 vols (Brockenhurst and Canterbury, 1892–3), vol. 8, p. 40.
34 Cited in Auguste Viatte, *Les Sources occultes du romantisme*, 2nd edn, 2 vols (Paris, 1965), vol. 2, p. 196.
35 Peter Washington, *Madame Blavatsky's Baboon. Theosophy and the Emergence of the Western Guru* (London, 1993), p. 17.
36 F. M. Barnard (ed.), *Herder on Political and Social Culture* (Cambridge, 1969), p. 278.
37 George Cheyne, *The English Malady* (London, 1733), pp. 68, 308.
38 George Cheyne, *An Essay of Health and Long Life*, 7th edn (London, 1725), p. 83.
39 Cited in Darnton, *Mesmerism and the End of the Enlightenment in France*, p. 184.
40 Gideon Harvey, *The Family Physician and the House-Apothecary*, 2nd edn (London, 1678), sig. A2^r.
41 Cited in Erich P. Hofacker, *Christian Morgenstern* (Boston, MA, 1978), p. 111.
42 Novalis, 'Fragmente', in *Hymns to the Night and Other Selected Writings*, trans. Charles E. Passage (Indianapolis, 1960), p. 71.
43 Honoré de Balzac, *Séraphîta*, trans. Clara Bell (Sawtry, 1995), p. 92.
44 Paracelsus, *Selected Writings*, p. 155.
45 Nolle, *Hermetical Physic*, p. 587.
46 Thomas Vaughan, 'Affliction (I)', in *The Complete Poems*, ed. Alan Rudrum (Harmondsworth, 1983), p. 219.
47 Ann, Lady Conway, *The Principles of the Most Ancient and Modern Philosophy Concerning God, Christ, and the Creatures* (London, 1692), p. 87.
48 George Cheyne, 'Philosophical Conjectures About the Nature and Qualities of the Original Animal Body', in *An Essay on Regimen. Together with Five Discourses, Medical, Moral, and Philosophical* (London, 1740), p. 25.
49 Rosalie Osmond, *Mutual Accusation. Seventeenth-Century Body and Soul Dialogues in their Literary and Theological Context* (Toronto, 1990), pp. 12–13.
50 Cheyne, 'Philosophical Conjectures About the Nature and Qualities of the Original animal Body', p. 12.
51 C. F. Mullett (ed.), *The Letters of Dr George Cheyne to Samuel Richardson* (Columbia, MO, 1943), pp. 88, 100.
52 Paracelsus, *Essential Readings*, p. 67.
53 Cheyne, 'Philosophical Conjectures About the Nature and Qualities of the Original Animal Body', p. 43.
54 Samuel Butler, *Characters and Passages from the Note-Books*, ed. A. R. Waller (Cambridge, 1908), p. 100.
55 Viatte, *Les Sources occultes du romantisme*, vol. 1, p. 111.
56 D. P. Walker, *Spiritual and Demonic Magic from Ficino to Campanella*, paperback edn (Notre Dame, 1958), p. 13.
57 Cited in Pachter, *Magic into Science*, p. 129.

58 Michael Sendivogius, 'The New Chemical Light', in Bryce (ed.), *Concerning the Secrets of Alchemy and other Tracts from the Hermetic Museum*, p. 157.
59 Cheyne, 'Philosophical Conjectures About the Nature and Qualities of the Original Animal Body', p. 44.
60 Cited in Pachter, *Magic into Science*, p. 210.
61 Paracelsus, *Essential Readings*, p. 82.
62 Cheyne, *The English Malady*, p. 154.
63 Marcus Woodward (ed.), *Gerard's Herbal. The History of Plants* (London, 1994), p. 1.
64 John Passmore, *Man's Responsibility for Nature. Ecological Problems and Western Traditions* (London, 1974), p. 6; Keith Thomas, *Man and the Natural World. Changing Attitudes in England, 1500–1800* (London, 1983), p. 289.
65 Edward Taylor, *Jacob Behmen's Theosophick Philosophy Unfolded* (London, 1691), pp. 28–9.
66 Jacob Boehme, *The Fifth Book of the Author [On the Incarnation of Jesus Christ]*, trans. John Sparrow (London, 1659), 1: 4: 55.
67 Samuel Pordage, *Mundorum Explicatio. Or, The Explanation of an Hieroglyphical Figure* (London, 1661), p. 59.
68 Cited in James Garden, *An Apology for M. Antonia Bourignon* (London, 1699), p. 46.
69 Cheyne, *The English Malady*, p. 368.
70 Cited in Viatte, *Les Sources occultes du romantisme*, vol. 2, pp. 156–7.
71 H. P. Blavatsky, *The Key to Theosophy* (Pasadena, CA, 1987), p. 260.
72 Cited in Stoddard Martin, *Orthodox Heresy. The Rise of 'Magic' and its Relation to Literature* (London, 1989), p. 144.
73 Thomas Edwards, *Gangraena*, 3 Parts (London, 1646), Part 1, pp. 34, 80.
74 Letter to Henry Brooke, in Christopher Walton (ed.), *Notes and Materials for an Adequate Biography of the Celebrated Divine and Theosopher, William Law* (London, 1854), pp. 595–6.
75 Christopher Hill, 'The Mad Hatter', in *Puritanism and Revolution. Studies in the Interpretation of the English Revolution in the 17th Century*, paperback edn (London, 1968), pp. 303–10.
76 Roger Crab, *The English Hermite and Dagon's Downfall*, ed. Andrew Hopton (London, 1990), p. 12.
77 *Ibid.*, pp. 14, 17.
78 Anonymous, *The Post-Boy Robb'd of the Mail: Or, The Pacquet Broke Open* (London, 1706), p. 230.
79 [Thomas Tryon], *Monthly Observations for the Preserving of Health* (London, 1688), p. 3.
80 Thomas Tryon, *Letters Upon Several Occasions* (London, 1700), p. 5.
81 *Ibid.*, p. 36.
82 Tryon, *Monthly Observations for the Preserving of Health*, p. 9.
83 *Ibid.*, p. 82.
84 Tryon, *Letters Upon Several Occasions*, p. 17.
85 Tryon, *Monthly Observations for the Preserving of Health*, p. 14.
86 Tryon, *Monthly Observations for the Preserving of Health*, p. 29. Saturn and Mars symbolise the first two qualities of Eternal Nature, the conflicting qualities of contraction and expansion with which the Behmenist dialectic begins.
87 Tryon, *Letters upon Several Occasions*, p. 37.
88 *Ibid.*, p. 82.
89 *Ibid.*
90 *Ibid.*, p. 86.
91 *Ibid.*, p. 63.

92 *Ibid.*, p. 70.
93 *Ibid.*, pp. 16–17.
94 *Ibid.*, p. 18.
95 *Ibid.*, p. 22.
96 Thomas Tryon, *A Treatise of Dreams & Visions* (London, 1689), p. 292.
97 George Cheyne, 'Philosophical Conjectures About the Preference of Vegetable to Animal Food', in *An Essay on Regimen*, p. 71.
98 Cheyne, *The English Malady*, sig. A2^r.
99 Cheyne, *An Essay on Regimen*, pp. xiii–xiv.
100 *Ibid.*, p. xvii.
101 *Ibid.*, pp. xv–xvi.
102 Cheyne, 'Philosophical Conjectures About the Preference of Vegetable to Animal Food', p. 55.
103 Akihito Suzuki, 'Anti-Lockean Enlightenment?: Mind and Body in Early Eighteenth-Century English Medicine', in Roy Porter (ed.), *Medicine in the Enlightenment* (Amsterdam, Atlanta, GA, 1995), pp. 336–59, p. 350.
104 Cheyne, *The English Malady*, p. 305.
105 Cheyne, 'Philosophical Conjectures About the Preference of Vegetable to Animal Food', pp. 55, 61.
106 Mark Holloway, *Heavens on Earth. Utopian Communities in America, 1680–1880* (London, 1951), pp. 130–2; Martha Saxton, *Louisa May. A Modern Biography of Louisa May Alcott* (London, 1978), ch. 9.
107 *The New Age and Concordium Gazette*, 6 May 1843.
108 Thomas Frost, *Forty Years Recollection – Literary and Political* (London, 1880), pp. 46–7.
109 George Hollyoake, *The History of Cooperation* (London, 1906), p. 152.
110 Anonymous, 'The Glory of the World', p. 17.
111 Anonymous, 'The Sophic Hydrolith', p. 99.
112 Anonymous, 'The Glory of the World', p. 17.
113 *Ibid.*, p. 70.
114 Agrippa, *Three Books of Occult Philosophy*, p. 270.
115 Anonymous, 'The Book of Lambspring', in Bryce (ed.), *The Book of Lambspring and The Golden Tripod*, p. 10.
116 Richard Coppin, *Divine Teachings*, three parts (London, 1649), Part 3, p. 3.
117 Hannaway, *The Chemists and the Word*, p. 47.
118 Vaughan, *Anthroposophia Theomagica*, pp. 55, 58–9.
119 G. H. Sabine (ed.), *The Works of Gerrard Winstanley* (Ithaca, NY, 1941), p. 20.
120 George Foster, *The Sounding of the Last Trumpet* (London, 1650), p. 20.
121 Joseph Dan, *Gershom Scholem and the Mystical Dimension of Jewish History* (New York, 1987), pp. 140 ff.
122 Christian D. Ginsberg, *The Kabbalah. Its Doctrines, Development and Literature* (London, 1956), pp. 124–5.
123 Cited in Viatte, *Les Sources occultes du romantisme*, vol. 1, p. 135.
124 Washington, *Madame Blavatsky's Baboon.*
125 Raine, *The Human Face of God*, pp. 204, 226.
126 William Blake, 'A Vision of the Last Judgement', in *Complete Writings*, p. 616.
127 See below, pp. 131–2.
128 Peter Sterry, *The Clouds in which Christ Comes* (London, 1648), p. 50.
129 Colleen McDanell and Bernhard Lang, *Heaven. A History* (New Haven, 1988), p. 183; G. Torbridge, *Swedenborg. Life and Teaching* (London, 1945), pp. 329 ff.; Erland J. Brock, E. Bruce Glenn, Caroll C. Odhner *et al.* (eds), *Swedenborg and his Influence* (Bryn Athyn, PA, 1988).

130 Emanuel Swedenborg, *The Delights of Wisdom Relating to Conjugial Love* (London, 1981), sect. 37.
131 McDannell and Lang, *Heaven*, pp. 200–1.
* 132 Michel de Montaigne, *The Essayes of Michael Lord of Montaigne*, trans. John Florio, ed. Henry Morley (London, 1886), pp. 92–8.
133 Aphra Behn's *Oroonoko* (London, 1688) is an obvious exception.
134 See, for example, Charles White, *An Account of the Regular Gradation in Man* (London, 1779), p. 61.
135 Swedenborg, *The Delights of Wisdom Relating to Conjugial Love*, sect. 37.
136 Emanuel Swedenborg, *Heaven and its Wonders, and Hell, from Things Seen and Heard* (London, 1899), sect. 370.
137 Swedenborg, *The Delights of Wisdom Relating to Conjugial Love*, sect. 49–50.
138 *Ibid.*, sect. 54^5.
139 *Ibid.*, sect. 52.
140 Swedenborg, *Heaven, and its Wonders*, sect. 380.
141 Swedenborg, *The Delights of Wisdom Relating to Conjugial Love*, sect. 44$^{8-9}$.
142 Schenk, *The Mind of the European Romantics*, ch. 16.
143 McDannell and Lang, *Heaven*, pp. 261 ff.
144 Anne Brontë, *The Tenant of Wildfell Hall*, ed. G. D. Hargreaves (Harmondsworth, 1979), p. 409.
145 McDannell and Lang, *Heaven*, pp. 54 ff.
146 Gibbons, *Gender in Mystical and Occult Thought*, p. 200.
147 Jane Lead, *The Wonders of God's Creation in the Variety of Eight Worlds* (London, 1695), pp. 39 ff.
148 Viatte, *Les Sources occultes du romantisme*, vol. 1, p. 206.
149 *Ibid.*, vol. 2, pp. 194–6.
150 William Blake, letter to William Hayley, 6 May 1800, in *Complete Writings*, p. 792.
151 Auguste Viatte, *Victor Hugo et les illuminés de son temps*, 2nd edn (Geneva, 1973).
152 G. K. Nelson, *Spiritualism and Society* (London, 1969), pp. 48–53; Janet Oppenheim, *The Other World. Spiritual and Psychical Research in England, 1850–1914* (Cambridge, 1985), pp. 210 ff.
153 Nelson, *Spiritualism and Society*, pp. 93–5; Washington, *Madame Blavatsky's Baboon*, pp. 10–12.
154 Blavatsky, *The Key to Theosophy*, p. 28.
155 Arnold Goldman, 'Yeats, Spiritualism, and Psychical Research', in George Mills Harper (ed.), *Yeats and the Occult* (London, 1975), pp. 108–29.
156 Cited in C. G. Jung, *Psychology and Alchemy* (London, 1980), p. 374.
157 Marsilio Ficino, 'Five Questions Concerning the Mind', in Ernst Cassirer, Paul Oskar Kristaller and John Herman Randall, Jr (eds), *The Renaissance Philosophy of Man* (Chicago, 1948), pp. 193–212, p. 211.
158 Henry Vaughan, 'Resurrection and Immortality', in *The Complete Poems*, pp. 152–3.
159 Lead, *The Wonders of God's Creation Manifested in the Variety of Eight Worlds*, pp. 35–6.
160 Basil Valentine, 'The Golden Tripod', p. 67.
161 Jacob Boehme, 'Of the Supersensual Life', in *The Way to Christ Discovered* (London, 1648), 46.
162 Viatte, *Les Sources occultes du romantisme*, vol. 1, p. 161.
163 Cited in Stafford, *Body Criticism*, pp. 285–6.
164 Christopher McIntosh, *Eliphas Lévi and the French Occult Revival* (London, 1972), p. 60.

165 Mead, *The Doctrine of the Subtle Body in Western Tradition*, pp. 82 ff.
166 Jean Calvin, *The First Epistle of Paul the Apostle to the Corinthians*, ed. David W. Torrance and Thomas F. Torrance (Edinburgh, 1960), pp. 336–8.
167 Richard Overton, *Mans Mortalitie*, ed. Harold Fish (Liverpool, 1968); John Milton, 'A Treatise of Christian Doctrine', in *The Prose Works of John Milton*, ed. J. A. St John, 5 vols (London, 1848–53), vol. 4, chs. 7, 12; Thomas Hobbes, *Leviathan*, ed. C. B. Macpherson (Harmondsworth, 1968), pp. 484, 630. See also Norman T. Burns, *Christian Mortalism from Tyndale to Milton* (Cambridge, MA, 1972); B. W. Young, ' "The Soul-Sleeping System": Politics and Heresy in Eighteenth-Century England', *Journal of Ecclesiastical History*, 45, 1 (1994), pp. 64–81.
168 Alexandre Koyré, *La Philosophie de Jacob Boehme* (Paris, 1929), p. 315; John Stoudt, *Sunrise to Eternity. A Study of Jacob Boehme's Life and Thought* (Philadelphia, 1957), pp. 300–4.
169 Denis Saurat, *Literature and Occult Tradition. Studies in Philosophical Poetry* (London, 1930), pp. 36–9.
170 Cited in Wouter Hanegraaff, *New Age Religion and Western Culture. Esotericism in the Mirror of Secular Thought* (Leiden, 1996), pp. 439–40.
171 W. B. Yeats, *The Letters of W. B. Yeats*, ed. Allan Wade (London, 1954), p. 469.

6   The mind in occult thought

1 Henry Cornelius Agrippa, *On the Vanitie and Uncertaintie of Artes and Sciences* (London, 1575), p. 5.
2 Thomas Vaughan, *Anthroposophia Theomagica: Or A Discourse of the Nature of Man and his State after Death* (London, 1650), p. 1.
3 Frances Yates, *Giordano Bruno and the Hermetic Tradition* (London, 1964), p. 131.
4 John S. Mebane, *Renaissance Magic and the Return of the Golden Age. The Occult Tradition and Marlowe, Jonson and Shakespeare* (Lincoln, NE, 1989), pp. 61 ff.
5 F. C. Happold, *Mysticism. A Study and an Anthology*, rev. edn (Harmondsworth, 1970), p. 27.
6 Lewis White Beck, *Early German Philosophy. Kant and his Predecessors*, paperback edn (Bristol, 1996), p. 95.
7 Russell H. Hvolbek, 'Being and Knowing: Spiritual Epistemology and Anthropology from Schwenckfeld to Boehme', *The Sixteenth Century Journal*, 22, 1 (1991), pp. 97–110.
8 Christian D. Ginsberg, *The Kabbalah. Its Doctrines, Development and Literature* (London, 1956), p. 119.
9 Dan Cohn-Sherbok and Lavinia Cohn-Sherbok, *Jewish and Christian Mysticism. An Introduction* (New York, 1994), p. 39.
10 C. J. Barker, *Pre-Requisites for the Study of Jacob Boehme* (London, 1920), p. 22.
11 Johann Reuchlin, *On the Art of the Kabbalah. De arte cabalistica*, trans. Martin Goodman and Sarah Goodman (Lincoln, NA, 1993), p. 57.
12 Paracelsus, *Selected Writings*, ed. Jolande Jacobi (London, 1951), p. 213.
13 Jacob Boehme, *The Fifth Book of the Author [On the Incarnation of Jesus Christ]*, trans. John Sparrow (London, 1659), 3: 1–5.
14 Walter Charleton, 'Epistle Dedicatory' to J. B. van Helmont, *A Ternary of Paradoxes* (London, 1650), sigs. f2^{v}–f3^{r}.

15 William Blake, 'Jerusalem', in *Complete Writings*, ed. Geoffrey Keynes (Oxford, 1966), p. 663.
16 Auguste Viatte, *Les Sources occultes du romantisme*, 2 vols (Paris, 1966), vol. 1, pp. 17–19.
17 *Ibid.*, vol. 1, p. 127.
18 Cited in Alan Menhennet, *The Romantic Movement* (London, 1981), p. 17.
19 Beck, *Early German Philosophy*, pp. 368–72.
20 F. W. J. Schelling, *On the History of Modern Philosophy*, ed. Andrew Bowie (Cambridge, 1994), pp. 165–8, 172.
21 Beck, *Early German Philosophy*, p. 366.
22 F. M. Barnard (ed.), *Herder on Social and Political Culture* (Cambridge, 1969), pp. 192, 199, 308.
23 Schelling, *On the History of Modern Philosophy*, pp. 170–1.
24 Synesius, 'On Visions', in G. R. S. Mead, *The Doctrine of the Subtle Body in Western Tradition*, 2nd edn (London, 1967), pp. 68–81, p. 69.
25 Beck, *Early German Philosophy*, pp. 36–8.
26 Henry Cornelius Agrippa, *Three Books of Occult Philosophy*, trans. I. F., ed. Donald Tyson (St Paul, MN, 1993), p. 609.
27 Owen Hannaway, *The Chemists and the Word. The Didactic Origins of Chemistry* (Baltimore, 1975), p. 26.
28 Alexandre Koyré, *Mystiques, alchimistes spirituels. Schwenckfeld, Sebastian Franck, Weigel, Paracelse* (Paris, 1955), pp. 93 ff.; Beck, *Early German Philosophy*, pp. 153–4.
29 Beck, *Early German Philosophy*, p. 154.
30 *Ibid.*, p. 154.
31 Jacob Bauthumley, *The Dark and Light Sides of God* (London, 1650), p. 1.
32 Vaughan, *Anthroposophia Theomagica*, p. 45.
33 John Furly, *A Testimony to the True Light* (n.p., n.d.), pp. 4, 6.
34 Vaughan, *Anthroposophia Theomagica*, pp. 38–9.
35 Reuchlin, *On the Art of the Cabala*, pp. 49–51.
36 Barbara Maria Stafford, *Body Criticism. Imaging the Unseen in Enlightenment Art and Medicine* (Cambridge, MA, 1991), p. 236.
37 Richard Kearney, *The Wake of Imagination. Ideas of Creativity in Western Culture* (London, 1988), pp. 43 ff.
38 *Ibid.*, pp. 87 ff.
39 Plotinus, *Enneads*, trans. Stephen MacKenna (London, 1956), 5, 5.
40 Kearney, *The Wake of Imagination*, pp. 112–13.
41 *Ibid.*, pp. 103–4.
42 Thomas Hobbes, *Leviathan*, ed. C. B. Macpherson (Harmondsworth, 1968), p. 88.
43 Cited in Desirée Hirst, *Hidden Riches. Traditional Symbolism from the Renaissance to Blake* (London, 1964), pp. 65–6.
44 M. H. Abrams, *The Mirror and the Lamp. Romantic Theory and the Critical Tradition*, paperback edn (Oxford, 1971), p. 43.
45 *Ibid.*, pp. 160–2.
46 Francis Okeley, 'A Brief Explication of Some Latin and Other Words used by this Author', appended to Jacob Boehme, *The Way to Christ Discovered* (Bath, 1775), pp. 395–433.
47 Francis Lee, letter to Henry Dodwell, 9 April 1699, in Christopher Walton (ed.), *Notes and Materials for an Adequate Biography of the Celebrated Divine and Theosopher, William Law* (London, 1854), p. 199.
48 Cited in Koyré, *Mystiques, spirituels alchimistes*, p. 58.
49 C. G. Jung, *Psychology and Alchemy* (London, 1980), p. 167.

50 C. G. Jung, *Alchemical Studies* (London, 1967), p. 137.
51 Koyré, *Mystiques, alchimistes spirituels*, pp. 31–2.
52 Mungo Murray, letter to Colin Campbell, 1701, cited in David E. Shuttleton, '"My Own Crazy Carcass": The Life and Works of Dr George Cheyne (1672–1743)', unpublished Ph.D. thesis (University of Edinburgh, 1992), p. 287.
53 Cited in Henry M. Pachter, *Magic into Science. The Story of Paracelsus* (New York, 1951), p. 232.
54 Charles Webster, 'Paracelsus Confronts the Saints: Miracles, Healing and the Secularization of Magic', *Social History of Medicine*, 7, 3 (December 1995), pp. 403–21, p. 414.
55 Nolle, *Hermetical Physick*, pp. 591–2.
56 Agrippa, *Three Books of Occult Philosophy*, pp. 199, 204–5.
57 Jacob Boehme, *Of Christs Testaments*, trans. John Sparrow (London, 1652), 4: 23.
58 Okeley, 'A Brief Explication', p. 418.
59 Boehme, *The Fifth Book of the Author*, 1: 3: 69.
60 Francis Lee, *Dissertations Theological, Mathematical, and Physical*, 2 vols (London, 1752), vol. 1, pp. 200–1.
61 Paracelsus, *Essential Readings*, ed. Nicholas Goodrick-Clarke (Wellingborough, 1990), p. 58.
62 Stafford, *Body Criticism*, pp. 306 ff.
63 *Ibid.*, p. 312.
64 Paracelsus, *Selected Writings*, p. 506.
65 Nolle, *Hermetical Physick*, p. 574.
66 Johann Caspar Lavater, *Essays on Physignomy. Designed to Promote the Knowledge and the Love of Mankind*, trans. Henry Hunter, 3 vols (London, 1792), vol. 3, pp. 185–6.
67 Van Helmont, *A Ternary of Paradoxes*, p. 70.
68 See above, pp. 20–1.
69 Kearney, *The Wake of Imagination*, p. 39.
70 Brian P. Copenhaver (ed.), *Hermetica. The Greek Corpus Hermeticum and the Latin Asclepius in a New English Translation*, paperback edn (Cambridge, 1995), p. 18.
71 George Cheyne, *Philosophical Principles of Religion, Natural and Revealed* (London, 1715), p. 46.
72 Boehme, *The Fifth Book of the Author*, 1: 1: 12, 2: 1: 41.
73 *Ibid.*, 2: 1: 47.
74 *Ibid.*, 1: 1: 65.
75 *Ibid.*, 1: 1: 27.
76 Thomas Tryon, *A Treatise of Dreams & Visions* (London, 1689), p. 259.
77 Agrippa, *Three Books of Occult Philosophy*, pp. 609, 3.
78 Paracelsus, *Selected Writings*, p. 107; Koyré, *Mystiques, alchimistes spirituels*, p. 58.
79 Koyré, *Mystiques, alchimistes spirituels*, pp. 62–3.
80 Robert Darnton, *Mesmerism and the End of the Enlightenment in France* (Cambridge, MA, 1968), p. 64.
81 Ernest Lee Tuveson, *The Avatars of Thrice-Great Hermes. An Approach to Romanticism* (Lewisberg, 1984), p. 19.
82 D. P. Walker, *Spiritual and Demonic Magic from Ficino to Campanella*, paperback edn (Notre Dame, 1975), p. 32.
83 *Ibid.*, p. 201.
84 Cited in Christopher McIntosh, *Eliphas Lévi and the French Occult Revival* (London, 1972), p. 149.

85 W. B. Yeats, 'Is the Order of R.R. & A.C. to Remain a Magical Order?' (1901), in George Mills Harper, *Yeats's Golden Dawn* (London, 1974), Appendix K, p. 265.

86 Vaughan, *Anthroposophia Theomagica*, p. 58.

87 Tryon, *A Treatise of Dreams & Visions*, p. 260.

88 Okeley, 'A Brief Explication', p. 418.

89 Agrippa, *Three Books of Occult Philosophy*, p. 206.

90 Paracelsus, *Selected Writings*, pp. 105–6.

91 Okeley, 'A Brief Explication', p. 418.

92 Cited in Phyllis Mack, *Visionary Women. Ecstatic Prophecy in Seventeenth-Century England* (Berkeley, CA, 1992), pp. 62–3.

93 Francis Lee, letter to Dodwell, in Walton (ed.), *Notes and Materials*, p. 199.

94 Cited in McIntosh, *Eliphas Lévi and the French Occult Revival*, p. 149.

95 William Blake, 'Milton', in *Complete Writings*, p. 522.

96 Blake, 'A Vision of the Last Judgement', in *Complete Writings*, p. 604.

97 Blake, 'Milton', p. 480.

98 Blake, 'The Ghost of Abel', in *Complete Writings*, p. 779.

99 Martin Ruland, *Lexicon alchemiae*, cited in Jung, *Psychology and Alchemy*, p. 277.

100 William Blake, annotations to Berkeley's *Siris*, in *Complete Writings*, p. 773.

101 Blake, 'Jerusalem', in *Complete Writings*, p. 624.

102 Blake, letter to Dr Trusler, 23 August 1799, in *Complete Writings*, p. 793.

103 W. B. Yeats, *Essays and Introductions* (London, 1961), p. 65.

104 See Lilian R. Furst, *Romanticism in Perspective. A Comparative Study of Aspects of the Romantic Movements in England, France and Germany* (London, 1979), pp. 119 ff.

105 Cited in Kearney, *The Wake of Imagination*, p. 176.

106 Cited in Gode-Von Aesch, *Natural Science in German Romanticism* (New York, 1966), p. 181.

107 Cited in H. G. Schenk, *The Mind of the European Romantics*, paperback edn (Oxford, 1979), p. 5.

108 William Wordsworth, Preface to *Poems* (1815), in *William Wordsworth*, ed. Stephen Gill, paperback edn (Oxford, 1990), p. 636.

109 I. A. Richards, *Coleridge on Imagination*, 3rd edn (London, 1962) provides a useful introduction to Coleridge's theory of imagination, but takes no account of its occult provenance.

110 Cited in Maurice Bowra, *The Romantic Imagination*, paperback edn (Oxford, 1961) p. 295, note.

111 Samuel Taylor Coleridge, *Biographia Literaria*, ed. George Watson (London, 1965), p. 167.

112 *Ibid.*, p. 83.

113 Kearney, *The Wake of the Imagination*, p. 156.

114 Earl A. Wasserman, 'Nature Moralized: The Divine Analogy in the Eighteenth Century', *ELH*, 20, 1 (March 1953), pp. 39–76, pp. 46 ff.

115 Rufus M. Jones, *Spiritual Reformers in the Sixteenth and Seventeenth Centuries* (London, 1928), pp. xlvii–xlviii.

116 Titus Burckhardt, *Alchemy. Science of the Cosmos, Science of the Soul*, trans. William Stoddart (Shaftesbury, 1986), pp. 23, 97, 123.

117 Anonymous, 'The Sophic Hydrolith', in Derek Bryce (ed.), *The Glory of the World and Other Alchemical Tracts* (Lampeter, 1987), pp. 96, 99–100.

118 Anonymous, 'The Glory of the World', in Bryce (ed.), *The Glory of the World and Other Alchemical Tracts*, p. 73.

119   Anonymous, 'An Open Entrance to the Closed Palace of the King', in Derek Bryce (ed.), *Concerning the Secrets of Alchemy and other Tracts from the Hermetic Museum* (Lampeter, 1989), p. 87.
120   William James, *The Varieties of Religious Experience*, ed. Arthur Darby Knock (London, 1960), p. 172.
121   Happold, *Mysticism*, pp. 47, 48.
122   Novalis, 'Fragmente', in *Hymns to the Night and Other Selected Writings*, trans. Charles E. Passage (Indianapolis, 1960), p. 67.
123   H. P. Blavatsky, *The Key to Theosophy* (Pasadena, CA, 1987), pp. 328, 52.
124   Cited in Auguste Viatte, *Victor Hugo et les illuminés de son temps*, 2nd edn (Geneva, 1973), p. 237.
125   Cited in Viatte, *Les Sources occultes du romantisme*, vol. 1, p. 231.
126   Jeanne Ancelet-Hustache, *Master Eckhart and the Rhineland Mystics*, trans. Hilda Graef (London, 1957), p. 66.
127   Victor Hugo, *Les Misérables*, 2 vols (Ware, 1994), vol. 1, p. 62.
128   Cited in Jones, *Spiritual Reformers in the Sixteenth and Seventeenth Centuries*, p. 23.
129   John Pordage, *Innocencie Appearing through the Dark Mists of Pretended Guilt* (London, 1655), p. 77.
130   E[dward] H[ooker], 'The Prefatori Epistl[e]' to John Pordage, *Theologia Mystica. Or the Mystic Divinity of the Æternal Invisibles* (London, 1683), p. 58.
131   Pordage, *Theologia Mystica*, p. 44.
132   Jane Lead, *The Heavenly Cloud Now Breaking* (London, 1681), pp. 10 ff.
133   Blake, 'Jerusalem', in *Complete Writings*, pp. 623, 675.
134   Cited in McIntosh, *Eliphas Lévi and the French Occult Revival*, pp. 78–9.
135   Evelyn Underhill, *Mysticism*, 14th edn (London, 1942), p. 68.
136   Cited in James, *The Varieties of Religious Experience*, p. 370, note.
137   S. L. McGregor Mathers, Preface to Christian Knorr von Rosenroth (ed.), *The Kabbalah Unveiled*, paperback edn (London, 1991), p. ix.
138   Cited in Underhill, *Mysticism*, p. 5, note.
139   Novalis, 'Geistliche Lieder', I, in Curt Grützmacher (ed.), *Novalis: Dichtungen* (Munich, 1986), p. 69.
140   Cited in Gode-Von Aesch, *Natural Science in German Romanticism*, p. 83.

7   Occultism and analytical psychology

1   Ethan Allen Hitchcock, *Remarks Upon Alchemy and the Alchemists* (Boston, 1857).
2   William F. Huffmann, *Robert Fludd and the End of the Renaissance* (London, 1988), p. 62.
3   Luther H. Martin, 'A History of the Psychological Interpretation of Alchemy', *Ambix*, 22, 1 (March 1975), pp. 10–20.
4   Ioan P. Couliano, *Eros and Magic in the Renaissance*, trans. Margaret Cook (Chicago, 1987).
5   Daniel O'Keefe, *Stolen Lightning. The Social Theory of Magic* (Oxford, 1982), pp. 329–30.
6   Wilhelm Reich, *The Function of the Orgasm. Sex-Economic Problems of Biological Energy*, trans. Theodore P. Wolfe, paperback edn (London, 1970), pp. 358 ff.
7   Herbert Silberer, *Problems of Mysticism and its Symbolism*, trans. Smith Ely Jeliffe (New York, 1917).
8   Johann Fabricius, *Alchemy. The Medieval Alchemists and their Royal Art* (Copenhagen, 1976), pp. 10–11.

9 David Bakan, *Sigmund Freud and the Jewish Mystical Tradition*, paperback edn (London, 1990), p. 25.
10 C. G. Jung, *Memories, Dreams, Reflections*, ed. Aniela Jaffé, trans. Richard and Clara Winston, paperback edn (London, 1995), p. 398.
11 Bakan, *Sigmund Freud and the Jewish Mystical Tradition*, pp. xvii, xx.
12 *Ibid.*, pp. 58 ff.
13 *Ibid.*, p. 61.
14 *Ibid.*, p. 35.
15 *Ibid.*, p. 77.
16 *Ibid.*, pp. 253 ff.
17 *Ibid.*, p. 245.
18 *Ibid.*, p. 272.
19 Colin Campbell, *The Romantic Ethic and the Spirit of Modern Consumerism*, paperback edn (Oxford, 1989), pp. 72–3.
20 Jacques Ferrand, *A Treatise on Lovesickness*, trans. Donald A. Beecher and Massimo Ciavolella (Syracuse, NY, 1990), p. 236.
21 Iltha Veith, *Hysteria. The History of a Disease* (Chicago, 1965). See, for example, Edward Jorden, *A Brief Discourse of a Disease Called the Suffocation of the Mother* (London, 1603), p. 1.
22 Danielle Jacquart and Claude Thomasset, *Sexuality and Medicine in the Middle Ages*, trans. Matthew Adamson (Cambridge, 1988), pp. 84–6.
23 A. L. Rowse, *The Case Books of Simon Forman* (London, 1974); Michael Macdonald, *Mystical Bedlam. Madness, Anxiety and Healing in Seventeenth-Century England* (Cambridge, 1981).
24 D. P. Walker, *Unclean Spirits. Possession and Exorcism in France and England in the Late Sixteenth and Early Seventeenth Centuries* (London, 1981).
25 Roy Porter, *Mind Forg'd Manacles. A History of Madness in England from the Restoration to the Regency*, paperback edn (Harmondsworth, 1990), pp. 72–3.
26 *Ibid.*, pp. 47 ff.
27 Cynthia Eagle Russett, *Sexual Science. The Victorian Construction of Womanhood* (Cambridge, MA, 1989), p. 48.
28 Friedrich Meinecke, *Historism. The Rise of a New Historical Outlook*, trans. J. E. Anderson (London, 1972), p. 149.
29 Christopher Janaway, *Schopenhauer* (Oxford, 1994), pp. 48, 106–7.
30 Alexander Gode-Von Aesch, *Natural Science in German Romanticism* (New York, 1966), p. 167.
31 H. G. Schenk, *The Mind of the European Romantics*, paperback edn (Oxford, 1966), pp. 7–8.
32 Sigmund Freud, *The Interpretation of Dreams*, trans. James Strachey, paperback edn (Harmondsworth, 1976), p. 130.
33 Cited in Schenk, *The Mind of the European Romantics*, p. 8.
34 Cited in Frank Miller Turner, *Between Science and Religion. The Reaction to Scientific Naturalism in Late Victorian England* (New Haven, 1974), pp. 121–2.
35 *Ibid.*, p. 127.
36 *Ibid.*, p. 132.
37 C. G. Jung, *Mysterium Conunctionis. An Inquiry into the Separation and Synthesis of Psychic Opposites in Alchemy*, trans. R. F. C. Hull (London, 1963), p. xiii.
38 C. G. Jung, *Modern Man in Search of a Soul*, paperback edn (London, 1989), p. 181.
39 B. J. Gibbons, *Gender in Mystical and Occult Thought. Behmenism and its Development in England* (Cambridge, 1996), p. 206.
40 Jung, *Memories, Dreams, Reflections*, p. 366.

41 *Ibid.*, p. 73.
42 John W. Gruchy, 'Jung and Religion: A Theological Assessment', in Renos K. Papadopoulos and Graham S. Saayman (eds), *Jung in Modern Perspective* (Hounslow, 1984), pp. 193–203, pp. 199, 201.
43 Jung, *Memories, Dreams, Reflections*, pp. 48–9, 86; Frieda Fordham, *An Introduction to Jung's Psychology*, 3rd edn (Harmondsworth, 1966), p. 14.
44 Cited in Morton T. Kelsey, 'Jung as Philosopher and Theologian', in Papadopoulos and Saayman (eds), *Jung in Modern Perspective*, pp. 182–92, p. 186.
45 C.G. Jung, 'Approaching the Unconscious', in John Freeman (ed.), *Man and his Symbols*, paperback edn (London, 1978), pp. 1–94, p. 6.
46 Fordham, *An Introduction to Jung's Psychology*, pp. 17 ff.
47 W. P. Witcutt, *Blake. A Psychological Study* (London, 1946), ch. 3. On the Jungian interpretation of Blake, see also June Singer, *The Unholy Bible. Blake, Jung and the Collective Unconscious* (Boston, MA, 1986). For a neo-Freudian analysis, see Diana Hume George, *Blake and Freud* (Ithaca, NY, 1980).
48 Jung, *Modern Man in Search of a Soul*, p. 107.
49 C. G. Jung, *Psychology and Alchemy*, trans. R. F. C. Hull, 2nd edn (London, 1968), p. 152.
50 *Ibid.*, pp. 25–6.
51 *Ibid.*, p. 125.
52 *Ibid.*, pp. 150–1.
53 Jung, *Modern Man in Search of a Soul*, p. 18.
54 Jung, *Psychology and Alchemy*, p. 19.
55 *Ibid.*, p. 112.
56 Jung, *Mysterium Coniunctionis*, p. 41.
57 Alice Echolls, 'The New Feminism of Yin and Yang', in Anne Snitow, Christine Stansell and Sharon Thompson (eds), *Desire. The Politics of Sexuality* (London, 1983), pp. 439–59.
58 Witcutt, *Blake*, pp. 16–17.
59 Jung, *Modern Man in Search of a Soul*, p. 76.
60 C. G. Jung, *Alchemical Studies*, trans. R. F. C. Hull (London, 1968), p. 11.
61 Jung, *Modern Man in Search of a Soul*, p. 215.
62 Jung, *Alchemical Studies*, p. 249.
63 Fordham, *An Introduction to Jung's Psychology*, p. 64.
64 Jung, *Psychology and Alchemy*, pp. 10–11.
65 Marie-Louise von Franz, 'The Process of Individuation', in Freeman (ed.), *Man and his Symbols*, pp. 157–254, p. 163.
66 Jung, *Alchemical Studies*, pp. 47–8.
67 Brian Morris, *Anthropological Studies of Religion. An Introductory Text* (Cambridge), p. 166.
68 Jung, *Psychology and Alchemy*, p. 347.
69 Jung, 'Approaching the Unconscious', p. 6.
70 Philip A. Faber and Graham S. Saayman, 'On the Relation of the Doctrines of Yoga to Jung's Psychology', in Popadopoulos and Saayman (eds), *Jung in Modern Perspective*, pp. 165–81, p. 170.
71 Jung, *Alchemical Studies*, p. 249.
72 Jung, *Psychology and Alchemy*, p. 229.
73 Martin, 'A History of the Psychological Interpretation of Alchemy', p. 15.
74 Fabricius, *Alchemy*, p. 35.
75 Titus Burckhardt, *Alchemy*, trans. William Stoddart, paperback edn (Shaftesbury, 1986), pp. 8–9; Seyyed Hossein Nasr, *Man and Nature. The Spiritual Crisis in Modern Man*, paperback edn (London, 1990), pp. 113, 139.

76 Henry Crabb Robinson, *Diary, Reminiscences, and Correspondence*, ed. Thomas Sadler, 3 vols (London, 1869), vol. 2, p. 305.
77 Gruchy, 'Jung and Religion', p. 195.
78 Cf. Wouter Hanegraaff, *New Age Religion and Western Culture. Esotericism in the Mirror of Secular Thought* (Leiden, 1996), pp. 497 ff.

8 Society, religion and history in occult thought

1 Anonymous, 'The Sophic Hydrolith', in Derek Bryce (ed.), *The Glory of the World and Other Alchemical Tracts* (Lampeter, 1987), pp. 92, 126.
2 Anonymous, 'An Open Entrance to the Closed Palace of the King', in Derek Bryce (ed.), *Concerning the Secrets of Alchemy and Other Tracts from the Hermetic Museum* (Lampeter, 1989), p. 77.
3 Anonymous, 'The Sophic Hydrolith', p. 105.
4 Thomas Charnock, 'The Breviary of Natural Philosophy', in Elias Ashmole (ed.), *Theatrum Chemicum Britannicum* (London, 1652), p. 291.
5 Anonymous, 'The Sophic Hydrolith', p. 91.
6 Wilfred R. Theissen (ed.), 'John Dastin's Letter on the Philosophers' Stone', *Ambix*, 32, 2/3 (November 1986), pp. 78–87, p. 82.
7 Anonymous, 'Hermes Bird', in Ashmole (ed.), *Theatrum Chemicum Britannicum*, p. 212.
8 William Bloomfield, 'Bloomfields Blossoms: or, the Camp of Philosophy', in Ashmole (ed.), *Theatrum Chemicum Britannicum*, p. 219.
9 Pierce the Black Monk, 'Upon the Elixir', in Ashmole (ed.), *Theatrum Chemicum Britannicum*, pp. 271–2.
10 George Ripley, 'The Compound of Alchemy', in Ashmole (ed.), *Theatrum Chemicum Britannicum*, p. 117.
11 Anonymous, 'The Sophic Hydrolith', p. 103.
12 *Ibid.*, p. 92.
13 H[enry] P[inell] (ed.), *Five Treatises of the Philosophers Stone*, dedicatory epistle, sig. A3^v.
14 Pierce the Black Monk, 'Upon the Elixir', pp. 271–2.
15 Bloomfield, 'Bloomfields Blossoms', p. 319.
16 Eyrenaeus Philoctetes, *Philadelphia, Or Brotherly Love To the Studious in the Hermetick Art* (London, 1694), p. 2.
17 Thomas Tryon, *Letters Upon Several Occasions* (London, 1700), p. 69.
18 William Law, *The Works of the Reverend William Law*, 9 vols (Brockenhurst and Canterbury, 1892–3), vol. 8, p. 5; vol. 4, p. 10.
19 A. Keith Walker, *William Law. His Life and Thought* (London, 1973), p. 170.
20 Law, *The Works*, vol. 4, p. 68.
21 H. P. Blavatsky, *The Key to Theosophy* (Pasadena, CA, 1987), p. 39.
22 William Blake, 'William Bond', in *Complete Writings*, ed. Geoffrey Keynes, rev. edn (Oxford, 1966), p. 436.
23 Blake, 'For the Sexes. The Gates of Paradise', in *Complete Writings*, p. 761.
24 Blake, 'Jerusalem', in *Complete Writings*, p. 621.
25 Blake, 'The Everlasting Gospel', in *Complete Writings*, p. 754.
26 E. P. Thompson, *Witness Against the Beast. William Blake and the Moral Law*, paperback edn (Cambridge, 1994).
27 D. P. Walker, *The Decline of Hell. Seventeenth-Century Discussions of Eternal Torment* (London, 1964), ch. 13.
28 Christian D. Ginsberg, *The Kabbalah. Its Doctrines, Development and Literature* (London, 1956), p. 126.

29 Arthur D. Imerti, Introduction to Giordano Bruno, *The Expulsion of the Triumphant Beast* (Lincoln, NA, 1992), p. 12. Dorothea Singer, on the other hand, argues that 'Bruno was in his incurable mental detachment in fact completely indifferent to the quarrels between Catholic and Protestant': *Giordano Bruno. His Life and Thought*, reprint (New York, 1968), p. 14.

30 James Freake, preface to Henry Cornelius Agrippa, *Three Books of Occult Philosophy*, ed. Donald Tyson (St Paul, MN, 1993), p. lviii.

31 Anonymous, 'Confessio Fraternitatis', in Frances Yates, *The Rosicrucian Enlightenment*, paperback edn (London, 1972), p. 304.

32 Quirinus Kuhlmann, *The General London Epistle of Quirinus Kuhlmann, A Christian* (London, 1679), p. 10.

33 Thomas Vaughan, *Anthroposophia Theomagica: Or A Discourse of the Nature of Man and his State after Death* (London, 1650), p. 62.

34 Lewis White Beck, *Early German Philosophy. Kant and his Predecessors*, paperback edn (Bristol, 1996), pp. 133, 148–9.

35 John G. Burke, 'Hermetism as a Renaissance World View', in Robert S. Kinsman (ed.), *The Darker Vision of The Renaissance. Beyond the Fields of Reason* (Berkeley, CA, 1974), pp. 95–117, p. 114.

36 Herman de la Fontaine Verwey, 'The Family of Love', *Quaerendo*, 6, 3 (1976), pp. 219–71, p. 248.

37 Tryon, *Letters Upon Several Occasions*, p. 62.

38 William Law, *The Works*, vol. 9, pp. 215–64.

39 William Law, letter to George Cheyne, cited in David E. Shuttleton, ' "My Own Crazy Carcase": The Life and Works of Dr George Cheyne (1672–1743)', unpublished Ph.D. thesis, University of Edinburgh, 1992, p. 298.

40 Auguste Viatte, *Les Sources occultes du romantisme*, 2nd edn, 2 vols (Paris, 1965), vol. 1, pp. 154 ff.

41 H. G. Schenk, *The Mind of the European Romantics*, paperback edn (Oxford, 1966), pp. 113–14.

42 Samuel Taylor Coleridge, *Biographia Literaria*, ed. George Watson, rev. edn (London, 1975), p. 288.

43 Victor Hugo, *Les Misérables*, 2 vols (Ware, 1994), vol. 1, p. 37.

44 D. P. Walker, *Spiritual and Demonic Magic from Ficino to Campanella*, paperback edn (Notre Dame, 1975), p. 93.

45 Cited in J. H. Josten, 'An Unknown Chapter in the Life of John Dee', *Journal of the Warburg and Courtauld Institute*, 28 (1965), p. 245.

46 Thomas Bromley, *The Way to the Sabbath of Rest* (London, 1650), sig. A2^r.

47 John Pordage, *Innocencie Appearing Through the Dark Mists of Pretended Guilt* (London, 1655), sig. A2^r.

48 Richard Roach, 'An Acc^t of ye Rise & Progress of the Philadelphian Society', MS Rawlinson, D833, fos. 63–5, fo. 63^v.

49 Anonymous, *The State of the Philadelphian Society* (London, 1697), p. 7.

50 Viatte, *Les Sources occultes du romantisme*, vol. 1, p. 289.

51 Franz von Baader, *Les Enseignements secrets de Martines de Pasqually* (Paris, 1900), p. 5.

52 Kathleen Raine, *Yeats, the Tarot and the Golden Dawn* (Dublin, 1972), p. 6.

53 Ben Jonson, *The Alchemist*, II: i: 89 ff.

54 Antoine Faivre, *L'Esotérisme au XVIIIe siècle en France et en Allemagne* (Paris, 1973), p. 182; Allison Coudert, *Alchemy. The Philosopher's Stone* (London, 1980), p. 141.

55 Cited in Viatte, *Les Sources occultes du romantisme*, vol. 1, p. 187.

56 Anonymous, 'The Sophic Hydrolith', pp. 87, 89.

57 Cited in Charles A. Muses, *Illumination on Jacob Boehme. The Work of Dionysius Andreas Freher* (New York, 1951), p. 13.

58 Leone Ebreo, *The Philosophy of Love (Dialoghi d'Amore)*, trans. F. Friedberg-Seeley and Jean H. Barnes (London, 1937), pp. 345 ff.; Blaise de Vignère, *A Discourse of Fire and Salt* (London, 1649), p. 12.

59 William F. Huffman, *Robert Fludd and the End of the Renaissance* (London, 1988), p. 212; Robert Fludd, *Mosaicall Philosophy* (London, 1659), p. 42.

60 P[inell] (ed.), *Five Treatises of the Philosopher's Stone*, dedicatory epistle, sig. A2^v.

61 Cited in Hirst, *Hidden Riches*, p. 78.

62 Frances A. Yates, *Giordano Bruno and the Hermetic Tradition* (London, 1964), pp. 7 ff.

63 John French, preface to *The Divine Pymander of Hermes Trismegistus*, trans. John Everard (London, 1650), sigs. A5^v–A6^v; John Everard, cited in Nigel Smith, *Perfection Proclaimed. Language and Literature in English Radical Religion, 1640–1660* (Oxford, 1989), p. 114.

64 Jean Seznec, *The Survival of the pagan Gods. The Mythological Tradition and its Place in Renaissance Humanism and Art*, trans. Barbara S. Sessions, paperback edn (Princeton, NJ, 1995); Frances A. Yates, *Astraea. The Imperial Theme in the Sixteenth Century*, paperback edn (London, 1993), p. 35; Hirst, *Hidden Riches*, pp. 16–17.

65 Andrew Michael Ramsay, *The Travels of Cyrus; With Discourses upon the Theology and Mythology of the Pagans*, 2 vols (London, 1730), vol. 1, pp. 187, xviii.

66 Brian P. Copenhaver, *Hermetica. The Greek Corpus Hermeticum and the Latin Asclepius*, paperback edn (Cambridge, 1995), Introduction, p. li.

67 Cited in Viatte, *Les Sources occultes du romantisme*, vol. 2, pp. 172–3.

68 Novalis (Friedrich von Hardenberg), 'Geistliche Lieder', I: 23–4, in *Gedichte. Die Lehrlinge zu Sais*, ed. Johannes Mahr (Stuttgart, 1984), p. 103; cf. A. Leslie Wilson, *A Mythical Image. The Ideal of India in German Romanticism* (Durham, 1964), p. 54.

69 Alist [Francis Barham], 'Theosophy', *Notes and Queries*, 2nd ser., 74 (1857), pp. 423–4.

70 Agrippa, *Three Books of Occult Philosophy*, p. 450.

71 Jacob Boehme, *The Aurora. That is the Day-Spring*, trans. John Sparrow (London, 1656), 11: 58–9.

72 Cited in Viatte, *Les Sources occultes du romantisme*, vol. 1, p. 121.

73 William Blake, 'A Vision of the Last Judgement', in *Complete Writings*, p. 610.

74 John Mee, *Dangerous Enthusiasm. William Blake and the Culture of Radicalism in the 1790s*, paperback edn (Oxford, 1994), p. 125; Hirst, *Hidden Riches*, p. 176.

75 Basil Willey, *The Seventeenth-Century Background*, paperback edn (Harmondsworth, 1972), ch. 7.

76 Alexander Pope, *The Dunciad*, IV: 478, in *The Works of Alexander Pope*, ed. Sir Adolphus William Ward (London, 1961), p. 418; Thomas Altizer, *The New Apocalypse. The Radical Christian Vision of William Blake* (Michigan, 1967), p. xi.

77 R. D. Stock, *The Holy and Daemonic from Sir Thomas Browne to William Blake* (Princeton, NJ, 1982), pp. 77–9, 100.

78 Robert E. Sullivan, *John Toland and the Deist Controversy. A Study in Adaptations* (Cambridge, MA, 1982), ch. 6.

79 Arthur D. Imerti, Introduction to Giordano Bruno, *The Expulsion of the Triumphant Beast*, paperback edn (London, 1992), p. 42.

80 Christopher McIntosh, *Eliphas Lévi and the French Occult Revival* (London, 1972), pp. 46–7.
81 Viatte, *Les Sources occultes du romantisme*, vol. 2, pp. 175–7.
82 Papus, *The Tarot of the Bohemians*, trans. A. P. Morton, paperback edn (London, 1994), p. 6.
83 Edouard Schuré, *The Great Initiates. Sketch of the Secret History of Religions*, trans. Fred Rothwell, 2 vols (London, 1912).
84 Peter Washington, *Madame Blavatsky's Baboon. Theosophy and the Emergence of the Western Guru*, paperback edn (London, 1996), p. 33.
85 Blavatsky, *The Key to Theosophy*, p. 3.
86 Denis Saurat, *Literature and Occult Tradition. Studies in Philosophical Poetry* (London, 1930), p. 67.
87 On the orientalising of Western occultism, see Washington, *Madame Blavatsky's Baboon*.
88 Stoddard Martin, *Orthodox Heresy. The Rise of 'Magic' as Religion and its Relation to Literature* (London, 1989), p. 99.
89 Kathleen Raine, 'Hades Wrapped in Cloud', in George Mills Harper (ed.), *Yeats and the Occult* (London, 1975), pp. 80–107, p. 105.
90 W. P. Swainson, *Jacob Boehme. The Teutonic Philosopher* (London, 1921), p. 25.
91 Peter Malekin, Introduction to his translation of Jacob Boehme, *The Key and Other Writings* (Durham, 1998), pp. 9, 15, 17, 21, 30–1.
92 William James, *The Varieties of Religious Experience*, paperback edn (London, 1960), p. 404.
93 Matthew Sylvester (ed.), *Reliquiae Baxterianae*, 3 Parts (London, 1696), Part 1, p. 78.
94 Brian Easlea, *Witch Hunting, Magic and the New Philosophy. An Introduction to the Debates of the Scientific Revolution* (Brighton, 1980), p. 106.
95 Imerti, Introduction to Bruno, *The Expulsion of the Triumphant Beast*, p. 39.
96 Beck, *Early German Philosophy*, p. 147.
97 Paracelsus, *Essential Readings*, ed. Nicholas Goodrick-Clarke (Wellingborough, 1990), pp. 150–1.
98 Anonymous, 'Confessio Fraternitatis', p. 304.
99 Anonymous, *The Hermetick Romance: Or the Chymical Wedding*, trans. E. Foxcroft (London, 1690), p. 14.
100 On the occult background of Interregnum spiritualism, see Serge Hutin, *Les Disciples anglais de Jacob Boehme* (Paris, 1960), ch. 3; T. Wilson Hayes, *Winstanley the Digger. A Literary Analysis of Radical Ideas in the English Revolution* (Cambridge, MA, 1979); B. J. Gibbons, *Gender in Mystical and Occult Thought. Behmenism and its Development in England* (Cambridge, 1996), ch. 6.
101 Abiezer Coppe, *A Second Fiery Flying Roule* (London, 1649), p. 20, mispaginated as p. 21.
102 Roger Crab, *Dagon's Downfall; Or, The Great Idol Digged Up Root and Branch* (London, 1657), p. 6.
103 G. H. Sabine (ed.), *The Works of Gerrard Winstanley* (Ithaca, NY, 1941), p. 251.
104 McIntosh, *Eliphas Lévi and the French Occult Revival*, ch. 6.
105 Viatte, *Les Sources occultes du romantisme*, vol. 1, p. 248.
106 McIntosh, *Eliphas Lévi and the French Occult Revival*, p. 40.
107 Cited in Viatte, *Les Sources occultes du romantisme*, vol. 1, p. 248.
108 Robert Darnton, *Mesmerism and the End of the Enlightenment in France* (Cambridge, MA, 1968), pp. 62–4.

109 G. D. H. Cole, *A History of Socialist Thought. The Forerunners, 1789–1850* (London, 1953), p. 97.
110 Mark Holloway, *Heavens on Earth. Utopian Communities in America, 1680–1880* (London, 1951), pp. 37 ff.
111 Gibbons, *Gender in Mystical and Occult Thought*, pp. 158 ff.
112 Henri Desroche, *The American Shakers. From Neo-Christianity to Presocialism*, trans. John K. Savakool (Amherst, 1971).
113 Denis Hardy, *Alternative Communities in Nineteenth-Century England* (London, 1979), pp. 58–62
114 Holloway, *Heavens on Earth*, pp. 130–2.
115 G. K. Nelson, *Spiritualism and Society* (London, 1969), pp. 18 ff.
116 Gareth Stedman Jones and Ian Patterson, Introduction to Charles Fourier, *The Theory of the Four Movements* (Cambridge, 1996), p. xxvi.
117 Ralph P. Locke, *Music, Musicians and the Saint-Simonians* (Chicago, 1986), p. 6.
118 Hugo, *Les Misérables*, vol. 2, pp. 836, 839.
119 McIntosh, *Eliphas Lévi and the French Occult Revival*, ch. 8.
120 Blavatsky, *The Key to Theosophy*, p. 79.
121 Washington, *Madame Blavatsky's Baboon*, ch. 7.
122 [Moses de Leon], *The Zohar*, trans. Harry Sperling and Maurice Simon, 5 vols (London, 1931–4), vol. 1, p. 56.
123 Michael Ferber, *The Poetry of William Blake* (Harmondsworth, 1991), p. 34.
124 William Blake, 'The Human Abstract', in *Complete Writings*, p. 217.
125 Reuchlin, *On the Art of the Kabbalah*, p. 107.
126 Boehme, *The Aurora*, p. 416.
127 Gibbons, *Gender in Mystical and Occult Thought*, pp. 4–5.
128 Michael M. Schüler, 'Some Spiritual Alchemies of Seventeenth-Century England', *Journal of the History of Ideas*, 41 (1980), pp. 293–318; Andrew Mendelsohn, 'Alchemy and Politics in England, 1649–1665', *Past and Present* 135 (1992), pp. 30–78.
129 Christopher Hill, *The World Turned Upside Down. Radical Ideas During the English Revolution*, paperback edn (Harmondsworth, 1975), pp. 224–6, 289–90.
130 Gibbons, *Gender in Mystical and Occult Thought*, pp. 7–13.
131 Mendelsohn, 'Alchemy and Politics in England', pp. 53 ff.
132 Douglas Brooks-Davies, *The Mercurian Monarch. Magical Politics from Spenser to Pope* (Manchester, 1983), p. 8.
133 Michael Hunter, *Elias Ashmole, 1617–1692. The Founder of the Ashmolean Museum and his World* (Oxford, 1983), pp. 11–12.
134 Vaughan, *Anthroposophia Theomagica*, p. 32.
135 Christopher McIntosh, *The Rosicrucians. The History, Mythology and Rituals of an Occult Order*, rev. edn (Wellingborough, 1987), pp. 44 ff.
136 *Ibid.*, vol. 2, pp. 199–201; Antoine Faivre, *L'Esotérisme au XVIIIe siècle en France et en Allemagne* (Paris, 1973), pp. 84–5; Darnton, *Mesmerism and the End of the Enlightenment in France*, pp. 139–40.
137 Daniel O'Keefe, *Stolen Lightning. The Social Theory of Magic* (Oxford, 1982), p. 560.
138 Schenk, *The Mind of the European Romantics*, pp. 104–5.
139 Nicholas Goodrick-Clarke, *The Occult Roots of Nazism. Secret Aryan Cults and their Influence on Nazi Ideology* (London, 1992).
140 Michael Baigent and Richard Leigh, *Secret Germany. Stauffenberg and the Mystical Crusade against Hitler*, paperback edn (Harmondsworth, 1995).

141 Urszula Szulakowska, 'The Tree of Aristotle: Images of the Philosophers' Stone and their Transformation in Alchemy from the Fifteenth to the Twentieth Century', *Ambix*, 33, 2/3 (November 1986), pp. 55–77, pp. 54, 63.

142 Ernest Lee Tuveson, *The Avatars of Thrice Great Hermes. An Approach to Romanticism* (Lewisberg, 1982), pp. xi–xii.

143 Mendelsohn, 'Alchemy and Politics in England', p. 74.

144 Pordage, *Mundorum Explicatio*, p. 84, note; Antoine Faivre, *L'Esotérisme au XVIIe siècle en France et en Allemagne* (Paris, 1973), p. 98.

145 Jacob Boehme, *Mercurius Teutonicus, Or A Christian Information Concerning the Last Times* (London, 1649); Anonymous, *The State of the Philadelphian Society*, p. 26.

146 Fleischbein, cited in Viatte, *Les Sources occultes du romantisme*, vol. 1, p. 128.

147 Blake, *Complete Writings*, pp. 799, 810.

148 Martin, *Orthodox Heresy*, p. 167.

149 On medieval chiliasm, see Norman Cohn, *The Pursuit of the Millennium. Revolutionary Millenarians and Mystical Anarchists of the Middle Ages*, paperback edn (London, 1970).

150 Antoine Court de Gébelin, *Le Monde primitif*, 8 vols., vol. 8, p. lxix.

151 M. R. Wright (ed.), *Empedocles. The Extant Fragments* (New Haven, 1981), pp. 30–4.

152 Viatte, *Les Sources occultes du romantisme*, vol. 1, p. 254.

153 Fourier, *The Theory of the Four Movements*.

154 Blavatsky, *The Key to Theosophy*, p. 84.

155 Martin, *Orthodox Heresy*, pp. 145–50.

156 See above, p. 8.

157 Anonymous, *The State of the Philadelphian Society*, pp. 12, 27.

158 Michael Ferber, *The Social Vision of William Blake* (Princeton, NJ, 1985), pp. 213–21.

159 McIntosh, *Eliphas Lévi and the French Occult Revival*, p. 151.

160 Marjorie Reeves, *Joachim of Fiore and the Prophetic Future* (London, 1976).

161 Jane Lead, *The Wonders of God's Creation Manifested in the Variety of Eight Worlds* (London, 1696), p. 8.

162 McIntosh, *The Rosicrucians*, pp. 37–8.

163 A. L. Morton, *The Everlasting Gospel. A Study in the Sources of William Blake* (London, 1958).

164 Viatte, *Les Sources occultes du romantisme*, vol. 2, p. 87.

165 Nicholas Campion, 'Astrological Historiography in the Renaissance: The Works of Jean Bodin and Louis Le Roy', in Annabella Kitson (ed.), *History and Astrology. Clio and Urania Confer* (London, 1989), pp. 89–136.

166 *Ibid.*, p. 92.

167 Eugenio Garin, *Astrology of the Renaissance. The Zodiac of Life*, trans. Carolyn Jackson and June Allen (London, 1983), pp. 15 ff.

168 W. H. Walsh, *An Introduction to Philosophy of History*, paperback edn (Bristol, 1992), pp. 155–8; Raymond Aaron, *Main Currents in Sociological Thought*, 2 vols (Harmondsworth, 1968), vol. 1, ch. 2.

169 George G. Iggers (ed.), *The Doctrine of Saint-Simon. An Exposition. First Year, 1828–1829* (New York, 1972), pp. 4–5 and *passim*.

170 Auguste Viatte, *Victor Hugo et les illuminés de son temps*, 2nd edn (Geneva, 1973), pp. 58 ff.

171 Cited in Locke, *Music, Musicians and the Saint-Simonians*, p. 61.

172 *Ibid.*, pp. 90–1, 171 ff., 63, 87 ff.

173 Gibbons, *Gender in Mystical and Occult Thought*, ch. 7.

174 Isaiah Berlin, *Vico and Herder. Two Studies in the History of Ideas* (London, 1976), p. 16, note.
175 Wouter J. Hanegraaff, *New Age Religion and Western Culture. Esotericism in the Mirror of Western Thought* (Leiden, 1996), p. 413.
176 F. M. Barnard (ed.), *Herder on Social and Political Culture* (Cambridge, 1969), p. 283.
177 Cited in Beck, *Early German Philosophy*, p. 386.
178 Cited in Friedrich Meinecke, *Historism. The Rise of a New Historical Outlook*, trans. J. E. Anderson (London, 1972), pp. 359, 315.
179 Barnard (ed.), *Herder on Social and Political Culture*, pp. 281, 185.
180 Walsh, *An Introduction to Philosophy of History*, p. 135.
181 Barnard (ed.), *Herder on Social and Political Culture*, pp. 256, 260, 267.
182 G. W. F. Hegel, *Vorlesungen über die Geschichte der Philosophie*, in Hegel's *Werke* (Frankfurt am Main, 1971), vol. 20, p. 94.
183 Peter Singer, *Hegel* (Oxford, 1983), p. 83.
184 Herbert Marcuse, *Reason and Revolution. Hegel and the Rise of Social Theory*, 2nd edn (London, 1967), p. 48.
185 See, for example, Jacob Boehme, *XL Questions Concerning the Soule*, trans. John Sparrow (London, 1647), 1: 178. The 'nothingness' of the godhead is, of course, an ancient mystical theme, symbolising its absolute ineffability.
186 Marcuse, *Reason and Revolution*, pp. 94–5.
187 Jacob Boehme, 'Theoscopia', in *Six Theosophic Points and Other Writings*, trans. John Rolleston Earle (London, 1919), 1: 8.
188 G. W. F. Hegel, *Lectures on the Philosophy of History*, trans. J. Sibree (New York, 1956), p. 27.
189 Singer, *Hegel*, pp. 34 ff.
190 Alexandre Koyré, *La Philosophie de Jacob Boehme* (Paris, 1929), p. xvi.
191 Hegel, *Vorlesungen über die Geschichte der Philosophie*, p. 92.
192 Friedrich Schlegel, cited in Gode-Von Aesch, *Natural Science in German Romanticism*, p. 185.
193 Cited in Thomas McFarland, *Coleridge and the Pantheist Tradition* (Oxford, 1969), p. 83.
194 David Walsh, *The Mysticism of Innerworldly Fulfilment. A Study of Jacob Boehme* (Gainesville, FL, 1983).
195 Cited in Gode-Von Aesch, *Natural Science in German Romanticism*, p. 94.
196 Cited in Nicholas V. Riasonovsky, *The Emergence of Romanticism* (Oxford, 1992), p. 59.
197 Christian Morgenstern, 'Mit dieser Faust hier greif ich in den Raum', in *Gesammelte Werke* (Munich, 1965), p. 108.
198 Gode-Von Aesch, *Natural Science in German Romanticism*, p. 211.

9 The occult and Western culture

1 I. M. Lewis, *Ecstatic Religion. An Anthropological Study of Spirit Possession and Shamanism*, paperback edn (Harmondsworth, 1975), p. 18.
2 *Ibid.*, p. 127.
3 Mary Douglas, *Natural Symbols. Explorations in Cosmology*, paperback edn (Harmondsworth, 1973), pp. 103, 113.
4 B. J. Gibbons, *Gender in Mystical and Occult Thought. Behmenism and its Development in England* (Cambridge, 1996), pp. 5, 11.
5 Christopher Marsh, *The Family of Love in English Society, 1550–1630* (Cambridge, 1994).

6 H. G. Schenk, *The Mind of the European Romantics*, paperback edn (Oxford, 1979), p. 13; Marilyn Butler, *Romantics, Rebels and Reactionaries. English Literature and its Background, 1760–1830*, paperback edn (Oxford, 1981), pp. 34–5.

7 Ellic Howe, *The Magicians of the Golden Dawn. A Documentary History of a Magical Order, 1887–1923* (London, 1972), p. 50.

8 On modern occultism, see Marcello Truzzi, 'The Occult Revival as Popular Culture', *The Sociological Quarterly*, 13 (Winter, 1972), pp. 16–36; Martin Marty, 'The Occult Establishment', *Social Research*, 37, 2 (1970), pp. 212–30; Nat Freedland, *The Occult Explosion* (London, 1972).

9 See, for example, Wouter J. Hanegraaff, *New Age Religion and Western Culture. Esotericism in the Mirror of Secular Thought* (Leiden, 1996).

10 Thomas Hardy Leahey and Grace Evans Leahey, *Pyschology's Occult Doubles. Psychology and the Problem of Pseudoscience* (Chicago, IL, 1983), p. xiii.

11 Dan Cohn-Sherbok and Lavinia Cohn-Sherbok, *Jewish and Christian Mysticism. An Introduction* (New York, 1994), p. 1.

12 See, for example, Pamela Berger, *The Goddess Obscured. Transformation of the Grain Protectress from Goddess to Saint* (London, 1988); Shirley Nicholson (ed.), *The Goddess Re-Awakening. The Feminine Principle Today* (Wheaton, IL, 1989); Caitlín Matthews, *Sophia. Goddess of Wisdom. The Divine Feminine from Black Goddess to World Soul* (London, 1991).

13 Gibbons, *Gender in Mystical and Occult Thought*.

14 Stoddard Martin, *Orthodox Heresy. The Rise of 'Magic' as Religion and its Relation to Literature* (London, 1989), 115.

15 Desirée Hirst, *Hidden Riches. Traditional Symbolism from the Renaissance to Blake* (London, 1964), p. 20.

16 William Blake, 'A Descriptive Catalogue', in Sir Geoffrey Keynes (ed.), *Complete Writings*, paperback edn (Oxford, 1966), 578.

17 Christopher McIntosh, *The Rosicrucians. The History and Mythology of an Occult Order*, rev. edn (Wellingborough, 1987), p. 84.

18 Elias Ashmole (ed.), *Theatrum Chemicum Britannicum* (London, 1652), Prolegomena, sig. A3^{r}.

19 David Walsh, *The Mysticism of Innerworldly Fulfillment. A Study of Jacob Boehme* (Gainesville, FL, 1983), p. ix.

20 Jean Delumeau, *Catholicism Between Luther and Voltaire. A New View of the Counter-Reformation* (London, 1977).

21 Lewis White Beck, *Early German Philosophy. Kant and his Predecessors*, paperback edn (Bristol, 1996), p. 100.

22 Herbert Lüthy, 'Variations on a Theme by Max Weber', in Menna Prestwich (ed.), *International Calvinism, 1541–1715* (Oxford, 1985), pp. 369–90, p. 382.

23 Max Weber, *The Protestant Ethic and the Spirit of Capitalism*, ed. Anthony Giddens, paperback edn (London, 1985), pp. 128–9.

24 Ernst Stoeffler, *The Rise of Evangelical Pietism* (Leiden, 1973), p. 8.

25 Friedrich Nietzsche, *Twilight of the Gods. The Anti-Christ*, trans. R. J. Hollingdale (Harmondsworth, 1968), p. 87.

26 Mircea Eliade, *The Sacred and the Profane. The Nature of Religion*, trans. William R. Trask (San Diego, 1959).

27 Amos Funkenstein, 'The Body of God in 17th Century Theology and Science', in Richard H. Popkin (ed.), *Millenarianism and Messianism in English Literature and Thought, 1650–1800* (Leiden, 1988), pp. 149–75, p. 175.

28 C. B. Macpherson, *The Political Theory of Possessive Individualism* (Oxford, 1964).

29 Edgar Wind, *Pagan Mysteries in the Renaissance* (Harmondsworth, 1967), p. 11.
30 Johann Reuchlin, *On the Art of the Kabbalah. De arte cabalistica*, trans. Martin Goodman and Sarah Goodman (Lincoln, NE, 1993), p. 187.
31 Frances A. Yates, *The Rosicrucian Enlightenment* (London, 1972); McIntosh, *The Rosicrucians*.
32 Christopher McIntosh, *Eliphas Lévi and the French Occult Revival* (London, 1972), p. 20.
33 Bronislaw Malinowski, *Magic, Science and Religion* (New York, 1954), pp. 79 ff.
34 Ernst Cassirer, *An Essay on Man* (New York, 1970), p. 101.
35 Daniel O'Keefe, *Stolen Lightning. The Social Theory of Magic* (Oxford, 1982), p. 420.
36 Schenk, *The Mind of the European Romantics*, ch. 15.
37 F. M. Barnard (ed.), *Herder on Social and Political Culture* (Cambridge, 1969), Introduction, p. 53.
38 Peter Singer, *Hegel* (Oxford, 1983), ch. 3.
39 Heinrich Heine, *Die romantische Schule*, ed. Helga Weidmann (Stuttgart, 1976), p. 21.
40 Norbert Elias, *The Civilizing Process. The History of Manners and State Formation and Civilization*, trans. Edmund Jephcott, paperback edn (Oxford, 1994), pp. 9 ff.
41 On the role of middle-class women and the young as carriers of the Romantic tradition, see Colin Campbell, *The Romantic Ethic and the Spirit of Modern Consumerism*, paperback edn (Oxford, 1989), pp. 223 ff.

Index